Baja Fever

Journeys Into México's Intriguing Peninsula

BY

Greg Niemann

Mountain N' Air Books
P.O. Box 12540
La Crescenta, CA 91224

Baja Fever©
Gregory Niemann, author
Copyright in 1998 by Gregory Niemann
First edition, 1999 – Original Paperback

Published in the United States of America by
Mountain N' Air Books
P. O. Box 12540
La Crescenta, CA 91224
Phones: (800) 446-9696 or (818) 951 4150
Fax: (800) 303 5578 or (818) 951 4153

Cover photographs: Sunset over waters of the Sea of Cortéz, background, by Leila Niemann. Inserts by Gregory Niemann.
All photographs by the author, unless otherwise indicated.
Maps by Naomi Blackburn.
Cover and general book design by Gilberto d'Urso.

Library of Congress Catalog Card Number: 98-87785
Niemann, Gregory A. –1939

 Printed on recycled paper.

ISBN: 1-879415-19-4

All the geographical information compiled in this book is, to the best of our knowledge, accurate. We disclaim all liabilities in connection with the use of this information.

*"Baja Fever" is dedicated to my parents,
August H. (Gus) Niemann Jr. and Gladys C. Niemann,
who gave me my first dose of the "fever"
at a very young age.*

TABLE OF CONTENTS

Acknowlegments:

Thanks to Anne Batty, First Draft Editor of "Baja Fever," whose enthusiasm for this project kept it moving.

Thanks to reviewer Gene Kira, author of "King of the Moon" and co-author of "The Baja Catch" for his early direction. His editing suggestions made the finished book that much better.

Special thanks to those whose companionship made the stories of "The Baja Fever" a reality: my wife Leila Niemann (for her support, help and photos), son Ken Palfenier, fishing partner Don Lund, the folks at Cantamar, and especially those warm people of Baja who remain kind and gentle even when invaded by hordes of sometimes boorish gringos.

All of the stories are true and happened as reported to the best of my recollection. Where full names appear in the text, the people are real. Many of the other names have been changed.

Credits:

Baja Life:

Three of "The Baja Fever" stories appeared in shorter, slightly revised versions in *Baja Life* magazine: My story "The Hill Taunts Thousands" appeared as "The Tradition Rides On" in Issue #3, 1995. "The Most Inaccessible Place" appeared as "Mission San Francisco de Borja Adac" in Issue #5, 1996. "The Oasis of San Ignacio Kadakaaman" appeared as "Mission San Ignacio Kadakaaman" in Issue #7, 1997.

Thanks to the publisher *of Baja Communications Group* and *Baja Life* Editor/Managing Director Erik Cutter.

Discover Baja:

Six of "The Baja Fever" stories appeared in slightly revised versions in *Discover Baja* magazine. "Swimming With Sea Lions" appeared with the same title in the Nov/Dec 1996 issue. "Diving For Sea Urchins" appeared with the same title in the Jan/Feb 1997 issue. "The First Capital of the Californias" appeared as "Loreto: Mother of Missions" in the Jul/Aug 1997 issue. "A Loop Back in Time" appeared as "From Loreto to Comondus: A Mountain Odyssey" in the Sep/Oct 1997 issue. "Santa and the Clam Man" appeared with the same title in the Nov/Dec 1997 issue.

Thanks to the Discover Baja Travel Club, Hugh Kramer, President, and Lynn Mitchell, Editor.

San Clemente Journal:

Several of the stories or segments of them have appeared as part of my ongoing column "The Baja Beat" in the *San Clemente Journal*.

These include: "Where Lobster is King," "Behind the Intriguing Arch," "Baja's Beaches Lure Surfers," "Hollywood Comes To Baja," "The First Capital of the Californias," "The Oasis of San Ignacio Kadakaaman," and "Hot Sand/Cold Shops."

Thanks to Don Kindred, Publisher of *Community*, *Publications Network* and the *San Clemente Journal*, San Clemente, CA.

Baja Times:

For over a dozen years until they printed their last issue in December 1994, I contributed regularly to the *Baja Times*. Earlier, shorter versions of most of the mission stories first appeared in the Baja Times.

In addition, versions of the following *Baja Times* stories have been revised for "The Baja Fever": "Searching for Albacore," "Let's Go Bottom Fishing," "No Boat in the Bahia," "Seis Llantas," "Fish From Shore in Baja Hideaway," "Big Tuna Fight Back," "Huge Crowds Highlight Baja 1,000," and "Montana Grande Challenges Mountain Bikers.

Thanks to the *Baja Times* Publisher Carlos Chabert and Editorial Consultant John Utley for their help.

"By God's sweet wounds! It is so beautiful we will name it after all the saints! Take possession of it in the name of His Most Catholic Majesty, the King of Spain, and call it Bahia Todos Santos."
—*Sebastian Vizcaino, upon visiting the future site of Ensenada, Baja California on November 5, 1602 and naming it Todos Santos Bay.*

Tijuana
Tecate
Calexico
Mexicali
Yuma
Rosarito
Ensenada
La Bufadora
San Quintin
San Felipe
El Rosario
Puertecitos
Catavina
Canal de Ballenas
Isla Ángel de la Guarda
Bahía de los Angeles
Sierra de San Borja
Guerrero Negro
Bahia Tortugas
Díaz Ordaz
Laguna Ojo de Liebre
Santa Rosalía
San Ignacio
Laguna San Ignacio
Mulegé
Sierra de la Giganta
Bahía Concepción
Bahía de Ballenas
Loreto
Villa Insurgents
Isla Magdalena
Ciudad Constitución
San Carlos
Bahía Magdalena
San Juan de la Costa
Bahia de La Paz
Isla la Partida
Isla del Espirito Santo
Isla Santa Margarita
Pichilingue
La Páz
San Pedro
Buena Vista
Todos Santos
San José del Cabo
Cabo San Lucas

Gulf of California

Pacific Ocean

Baja Fever

HOOKED ON BAJA

INTRODUCTION

Before I was born, I was in Baja!

I'm not just referring to the exciting forays of my ancestors into that harsh and then unknown Mexican peninsula, although that interpretation could be valid too.

I was there with my mom, quite literally attached at the time. Curious to see the Baja landscape, I kicked and fought to no avail but to cause her discomfiture.

Though I wasn't born in Baja, it was close.

My mother's labor pains with me started early while the family was still in Ensenada. The Baja trip was immediately aborted and I was quickly whisked north across the border to make my arrival in the antiseptic sanctuary of a familiar hospital. I decided to cooperate and abate my early arrival in México, thus relinquishing what could have been a coveted dual citizenship.

I still cherish a small black and white photo of my older brother and sister standing on an old seawall at Ensenada, dated July 9,1939. I was born two days later.

I returned to Baja and other parts of México many times.

My earliest memories painted a picture of family fun: swimming in the ocean, camping on the beach, surf fishing, and a simple way of life. Even to a toddler it suggested a more relaxed, mellow and less-stressed family than in the city. My dad spent more time with us. We kids discovered he could unwind and, at least temporarily, shed his autocratic demeanor.

As I aged, I tried to look objectively at my father's strengths and weaknesses. While I tried to distance myself from some of his convictions, opinions and biases, I was attracted to his romantic spirit and sense of adventure.

Most importantly, I became enamored with a land that could make Papa get in the slow lane and relax.

Those pleasant memories of a restful family on the beach set the stage for a love affair with Baja that has survived and grown for almost three score years.

A Baja buff is a unique individual who suffers from the singular ailment of being attracted to this sometimes desolate, sometimes exotic foreign land. The Baja buff is lured to Baja and grows to love the place in spite of, and maybe because of, its imperfections. The Baja buff gets an uncomfortable, itchy feeling when he or she has been away too long. I call that feeling the "Baja Fever."

On the other hand many visitors don't like Baja, or even México, at all. They might be uncomfortable in a foreign land where the standard of living is not quite the same as home. This book is not for those who went, saw, and would rather be comfortably ensconced at the Hyatt Regency in Maui.

Most Baja buffs lack the vanity that feeds the fashion industry and its designer names. They rarely covet the newest, the most prestigious, and that which has herd-appeal. About the only type of one-upmanship you'll find among Baja buffs is when they mention the length of time they've been coming to Baja, or how many places they've been. It's common to discover an idyllic spot and discover Americans there who will try to "out-Baja" you:

"We've been coming here every year for (fill in the blank) years," you'll often hear, even if the people live in North Dakota and are making their annual sunshine migration.

I'm guilty of that attitude too. We don't want people we run across to think we're not seasoned Baja travelers: Expecting to be rendered the deference of a savvy sage, I might advise, "Yes I've been on that road, but it's been a few years," or "Make sure you top off with gas; sometimes they run out at Cataviña."

One must have "Baja credentials" I've noted, especially to be taken seriously as a writer of Baja lore. I figure that if being in Ensenada a few days before I was born doesn't "out-Baja" most people, the activities of my great-grandfather there surely must! I hope the readers will be as fascinated in learning about him and his antics as I was.

What is Baja?

What is Baja? Technically it is an 800-mile long peninsula separated from the mainland of México by the Gulf of California — or Sea of Cortéz, if you prefer. It is comprised of two Mexican states, Baja California (Sometimes called Baja California Norte), with Mexicali as capital, and Baja California Sur, capital city — La Páz.

The peninsula served as a stepping stone to the colonization of the U.S. state of California. Once the Spaniards left the Baja California peninsula to expand their efforts northward, the remote and arid peninsula was left to languish, virtually unpeopled and almost completely ignored by México and the United States alike.

Baja California (B.C.) did not become a Mexican state until 1952. The southern half of the peninsula, Baja California Sur (B.C.S.), entered statehood in 1974, less than a year after the first paved road linking north to south (Highway 1) was completed.

The reader will note the term "California" used differently in some of this book's historical references. Prior to the 1769 exploration into what is now the U.S. state, "California" only meant the peninsula.

Then the practice began of calling the north (now U.S.) Alta California (Upper California) and the peninsula Baja California (Lower California). "The Californias" referred to it all.

Baja is more than a place; it is a state of mind. American products that are labeled "Baja," from clothing to dune buggies, to big tires, to outdoor products suggest a free spirit, a sense of adventure.

Baja holds a fascination to many. In my lifetime I've watched that fascination expand beyond Californians, even beyond the American borders to include Europeans and others seeking the wide-open spaces in greater numbers. The Japanese, for example, keep returning to challenge in the famous Baja off-road races.

In recent years Tijuana, Rosarito, Ensenada and Cabo San Lucas have literally exploded in population, growth and services offered, both to accommodate a more demanding tourist and because of economic opportunities afforded in the border areas.

While the Baja of today is changing, outside of the border area and Cabo, that growth is slow compared to more populated parts of the world. Many coves, villages, ranchos and fish camps have seen very little deviation in their way of life over the past several decades.

My family's early romps into the wilds of Baja instilled Baja Fever in me, got me craving to see more, especially those out-of-the-way places.

Driving the Baja peninsula with my fishing buddy Don Lund, I'll often pull off the pavement to bounce up a dirt road to some mine, mission, cave, or little village I'd read about, or maybe just to see where the road goes. I felt guilty on our first trip, depriving him of fishing time for my selfish curiosity or article research. But when we returned home, the out-of-the-way places were all he talked about. He now eagerly awaits my side trips, knowing that they often might be a highlight of our trip.

I have always preferred those out-of-the-way places not spoiled by commercialism. In fact, when I see that RVs can drive to the same spot I am, or when I hear English spoken, especially by the locals, I figure I'm probably in the wrong place.

As a jumping-off point to explore Baja, I bought a small trailer at Cantamar over 26 years ago. Over the years that original humble refuge grew in land purchases and construction phases to a beautiful home a block away from the original. Aside from building that home, my wife Leila and I also built two rental properties, finally selling both and getting out of the time-demanding Baja vacation rental business in 1996.

Not a guide

This book is not a travel guide, but more a life-long accumulation of travel narratives and adventures in Baja, from Tijuana to Cabo San Lucas. While some stories are about fishing and bicycling, others cover snorkling, visiting missions or exploring those out-of-the-way places. Many stories, especially those on the missions, delve into the history and background of the area, what it was like then, and then again when I visited.

Some of the narratives have been gleaned from articles that have been published in both Baja-based and stateside newspapers and magazines over the years, including the *Baja Times, Baja Sun, Baja Life, Discover Baja and the off-road Cycle News* and *On-Dirt* magazines.

Baja is not for everyone. We've run into many tourists who get upset about an occasional lack of hot water, or a power outage, or the locals' lack of the English language or cultural differences. We wonder why they ever left home. They look for the same American-style amenities around the world.

We tried advertising our Cantamar rental in stateside magazines but soon gave that up. So many Americans expected the antiseptic world of a mega-resort, for $50 a night yet, that we finally refused to rent to anyone who had never been to México. We learned that México is not for everyone. We wanted to attract people who had stayed in hotels there and wanted to return to México. Our regulars came to love our rentals, but we refused to teach culture appreciation and optimism to a fearful non-traveler.

Some Baja buffs may note that places I describe in this book might not have appeared the same as when they visited. For example, many roads which were difficult to drive even three years ago might have been graded and be no problem today. For this reason, I have included the year I was there.

While Baja has been slow to change over the past 300 years, in some places mega-changes have occurred over the past five years. Even when I return to a place, I'm never able to find things exactly as they were.

Every person's Baja experience is different. I've seen this exemplified many times. A group of us could be together all weekend and the high-light for one might be the food in a particular restaurant. For another, it might be sharing candy with some friendly kids. For another it might be a hard-won purchase of a colorful souvenir following a long and fun bargaining session.

The more time one spends in Baja the more certain rituals appear less exotic. A first-time visitor is awed by many things we hardly notice, like scrawny dogs and bright purple houses, or mariachis serenading in res-taurants and people riding horseback down the main street.

This book is about my experiences, my Baja. Your Baja may be simi-lar, but is certain to be different.

So, sit back and enjoy a few of my forays into this compelling land to the south. Repeat visitors will relate with these stories; those who haven't yet been to Baja will hopefully have a better idea of what awaits them.

The second best thing to being in Baja is planning your next trip there. Perhaps reading about it might prompt those already bitten by the Baja bug back into action. Or maybe this book might be the "Bite of the Baja Bug" to yet others not yet afflicted: Baja Fever.

Bascom Ashbury Stephens

August H. "Gus" Niemann Jr.

Author's older sister Camilla and brother Fritz, taken in Ensenada on July 9th, 1939 – 2 days before the author was born. Photo by Gus Niemann

August H. Niemann Sr. fishing at Silver Lake in Los Angeles. -1918

Baja Fever

A Baja Heritage

"I had found what I wanted. I belonged to Baja and to those who felt that they belonged. Again it was the feeling that was the undeniable truth, the absolute certainty that this land was sacred to me."

—*Graham Mackintosh, 1988*
"Into A Desert Place,"
A 3,000 mile walk around the coast of Baja California

Cover of Bascom Stephen's book, "The Gold Fields of Lower California."

Baja Fever

THE POWER OF THE PEN

A BAJA GOLD RUSH — 1889

Baja California — The first known of California, it has remained the longest unknown!

In recent years, guide books, maps, magazines and videos have proliferated as more and more adventurers have documented their wanderings down the length and breadth of the Lower (Baja) California peninsula. Yet Baja still remains one of the more remote corners of the world.

Since the arrival of the first Europeans, all types of writers have been documenting their impressions and prejudices of Baja for future generations.

Most have strived to be accurate and informative, citing the good, interesting and worthwhile, highlighting those things that make Baja desirable, and at the same time documenting anything less desirable so that visitors will know what to expect.

Some, including the conqueror of México Hernan Cortes, have passed on hearsay. In his fourth Carta de Relación in 1524, Cortes wrote the King of Spain about this island allegedly populated by women about 10 days' journey away. He added, in speaking of native legends: "They also told me it is rich in pearls and gold. I will labor at making preparations to learn the truth and will write at length about it to your majesty."

Cortes himself went to Baja in 1535, just two years after the legendary "island" was discovered by his pilot Fortun Jimenez. Cortes spent time there and learned that those earlier reports contained a lot of fantasy.

It was due to a writer that the word "California" came into being. Writers at the time were quite aware that the word "colophon" meant the "end" of a book: title, name of publisher and other notes.

Colophon was the name of a Greek city in Iona whose people were proverbially at the end, the farthest away, the least civilized. In Spanish, the term became "Colophonia." The German spelling was very similar to California or Kalifornia.

A very popular novel at the time of México's conquest was "Sergas (The Exploits of) de Esplandian" by Garci Ordonez de Montalvo. The ingenious author called his fictional island at the end of the world, "very near the gates of the Terrestrial Paradise" — California. Apparently it was a play on words with California signifying "the end place."

Another writer took that book's fictional island and gave its name to the newly-discovered peninsula, thus relegating it one of the most recognizable names on the planet. It was Francisco Preciado who traveled with Francisco de Ulloa in 1539-1540 as they looped the Sea of Cortéz and then explored the Pacific Coast up to about the San Quintín bay area. In his diary which was later published in Europe, he recalled the fictional island from the earlier book and referred to the new peninsula as "California." It was the first reference in print to call the place California.

Some books suggest that the word California might have come from the Latin "callida fornax," meaning "hot furnace," referring to the blistering temperatures in Baja, but most scholars disregard this as mere supposition and embrace the "Sergas de Esplandian" origin.

WRITERS HAVE LAMBASTED EVERYTHING

Through the years, some writers have lambasted everything about Baja California: from the indigenous people, to what could be considered barren nothingness, to a paucity of water, to more current poor roads and trails.

One of these was the German Johann Jakob Baegert, a Jesuit missionary who spent the years 1751-1768 among the Baja Indians. He opens his 1771 book "Observations in Lower California" with this negative comment:

"Everything concerning California (Baja California) is of such little importance that it is hardly worth the trouble to take a pen and write about it. Of poor shrubs, useless thorn bushes and bare rocks, of piles of stone and sand without water or wood, of a handful of people who, besides their physical shape and ability to think, have nothing to distinguish them from animals, what shall or what can I report?"

Then there are those who have gone overboard in extolling undeserved merits to everything, painting a seductive picture so glowing and inviting that it borders on deception.

The hype offered by reporters and writers made the peninsula of Lower (Baja) California, by the mid-1880s, seem larger than life.

An Ensenada newspaper in 1888 reported that a sheaf of wild oats sent from Baja's El Sauzal measured four feet in length and contained so much grain that "immense fields of them go to waste for want of stock to eat them."

Americans north of the border heard tales of Baja's ideal climate, great natural mineral wealth, good tillable land for orchards, tall forests and abundant water, even with rivers to float the logs out of the mountains.

These legends and fantasies that were presented to excite a growing legion of Americans illustrate the remoteness of the peninsula. By the 1880's, it had been 350 years since Cortes first heard other enchanting and seductive rumors and still only a handful of people had ever been there. It comes as no surprise then that Baja is still a fantasyland for many - even now, after yet another 100 years.

By the late 1880s many Americans, especially Southern Californians, had taken to looking south across the border. Many considered Lower California an even more fertile and abundant land than the U.S. California with endless latent possibilities.

Consider these alluring comments about Baja from Bascom A. Stephens in his 1889 book "The Gold Fields of Lower California":

"...The boundary line (U.S.-México) does not change the climate and resources. Nature had not placed an oasis on the American side and a desert on the Mexican side. Alta California itself was once a part of México. The same mountains that are towers of strength to Southern California are the eternal fastnesses of the peninsula. The same balmy breezes blow softly amid her pines and waft the fragrance of her orange blossoms inland.

"The same characteristics of soil, climate and products exist south of the boundary line as north. It is a land of sunshine and silver, of fruits and flowers, of grain and gold, of gems and jewels, of the walnut and wine, of the olive and the orange, of banana and tobacco, of fish and fowl, of grand possibilities and certain probabilities of development.

"The 'great American desert,' which was driven westward so many years by the map-workers, who as late as 1700 made California an island, and who shoved their mystical waste on the peninsula, will have to find another abiding place — on the maps.

"The Colophon of the World — With a soil so rich and well watered, and so genial a clime, it is only a question of time, and not long either, when the great valleys and broad mesas of the peninsula will be occupied by a soil-delving and cultured people. Her grand harbors indicate her future greatness. With the country fully populated, and it can sustain a dense population, with its cities which will grow by its harbors, with a clime which is a help instead of a hindrance to work, it will, with Southern California, whose climate and soil are identical, be the colophon of the world — hindermost only in the sense of time. Here will be the grand culmination of the world's civilization. Here the arts and sciences will attain their highest perfection."

PROVOCATIVE PROPAGANDA

The aforementioned sounds like provocative Chamber of Commerce propaganda of the sort that might lure people to migrate, it should. In the late 19th century many books and pamphlets were published to attract thousands of Americans to settle in Southern California, and Stephens was the author of several of them.

The writer, Bascom Ashbury Stephens, was Secretary of the Historical Society of Southern California and published several books about the area, including "The Los Angeles City and County Guide Book," "The Resources of Los Angeles County," "A Succinct History of Los Angeles City," and "The History of San Diego County."

Taking a closer look at this character who let his pen do his talking, we find he was two years old when he arrived in California in 1857. A Santa Clara High School graduate, he founded the *Santa Clara Echo* (later called the *Journal*). He became an ordained Seventh Day Adventist minister, later quitting to return to journalism in 1880. As he aged, in religion he became an agnostic, and to quote him, "in politics an independent," although we'll learn this also wasn't always so.

He was a reporter for several Los Angeles papers, became city editor of the *Tucson Daily Citizen* in 1882, and publisher of the *Pomona Progress* and *Independent* in 1886-1887.

Stephens married in 1878 and he and the former Minerva Overshiner had three children: Bascom Albert, Minerva Eleanor, and William Ashbury. Daughter Minerva married August H. Niemann in 1903 and they had four children including August H. Niemann Jr. — my father! Bascom A. Stephens, this newspaperman who wrote so dramatically about imagined wonders of Baja, is in fact my great-grandfather.

My familial interest in Baja for over a century should "out-Baja" most, even though I question the wisdom and purpose behind some of my great-grandfather's later shenanigans.

International Company to Develop Baja

We must set the stage and give you a flavor of what was happening in Baja at the time. Between 1880 and 1889 the Mexican government granted several large concessions of land to foreigners to develop. The largest of these in Baja became the International Company of México, managed and financed by Americans.

The International Company chose Baja's two finest ports, Ensenada and San Quintín, and set about to develop them by offering future colonists lots of six ½, 25 and 50 acres at attractive terms. Ensenada, while the capital of the Norte district since 1882, was but a rancho before 1887 when it was being developed by the International Company.

Due to colonization, by January 1888 Ensenada had a population of 1375, of whom only 28 percent were Mexican!

In February 1889 gold was discovered in the mountains behind Ensenada. Within weeks thousands of prospectors invaded the place, 3,000 from San Diego alone. On one single day at the height of the boom 600 prospectors left San Diego for the gold fields. While the exciting placer strikes had all but petered out by the end of March, many prospectors lingered on to work the quartz mines at El Alamo.

Stephens was extremely quick, especially for 1889 technology, in getting a 48 page booklet out to the miners by March 9, especially when the gold rush started only three weeks previous. It was on February 23 when an Indian walked into an Ensenada store with a 10 ounce nugget of coarse gold. That show of gold set off the mining boom.

Stephens' book is curious. The first part is about the 1889 gold strike is a blow-by-blow daily accounting with maps and directions. He quotes reports from San Diego reporters and miners in the fields.

One part of the book is about mining, mining laws, equipment needed, etc. That material would have already been prepared by Stephens, and lifted from his earlier (1884) book "The Quijotoa Guide Book," outlining that Arizona gold strike in which he also took part.

But much of the book, including information for settlers, maps of the San Quintín area and much verbiage about colonization and Mexican Revenue Laws appears to be direct propaganda for the International Company.

About the company, Stephens says, "The International Company of México was organized in 1885. Among its members were E.T. Welles, L.R. Huller and George H. Sisson. Its concession has been turned over to a new management, with B. Scott, Esq. of Ensenada as general manager. It has a concession for all the public domain on the peninsula north of the 28th parallel.

"The title of the International Company is one in fee simple from the Mexican Government, which is pledged to warrant and defend the conveyance so made to the International Company, and is pronounced by the highest Mexican authority to be absolute and conclusive.

"By its efforts flourishing colonies exist at Ensenada, Colnett and San Quintín. A railroad coast survey has been made between San Diego and Ensenada."

In describing the route to the mines, Stephens notes two ways, overland or steamer. He reported that the International Company made three trips each week from San Diego to Ensenada with their two steamers.

A THREE YEAR BOOK SEARCH

It took me three years after I learned of its existence to track down this book. I was dismayed to find it so full of propaganda. But the exaggeration is to be expected in promotional material of this type at the time. It also explains how exaggeration has become a common trait among many members of my family, several of us in every generation.

The rainfall figures for Ensenada cited by Stephens are hard to believe and, if true, represent 10 real wet years in a row. Consider these figures he attributed to the daily record kept in Ensenada by Col. D.K. Allen, Land Inspector of the International Company:

Years	Inches
1878-79	15.50
1879-80	17.75
1880-81	15.25
1881-82	9.50
1882-83	42.00
1883-84	18.10
1884-85	32.05
1885-86	27.16
1886-87	24.10
1887-88	25.50
Total	226.90 Average 22.69

According to the most current guidebook "Baja California" published by the Automobile Club of Southern California, the average annual rainfall for Ensenada is 12½ inches. True, about every third or fourth year can be a wet one, but I've never seen the average doubled nine out of 10 years. Then again, look who was keeping the figures, an agent of the International Company.

Despite the best propaganda efforts of the International Company and their two steamships, they were having trouble attracting quality colonists to help settle their property. Also many Mexicans on the mainland were raising doubts about foreigners settling in Baja.

THE ENGLISH TAKE OVER

So the International Company sold out to an English firm headquartered in London. Now called the Mexican Land and Colonization Company, they began paying outstanding bills and developing Ensenada.

A subsidiary English company, the Lower California Development Company, took over 160,000 hectares in San Quintín and promised to settle 1,000 colonists there. They began to dig wells and create irrigation. They set about dredging the harbor and building a pier. They built a flour mill and exhibited machinery that they said was to start the construction of a Yuma-San Quintín railroad.

The enterprise failed, however, as much of this fanfare was a charade to attract investors. Neither this railroad nor the San Diego-Ensenada line was ever built, even to this day.

Those 200 colonists who did emigrate to San Quintín were further devastated by drought. Despite the prodigious amounts of rainfall reported, nature showed how fickle she can be — between the years 1892 and 1896 there was not one inch of rainfall in Ensenada or San Quintín!

The pen can hail and shout and whoop and yell. It can create attention and can afix names to places. The pen can, and often does, make something insignificant seem bigger than life.

The pen has helped make Baja, that California first known, less of an unknown. It could feed mining frenzies, create desire, attract settlers — but it couldn't make rain!

Ultimately, it was the harshness and unpredictability of Baja that thwarted the efforts of those settlers, lured to its "poor shrubs, useless thorn bushes and bare rocks" by those who painted such inviting pictures with the pen.

From the Pen to the Sword

Lower California — 1890

Journalists have, throughout history, been at the front of the action, documenting wars, riots and rebellions. The very nature of their jobs demands that they must be on the spot to gather reports for an insatiable public. The age-old question is, how close?

Sometimes it's a fine line between observer and participant. Does a writer on the sideline who helps a fallen motocross rider back on his feet cross that fine line? Is he affecting the outcome of the race? Should a news photographer create a posed picture?

Should journalists try to sway public opinion? Should the media be allowed to determine what is important and what is not?

The late nineteenth century marked the advent of what could be considered "creative" journalism. It was a muckraking time where the various newspapers virtually created sensations, mostly just to increase readership. One New York paper hired a female adventurer just to cover her record-breaking exploits.

Some historians attribute the Spanish-American War to the over-zealous inflammatory media. One publisher even commented to a reporter in Cuba: "You just keep the reports coming in; I'll keep the war going."

Sentiment to split state

In California during the late 1800s there was a strong sentiment to split the U.S. state and make Los Angeles the capital of the southern half. Many of the newspapermen, including my great-grandfather, Bascom A. Stephens, kept this idea in the public's minds through continuous articles and editorials.

A lot of people carried the idea one step further and wanted the United

States to annex Lower California and make it part of the new state of Southern California. After all, Americans were already colonizing Lower (Baja) California.

The idea of annexing Lower California, which flourished during the 1880s, was not a new one. The Mexican-American War, from 1846-1848, finally separated the Californias and created the present international border. As a result of that war, México ceded California and parts of Texas and New México to the U.S. but managed to keep Lower California.

It was not without the U.S. trying, however, as it took a Mexican counter-proposal in the negotiations leading up to the 1848 Treaty of Guadalupe Hidalgo to save what is now Baja. It stated:

"The cession of Lower California, of little importance to the Republic of North America (U.S.), offers great embarrassment to México, consider-ing the position of that Peninsula, facing our coast of Sonora, which is separated from it by the narrow Gulf of Cortéz. It will suffice that México would preserve Lower California, as it is necessary to have a part of Upper California, since otherwise that Peninsula would be without communica-tion by land with the rest of the Republic."

México's economy fell on hard times following the war and the coun-try was forced to sell Arizona and the southern part of New México to the U.S. in 1853.

Lower California was forgotten, which is not a surprise considering how far removed it was from the country's capital, México City. It became a difficult land, poor and beset with internal strife. With a population of only 7,000 on the entire peninsula in 1851, that number grew to about 20,000 by 1866. But most of those newcomers were not your ideal settlers as the lawlessness of Baja made it a haven for criminals, smugglers and other opportunists.

One such soldier of fortune was the American pirate William Walker, a small man with a big dream. In 1853 Walker left San Francisco in a ship with 45 armed men to capture Lower California.

After attacks in La Paz and Cabo San Lucas, he landed in Ensenada where he proclaimed himself President of his new Republic. Reinforced there with 230 other mercenaries, Walker and his men put down attempts to dislodge them. When a U.S. government ship came to Ensenada to persuade him to leave, he relocated his "capital" to San Vicente.

In March 1854 he lost most of his troops to suffering, thirst and aban-donment as he tried to cross the desert to capture the mainland state of Sonora. He was later captured near San Diego, tried and imprisoned for violating neutrality laws. He wasn't reformed, however, as he created a new army and took over the Central American country of Nicaragua. But that's Nicaragua's story.

The Lower California peninsula was coveted officially by the U.S. as well. In 1859 Mexican President Juaréz was sequestered up in Vera Cruz by Imperialist forces during an insurrectionary movement. U.S. President Buchanan sent Mr. McClane as minister to México to conclude a treaty and with vague promises of assistance and future support, to negotiate for the purchase of several Mexican provinces, including Lower California. The negotiations were soon confined to Lower California alone, but Juaréz refused to sell.

It is also reputed that in 1881 President Garfield through Secretary Blaine approached México on her willingness to sell the Peninsula.

In 1881 it is on record that California pioneer John C. Fremont, at the time territorial governor of Arizona, proposed to the U.S. government that the United States join with México and make Lower California an asylum for the warlike Apache Indians. Another idea that didn't quite make it.

JOURNALISTS PUSHED FOR CESSATION

During the mid-1880s the Southern California press was constantly pushing for this separation from Northern California with Los Angeles as capital, and the annexation of Lower California.

The following example was part of a lengthy editorial written by Captain John F. Janes in his San Pedro newspaper on December 22, 1883:

"I hope to see the day when Southern California will become a state and Los Angeles the capital, and her government buildings the pride of her people, and Lower California will be to her what Los Angeles County is to California today. Lower California we must have; it belongs naturally to Alta California. The United States must own the Peninsula as a protection against invasion, to reach from the Rio Grande to the Colorado River. Magdalena Bay as a Mexican mail depot and marine outfitting port would compel the United States to have a large naval fleet to watch and protect our coast and marine interests. Cape San Lucas, La Paz and Magdalena Bay, under the American government will secure us from invaders in case of war.

"The Peninsula in the hands of the Mexican government is worthless to them, and always will be. Her mountains and canyons are full of wealth, her valleys fertile, and only want American push and capital to show her natural resources. The government of this country must buy it, or we will have to take it for our own protection. Buy it if we can, if not we must take it. I have lived there and know the country."

Pretty inflammatory words for a journalist. And words like those incited some to act, including Colonel J. K. Mulky of Los Angeles.

In July 1888, Colonel J.E. Mulkey organized a secret society called the "Order of the Golden Field" with the sole purpose of claiming Lower (Baja) California. A San Francisco reporter who appeared supportive exposed the plan and it was disbanded.

FILIBUSTER OF 1890

Newspaperman Janes himself later became a participant in what historians refer to as the Filibuster of 1890.

The filibuster was a well-planned scheme by a number of Southern Californians, primarily newspapermen, to capture Lower California and erect there an independent government with a view to ultimate annexation to the United States.

It was a time when the writers decided to set aside their "pens" and grab their "swords." My great-grandfather would take the flowery praise of Baja that he wrote about in "The Gold Fields of Lower California" to the extreme—he was one of the key figures in the shadowy scheme to wrest the peninsula away from México.

Unfortunately, or rather fortunately for all concerned, the plan was discovered and the conspirators caught—but not before a great deal of very elaborate planning was completed.

The *San Diego Union*, on May 21, 1890, carried a vivid story about the planned filibuster, naming names, and citing details of the planned takeover. It noted Stephens' initial involvement in the initial expose':

"It will be remembered by some of those who read this that about six weeks ago B.A. Stephens arrived in San Diego, from Los Angeles, and formed an editorial connection with the Informant newspaper. Stephens is well known to Southern California newspapermen as one who has written a good deal in favor of the Annexation of the Peninsula and it is believed that he was at least fully cognizant of the Mulkey scheme. Stephens came to San Diego on the invitation of Augustus Merrill, editor of the *Informant*, and immediately upon his arrival was informed by Merrill of the details of the plan to take the peninsula.

"Merrill told Stephens that the Mexican Land and Colonization Company had pledged $100,000 to support the scheme and that other money would be raised by individuals who had interests that would be served by the annexation.

"After explaining some of the general features of the scheme, Merrill took Stephens to the office of the *San Diego Sun* and introduced him to Walter G. Smith, who confirmed the statements about the scheme as they had previously been outlined by Merrill.

"At the meeting of the trio at the *Sun* office a second conference was arranged at the Coronado Hotel on the next evening, Saturday, April 8. The conference was attended by Augustus Merrill, B.A. Stephens, Walter G. Smith and Colonel Edward Hill."

Conspiracy with the English Company

The conspirators discussed the financing noting that $25,000 immediate cash from private parties would be refunded out of the $100,000 the English Company would contribute later. They noted that the Company, with the exception of its President Sir Edward Jenkinson, was in favor of the scheme because under México they felt their property was near worthless.

The conspirators were working through Company Treasurer Mr. McQuilter and the Manager in Ensenada, Major Buchanan Scott.

They also discussed cost and shipment of arms, how the new government would be organized and plans to "take" the Peninsula.

They were going to fill the English Company warehouses with arms and provisions and then bring a large number of American laborers into México. On a certain night a grand fandango was to be given at the Hotel Iturbide in Ensenada, to which all Mexican officials would be invited. The conspirators would get them all drunk, bribe the Captain of the Guard, and on a given signal, the guards would be overpowered and the revolutionists would take possession.

The English Company even offered the use of their two steamers for the revolutionists.

The many planning meetings of the newspapermen conspirators outlined every detail of their new Republic. A flag was designed and each new department head set about to organize his own function.

Walter G. Smith, the *Sun* Editor, was to be the President of the new Republic, with the militaristic title of Governor-General. A former member of the New York legislature, he wrote a Declaration of Independence for Lower California and even read his inaugural address to the group.

The Commanding General was to be Merrill, a former member of the Grand Army and editor of the Informant, who drew up a plan for the military establishment of the new government.

Bascom A. Stephens would be Secretary-General. He wrote a draft of the Constitution for the Republic of Lower California. Historians have never been successful in locating a copy of this. I am still trying, although I wish I had known of its existence when my grandparents were still alive.

Ranford Worthing was to be Treasurer-General; Col. Edward Hill, War General; C.A. Harris, a newspaperman who worked with Merrill, Surveyor-General; and E.B. Higgins, a land-owner near San Quintín, as Industrial-General. Two other cabinet posts (Attorney-General and Postal-General) were not named pending acceptance of the parties involved.

Janes had earlier planned an independent foray to take Lower California but was talked into joining the San Diego newspapermen's group.

Back in San Pedro Janes wrote hints about the filibuster and both Merrill and Smith went to visit him to request his silence. Knowledge of the filibuster must have leaked because their visits to San Pedro were reported in the *San Diego Union*, causing fear in the hearts of the plotters.

Soon the *San Diego Union* got wind of the entire plot and exposed it in the aforementioned May 21 edition, thus forever making a moot issue as to whether or not the fandango caper would have worked.

The next day the *San Francisco Chronicle* outlined the detailed account and included biographies of the conspirators. Editorials in both papers called for the U.S. government to do something to those who openly defied the treaty relations between México and the United States.

During the hectic days following the divulgence, there was a lot of finger-pointing, with Janes accusing the other conspirators and vice-versa.

Smith was challenged to a duel by Mexican Colonel Manuel A. C. Ferrer for what he claimed an insult to México. The duel never took place.

The Mexican Land and Colonization Company of course denied any involvement, although the manager, Scott, was on the next boat to England. Lower California Governor Luis Torres displayed a willingness to work with the new Company officers and his belief that the filibustering conspiracy was "limited to a very few, irresponsible adventurers," helped México's President Porfirio Diaz determine that it was not a major incident.

While the filibuster caused a lot of general excitement in México City, President Diaz told an Associated Press correspondent that he placed little importance to the movement. He knew the United States Government would not allow the neutrality to be violated and the Mexican Government would protect her territory.

Thanks to the gracious attitudes of Governor Torres and President Diaz none of the conspirators was jailed for his involvement.

U.S. Secretary Blaine apologized to the Mexican government on behalf of the U.S. President, and responsible journalists across the country berated their fellow newspapermen for their hare-brained scheme.

Those journalists who remembered the power of the pen prevailed. That handful of writers who laid down the pen to seek a solution by the sword learned a valuable lesson, and it seems they were fortunate that the plan was exposed when it was.

It appears that my great-grandfather was a dreamer. Bascom A. Stephens did a great job as a Los Angeles reporter. Most of his books were a credit to his profession. But he allowed those dreams and fantasies of the riches of Lower California cloud his judgment. He believed his own propaganda. He had Baja Fever.

The lure of Lower California was as strong to him as was the lure of the mythical island peopled by Amazons. The lure was as strong to him then as it is now to the many thousands of us who visit for relaxation and introspection. Lower California, now just called "Baja," truly is the colophon of the world.

Gus Niemann and son Greg. - 1990's

Bonding with Bojo

"I was indeed a Baja buff. In my youth I had been drawn to Baja as my heroes had been drawn to Everest and the Amazon."

— *Jack Smith, "God and Mr. Gomez," 1974*

Greg and his older brother Fritz about the time they "played detectives."
Photo by Gus Niemann Jr.

THE DAY WE PLAYED DETECTIVE

ENSENADA, 1947

"There's another one," Fritz said, pointing to the sand in his authoritative manner that came with being the oldest kid in the family.

Indeed it was, another 2-3 foot long indentation in the sand where the thieves had temporarily dragged the fishing rods.

"For sure they went this way," I answered, recognizing the obvious sign.

I was only eight years old, and my 12-year-old brother was a smarter, wiser, more sophisticated grown-up. At least he was to me.

We were together in this, and this was not a game. We were hot on the trail of the family's stolen fishing rods. And the signs were leading up the beach from our camp to the small fishing village of Ensenada.

Each summer our whole family, Papa, Mama, and whomever of the nine kids born by then, spent two blissful weeks camping in the sand dunes at the mouth of an arroyo upon whose banks a slaughterhouse once stood. This out-of-the way location was then about two miles south of the town center. In later years the environs of the city of Ensenada grew to include our camping site. In my recent attempts to find the camp, I concluded that we were near where the current Cueva de los Tigres restaurant now stands.

We had the sandy draw to ourselves and camped under a flimsy shelter, a square palm-thatched palapa weathered by the elements. At the time we didn't even have a tent. Mama used boxes for a table and her "kitchen" was in the shade of the rustic palapa.

A privy was dug in a nearby sand dune; the ocean was our family room (this was in the days before anyone had TV anyway). But I most enjoyed the bedroom; we merely rolled the sleeping bags out, all in a row, in the sandy area next to the palapa. The millions of stars not visible from urban Los Angeles provided us with the evening entertainment as we drifted off to sleep. We especially delighted in seeing the meteors or shooting stars make fiery dashes across the black velvet sky.

Days were spent swimming, riding waves, beachcombing, exploring, playing "King of the Mountain" on the sandy hills and occasionally getting stuck by the tiny spines of the cholla cactus.

Mexican kids often joined us to play, just mysteriously appearing out of nowhere. At least I never figured out where "home" was to them. Unknown to us, we must have been watched by others, too, older and malevolent, but they kept their distance during the day.

We enjoyed the local kids. Despite a language barrier, Francisco, Juan, Lupíta and the others became part of our extended family and we played and learned from each other. We learned about the animals and plants, the shells and the tides. We taught words to each other. An important phrase for us became "Como se dice en Español?" which translates "How do you say this in Spanish?"

Another pastime was helping my dad and older brother catch fish. Our family was poor and the fish became an integral part of our summer diet.

Before our trip this year and with Papa's blessing and help, my resourceful older brother handcrafted two long surf-fishing rods. They were of fine bamboo supplied through the courtesy of Mrs. Hansen who lived down the street from our northeast Los Angeles home. Fritz mowed her lawn regularly so we didn't even need a dark night to forage in her huge backyard bamboo grove. She let him select two straight and sturdy specimens.

My dad bought the metal eyes and reel holders and thick colored twine. Then Fritz spent many hours sanding and staining the rods, meticulously tying on the eyes and cramp-ons with the twine, wrapping each with a pattern. One rod had yellow and blue wrapping, the other red and blue. Both had a thicker royal blue twine wrapped around the base for the handles. All my dad had to buy were a couple of reels and we were in business.

We caught fish daily with the two durable rods. I say "we" because sometimes my sisters and I would take turns fishing, usually to relieve Fritz and Papa. Sometimes we'd actually be holding the rods when something hit. It was a thrill I've never forgotten and still enjoy.

We caught perch, corvina and halibut. We also caught sting rays and shovelnose sharks. We kids became expert at digging up sand crabs for bait. Fishing became an integral part of each day.

That is, until the night the rods were stolen.

At night, the reels were taken off and put in the old family '36 Oldsmobile, and the fishing rods were laid to rest alongside the family for which they provided sustenance. Papa would carefully place the rods down next to his sleeping bag, in the narrow space between his and the next bag in line.

Then one morning we awoke to discover them gone, stolen right out from under our noses while we slept.

My brother is one determined individual, especially when it comes to one of his hard-earned possessions. After all the excitement died down, Fritz grabbed me and said, "Come on. It looks like their tracks go this way."

We walked down to the beach and saw two sets of footprints taking off to the north, towards town. Occasionally there was a depression or gouge in the soft sand near the prints. It happened frequently and we decided that the prints had to belong to the thieves because apparently they were allowing the rods to drag in the sand, thus making the depressions. Fritz and I decided to pursue them.

This was thrilling. We were the Hardy Boys out on a great adventure. We were going to nab the culprits. Who cared if we didn't have a weapon or a plan? We were determined.

Our minds conjured up the worst type of villains as we quickly hastened up the beach. The tide was coming in and in a few places their prints were obliterated altogether only to reappear farther up. We moved quickly while there was still the trace.

Folks who know present-day Ensenada have to imagine that in 1947 it was about the size that San Felipe is today, if that. Thus, when the tracks left the beach it was easy for us to see where they headed. At the time there were a number of deep sea fishing shops along what is now the tourist shopping street of Boulevard Lazaro Cardeñas. Fishermen arriving in town used to head straight for one of those shops to book trips and buy and rent equipment. Most of the outfitters are still in business, but have moved to the newer fishing piers.

We kids had been to town before. In fact, we had sometimes joined other Mexican kids who used to hang out on the old pier. When the full boats came in with exuberant, high spirited fishermen, we would line up and ask them for fish. That's how I learned the word "pescado," saying it imploringly to the fishermen, even though many were Americans. I was that incongruous blond kid in the crowd who would also sometimes be rewarded with a large fish I could proudly take back to camp.

We didn't go to the pier this day. The tracks led to the row of fishing shops.

We walked along the one main street in front of the shops, noticing that many rods were displayed in racks outside the front doors of these places.

It was the third shop where our hearts started beating a little faster. There they were, Fritz's custom rods, one with blue and yellow wrapping and the other with blue and red, in a rack by the door.

"Let's grab 'em," I said.

"No," countered a more conservative Fritz. "They'll say we're stealing them and we could go to jail. What about that?"

"Well, they stole 'em first," I said wanting a more swift justice.

"We better get Papa," advised the older, wiser sibling.

So we hurried back to camp and related excitedly that we had found the missing rods.

Papa and Fritz then jumped in the family Oldsmobile and rode off up the sandy arroyo heading to town seeking justice. I was devastated when it was determined that I was too young to go. "There might be a problem," I was told.

The shop owner turned out to be a big, gregarious, friendly Mexican whose immense stomach strained his shirt so that only one button was fastened. His natural smile turned to a frown as he listened with apathy to the tale of the stolen fishing rods.

He better represented the warmth of the Baja people than did those who dared enter our camp at night. He went outside, grabbed the rods and returned them with profuse apologies, saying that he had bought them from some young guys who had come in that morning.

My dad expressed concern that the shop owner would be out the money.

"No problema, Señor. This is a small town. I've seen those guys before and figured they were up to no good. I'll see them again and they'll be sorry," he said.

When my dad and brother returned from town with the rods and the good news, I sulked and refused to share in the joy. Finally I cried out, "I can track the thieves down and solve the crime, but I'm too young to go and get the fishing rods. I shoulda just taken them when I was there."

Maybe I should have, but then we wouldn't have met the owner, another caring Baja character who quickly became a friend of our family and remained so for years.

A Coming of Age in T.J.

Tijuana - 1956

I left the house in boots, grubby clothes and a backpack. I dared not dress in anything finer as it was to be a fishing weekend in the mountains — at least that's what we told our parents. But it was a seductive weekend of debauchery we teenagers really sought.

Our destination was an intriguing, exotic place, one which suggested sensuality and fascination, a most provocative town indeed — the Mexican border city of Tijuana!

We four teens were giddy heading south in Clem's old Studebaker. For 16- and 17-year-olds, this was definitely a grand adventure. For two of the guys it was a second trip, but it was my first.

South from Los Angeles, the freeway ended at Santa Ana. From there a two lane road wound through hills, up and down the main streets of all the coastal towns until we finally reached San Diego. It was mid-day Saturday before we approached the border.

Two-trip veteran Bill commented that last time he was here a San Ysidro liquor store had free passes to Tijuana's Caliente Racetrack. We stopped at the U.S. town on the border to see if they were still available.

A giant pad of these promotional freebies, good for $2 general admission at Caliente, rested on the liquor store counter. After we walked out, one lone pass was but half attached to the cardboard pad.

"Let's sell 'em," someone suggested.

"Great idea," countered another. Most of us worked after-school jobs but we were always broke. Grocery store baggers and the like, our average pay was only about 75 cents an hour.

After we anxiously crossed the border, tentative and nervous because of our age or lack of it, we made the immediate obligatory right turn and crossed the Tijuana River over the old, narrow concrete bridge. That put us on Avenida Revolution, then as well as now the tourist area. But we kept going that day, all the way out to the racetrack.

We each took some coupons and stood in front of the admission gate, where a sign clearly indicated a $2 admission. As gringos walked up, we approached and offered them a half price ticket at only $1.

While there were a few skeptics who doubted the veracity of our offer and preferred to pay full fare, we quickly sold most of the tickets, using the rest for our own admissions. It was good and fast income especially considering our menial after-school jobs.

The extra money also let us make a few bets on the ponies, something teenagers were not allowed to do at Hollywood Park or Santa Anita. In fact almost everything we did that weekend would be outlawed to teenagers in California. Therein was the attraction.

A park next to the racetrack was quite secluded and bordered with trees. We made note of it and decided to return there later, park the car and get some much-needed sleep. Also, if we got separated, this would be our rendezvous point. But for now, downtown awaited.

I quickly learned that Tijuana's Avenida Revolution was not the Baja of my youth; in fact this boulevard of temptation bore no resemblance to the sandy beach and rustic campsite south of Ensenada.

My father had mentioned that he and his brother had previously stopped in Tijuana in the early '30s during their several "jalopy jaunts" south of the border. This was, of course, before either was tempered by the restraints of marriage. But he did not go into any details.

Tijuana was still small in the mid-1950s, just a few curio shops and bars along the one main street. Unfortunately for most American visitors, even today that same street is the only thing most people see. They are unaware that Tijuana is currently a vibrant city of well over a million people, with shopping plazas, museums, cultural centers and art galleries.

Bars every few feet

But then, in 1956, it was bars we were looking for. And they lined the street every few feet. There was the Bambi Club, the San Souci, the Navy Club and so many more. Some were downstairs, some upstairs, but all were dark and full of delicious intrigue, especially for 16-year-olds.

Hawkers stood out front and barked, "Show time. Show time right now. Come on in. Pretty girls. Show starts now," and they'd usher us in.

A typical sign, found all over town, inviting visitors into Tijuana nightclubs.

We learned that regardless of when the hawkers indicated that show time was starting, we usually had a long wait before the music began and the lights got dimmer yet and semi-nude women stepped out onto the low stages.

We'd enter these bars, full of wonder, anticipation and excitement, all the while we tried to look blasé and sophisticated, which was hard to do when you were hyperventilating with excitement and also trying to focus your eyes in the darkness.

Once inside, we were immediately met by the aggressive bar girls. My first reaction was olfactory. They didn't smell like the girls at Benjamin Franklin High School in L.A. These professionals were drenched in heady overpowering perfumes that were actually quite tantalizing to a teenager.

They would grab your hands tightly or put their arm around your waist with practiced, suggestive squeezes. And they looked directly in your eyes suggesting femininity, promise and sex. It melted this randy kid.

Their job was to get you into a booth and get you to buy them a watered-down drink. All the while they would touch you, or caress you or kiss your neck. Of course, you were expected to buy beer too and watch the show and buy more drinks once the show got started.

WE WERE CHEAP

Their ploy would have worked too, as excited as I was, but we didn't have much money, we were cheap, and also had a little savvy.

So we would enter the booths with the girls. All the while they would plead for us to buy them drinks, touching us, stroking high up on our legs, trying to arouse us while hinting at more to come, if only we'd buy them a drink. We learned to touch back, to fondle the merchandise so to speak, and then emphatically say "No" to their drink demands. Spiteful, they'd jump up and leave, cursing at us and calling us "Cheapskates," so loud that no others would come over to be fondled.

We didn't care. There was always next door, or down the street. We loved the attention and the touching, but we were not about to buy watered-down drinks for these girls with our hard-earned, or hard-connived money.

We even rationed our own drinks if we could get away with it. The bouncers would usually insist that somebody order a drink, so one or two of us would buy a beer at each place, rotating at each bar. The night was long and even a beer at every other bar was plenty for us. We didn't want to get too drunk too soon.

The bars and nightclubs all smelled the same. They smelled of spilled beer which permeated the tables and floors, stale alcohol, cigarette smoke, the heady perfume and hair spray of the girls, mingled with body odors of the unwashed and the smell of excitement from those whose adrenalin was in overtime. Even the mildew from the old building itself added to the stench. All together it created a musky sensuality.

The floor shows were tame when compared to today's clubs in minimalls across America, from Portland to Atlanta, Denver to Dallas. In the sedate '50s motion pictures never even showed the skin now seen everywhere, even on network television. So seeing a flash of forbidden flesh was quite a thrill for us.

THAT IN-BETWEEN GENERATION

We were that forgotten, in-between generation. Our parents had lived through the Great Depression and we heard plenty about it during our formative years. Our older cousins and big brothers and friends' big brothers served during World War II.

During the later, tumultuous 1960s we had already returned from the military and were busy raising families. We have always more readily identified with the old-fashioned attitudes only a half generation older.

The difference in attitude between of those of us born just before WWII, and those born just after was so overwhelming that older brothers still have difficulty relating to younger ones. It was historic in that it was a most dramatic change in America. Post-war children were subjected to unbridled prosperity, and parents who had the means and inclination to spoil them. The formative years of these younger baby boomers was abet-

ted by the never-say-no-to-your-child mentality and advice of popular experts.

Our youngest brothers and sisters did not want for simple things like
we did. It was these younger brothers and sisters who got caught up in the
"me" decade and the Vietnam War that marked their growing up in a
permissive America. Our age group never heard of pot smokers or free
love, or LSD. We would never consider avoiding the draft or protesting
our government. Such attitudes, embraced by people only five and six
years our junior, were appalling to us. How did a country change so fast?

In the 1950s, sex was still treated with puritan restraints and our only
mood-altering substance was beer. One time we sneaked down to Main
Street, the sleaziest part of Los Angeles, to see a racy strip-tease show on a
big stage. A couple of baggy-dressed comedians telling corny, ribald vaude-
ville jokes were finally interrupted every now and then by much fanfare
and the opening of the curtain. A voluptuous woman would then take a
half hour and several different songs to take off gloves, hat, evening gown
and finally flash a pose in panties and pasties for a second or two. It was big
stuff at the time, but even we were disappointed in how tame it was.

T.J. DID NOT DISAPPOINT

We were sure T.J. would have everything. It did not disappoint.

We joined small groups of slightly-older sailors, who were not restricted
to day-time-only Tijuana visits in those days, in whooping and hollering
as scantily-attired girls in cumbersome high heels would take two steps
forward and two backward in time with the suggestive music. The stages
were like runways, only two feet high, and extending out over the tables.
After our initial five minute grope and groan session in the booths we'd
commandeer a stage-side seat.

A couple of times, in reckless abandon one of the sailors, sometimes
one of us, would make a spectacle by joining the girl on stage.

It was testosterone overflowing. It made for a fun and long night.

As the night wore on, we allowed the proverbial ubiquitous Tijuana
taxi driver to take us to a house with "lots of girls." The dirt road, just a
few blocks off the main street, was sandy and dark as we bounced up the
riverbed. The place now would be about the middle of the Rio Tijuana
Shopping Mall. Then amid the sagebrush a lone, wood-frame house ablaze
with lights and women lounging in the doorway greeted our headlights at
the end of the blackened road.

This was the place. Scared, bashful, shy, confident, swaggering, macho, nervous, excited, intoxicated and eager, we entered while the cabby waited.

Dawn was breaking by the time the taxi dropped us back off downtown. We found our car, drove to our shady park and tried to get a couple hours sleep crammed in that old Studebaker. That we actually dozed is tribute to how hard and long we partied.

I don't remember much about the ride home that weekend. I do remember telling my parents the fish weren't biting or some such gibberish. But as I looked at Papa, I couldn't help wondering if he and his brother ever visited the Bambi Club, or even if there was a Bambi Club back then. I never did find out.

Now, over 40 years later, I still remember many lurid details about that first of several exciting adventures into Tijuana, where my buddies and I grew up fast.

The Bambi Club is still open inTijuana.

Horses on the Bluff

Rosarito Beach — 1958

Vince and I scrambled up the rocky bluff from the beach. We looked back to enjoy the morning sun bouncing off the glossy ocean when the vibrant sounds of thundering hooves disturbed our reverie.

They were not buffalo, but about a dozen spirited horses galloping straight at us across the field. At first we thought they were wild, not seeing the Mexican kid astride one of the rear horses, whipping his steed with a piece of leather.

I remember wondering if they would ever stop their momentum before reaching and perhaps plunging over the cliff. But stop they did. Raising a tremendous cloud of dust the horses put on the brakes and stopped just a few feet from the precipice. Like the horses ridden by the female sidesaddle riders at a Charro rodeo, these horses raised their heads, put their feet together and lowered their rumps to brake on a dime. Most of these cow ponies, however, carried no rider and relied on instinct to bring them to that dramatic screeching halt.

Once we saw these animals headed directly at us, we crouched back behind the crest of the hill. When they stopped we dared lift our heads. Through the dust we were able to make out the kid who had driven this small herd to the brink of the cliff.

The boy, only about 10 years old, jumped off a horse that seemed way too big for him, walked up to us, smiled, and said in broken English, "You want ride horse."

Our relief at not being overrun by wild animals was another highlight of that impromptu camping trip to Baja. My older brother Fritz, then 22, and his buddy Dick were headed for the Rosarito Beach area and invited me and a buddy along.

49

Vince Baca, 18 like me, was eager to join us. He and I'd been to Tijuana a few times but together had never ventured south of there. In fact, I was a kid the last time I'd been below the border area.

It was the older guys' show, we learned, and Vince and I couldn't talk them into stopping at one of the Tijuana nightclubs on our way south. With regret, we drove right past the twinkling neon, busy streets and gaudy bars along Avenida Revolution.

Maybe nightclubs weren't on the agenda, but booze was.

We stopped in that last liquor store on the south side of Avenida Revolution just before the turn to the old road which wound south into the darkened hills. We bought some inexpensive rum, quart bottles of Coca Cola and a couple blue metal cups to mix our potions.

It was night as we drove through the little village of Rosarito Beach. Just south of town was a bar and a motel/trailer park (Rene's, a long-time landmark), and south of that, nothing for miles. We pulled off the road just below Rene's and made our way to the narrow beach.

There, at the base of the bluff we set up camp by pitching our sleeping bags on the ground away from the cobbles and the high tide line.

Then we sat around mixing liberal warm drinks (we forgot ice) into the utilitarian metal cups. As the night wore on the moon joined the millions of visible, brilliant stars in illuminating the landscape. Our campfire, which had aided the rum in providing warmth, also created dancing light to supplement the wondrous skies.

We were at once peaceful, powerful, content and happy to be alive. I don't believe Dick quite believed our stories about our earlier forays into Tijuana (He was quite a sheltered kid), but Vince and I enjoyed telling them anyhow.

It was a feeling of invincibility, of warmth, of a glad-to-be-in-Baja freedom, that we four reflected on as we kicked out the embers and snuggled in our bags for the night.

A pack of dogs woke us early. They barked and yipped and ran around in circles. They were lean and hungry strays staring, barking and snarling at us, standing their ground from only a few yards away.

A concerned Vince reminded all of us that roving packs of dogs like that can be vicious and dangerous. It got us all wondering.

I stretched from the warmth of my sleeping bag to grab a few cobbles lest they attack. But our alarm was for nought, as the dogs were probably more hungry than anything and once we started to ignore them, one by one they loped off down the beach.

It was still early when Vince and I climbed that bluff to survey our surroundings. We hadn't planned to go horseback riding, but this Mexican kid's hustle was irresistible.

"Okay," we said, and the boy set about finding just the right horses for us.

We boarded our selected beasts and clip-clopped off, leaving the adolescent holding the reins of his horse while the other horses stood around checking to see if anything interesting might be in the grass.

We rode all over Rosarito, down the beach and all around what was considered a town in those days. Aside from Rene's and the grand old Rosarito Beach Hotel, there was little else there.

Finally hungry, we rode to a small café across the street from the Rosarito Beach Hotel. It would later be the bus station in a city of over 100,000 people. Back then it was one of the few businesses in a small town.

We tied our horses to the post out front (we were not the only ones to do so) and pigged out on tacos and beans.

It was early afternoon before we returned the horses to the kid on the bluff. When we asked how much the rental was, he shrugged and said, "One dollar, Señor, one dollar each."

Vince and I looked at each other, smiled, and paid him. We also gave him some candy we'd bought in town and he quickly became the happiest kid in Rosarito Beach. They were simple times, those 1950s.

SONG OF THE SEA

CANTAMAR, B.C., MÉXICO — 1970-1998

"Hey compadre," the caller yelled into the phone that day in 1970, speaking with the enthusiasm that only Bob could generate, "I bought a trailer down in Baja, México."

Bob, as godfather to my son Steve, was in fact my compadre. This half Irish/half Mexican bundle of energy had inherited the "drink now/party now" instincts from both sides of his family and he constantly lived in the center of a whirlwind of activity. He'd earlier moved from L.A. to San Diego, and was now excitedly inviting us to check out his Baja trailer.

Baja — I'd only been a few times in the past decade, but many happy summer vacations were spent there in the mid-1940s. We used to camp on the beach in a sandy draw south of Ensenada. Sleeping bags on the sand faced the dark sky which was dappled with millions of stars. I was a child in a fantasy world. My brothers and sisters and I played with Mexican kids who taught us the rudiments of the language, starting with the obligatory cuss words.

My bathing suit became an appendage, never leaving my body for a full two weeks. I'd later return to school with dark bronze skin and bright sun- and salt-bleached blond hair. My memories were fond ones so Bob's invite was well received.

His new enterprise was in a trailer park about 12 miles south of Rosarito Beach. It had been developed in recent years by Alejandro Borja, who called it Cantamar, or "Song of the Sea."

Borjas pioneer Baja coast

"Borja" is the Spanish spelling of the notable Italian "Borgia" family which had an arm of the family in Spain. Señora Maria de Borja, the General Duchess of Gandia, had heard about the difficulties of the Spanish missionaries in developing the rugged Baja peninsula and donated a sizable sum for the establishment of three missions.

Soldiers named Borja from her household helped settle the peninsula for Spain. Many of the early Spanish families including the Borjas are still in evidence throughout Baja.

The Borja pioneering spirit survived and Alejandro Borja had been successful with several Pemex gasoline station franchises in Tijuana before he looked south about 30 miles (K-46) for a summer home.

Cantamar was developed because of the can-do spirit of Señor Borja. His first well at Cantamar was salty. Not dismayed, he sunk four more wells. All were salty. Rather than quit, he tried one more time. Aqua Dulce. Sweet water. The sixth well, and $15,000, brought results.

Someone suggested that Borja turn his summer home into a tourist community. "Some Americans came to me and asked if they could park their trailers, so I said to my wife, 'maybe it's a good business,'" the hard-working, far-sighted businessman recalled.

By August, 1960, three trailer spaces were leased. During the sixties, Borja built a 24 unit motel on the beach, a nearby swimming pool in which a waterfall cascading over lava stones actually cooled the generator that provided power to the whole place.

His Cantamar Pemex station became the only gas station between Rosarito and the outskirts of Ensenada and would be for over 30 years.

Borja can be called a dreamer, but not without being called a doer in the same breath. He gets grandiose ideas, and then goes ahead with them. The restaurant/bar he built at the entrance to the trailer park could not be complete without a large lighthouse, visible from miles away.

He wanted to light it, but was told by the government that once lit, it would have to be registered and maintained as a working lighthouse. Better to keep it unlit.

Original trailer spaces were cement slabs set at a diagonal off of four dirt roads sandwiched between the old road (libre) and the ocean. Alongside each slab was a dirt space to park one's car.

BUSTLING WITH ACTIVITY

My first visit found the place bustling with activity. It seems that many of the trailer owners, who paid the Borja family monthly space rent, decided to use their designated parking space to enhance their trailers. Thus the sound of hammering and sawing went on continually in the early years as enclosed patios were constructed. Soon most trailers had an adjoining cabaña or screened patio. By early 1971, three enterprising owners had even constructed small second floor rooms above their trailers.

After our indoctrination weekend, Bob let us use the place for a week. It was an idyllic and restful week, in contrast to the loud, continual party of our previous visit. My ex-wife and I found we liked it, both the party time and the respite, and looked forward to going again.

We were literally shocked into our next visit as a 6.4 earthquake rumbled through northeast Los Angeles in February 1971 causing enough damage to our house to scare us out of there for a few days.

"Hey Bob," I nervously asked, "Any chance of using your place in Baja for a few days?"

And so it was that my family and my former in-laws sought refuge from the nerve-wracking aftershocks in the little trailer community of Cantamar.

That's when we saw the sign: "For sale." It was a dreary looking silver trailer with an unpainted and ugly concrete block structure as an accompanying cabaña. Owned by two elderly men, its interior was dank, dusty and full of cobwebs.

But to us it was beautiful. We could paint it; we could make it habitable. My in-laws even decided to go in as half owners. We decided to make the sellers an offer. They'd wanted $1,000 for the trailer and structure and I would take over paying space rent to the Borjas, which at the time was $35 per month.

We drove out to the San Gabriel Valley somewhere and met the old men. They were unshaven and reeked of alcohol. The smell of cash had them salivating. Thus, negotiating we were able to buy the trailer and cabaña at Cantamar for $700 cash. Similar places, although cleaner, were going for around $2,000 at the time.

It's a satisfying type of work polishing and cleaning a new possession. We painted and added curtains. We sawed off the trailer hitch, added a small wall, and had concrete poured for a small patio.

Soon my in-laws lost interest and we became the sole owners. I thank them for their early excitement, as without it, we probably would not have made the decision to buy at all.

I wonder what Great-grandpa Bascom Stephens would have thought, that 80 years after his attempt to colonize Baja, that a descendent of his might finally do so. He probably would have approved.

My dad was tougher to please. He chided me for being in a sissy development, yet bragged to others how I had a place in México. Go figure!

A ROWDY CAMP CALLED CANTAMAR

The early 1970s were rowdy times at the camp called Cantamar. The dusty trailer village befit its residents. Alcohol was the common bond for many.

Gallon jugs of vodka and tequila and such were so cheap in México, heavy tipplers were attracted to all the rustic Baja campos, including Cantamar. Some weekends, many people on our street would never make it to the ocean, 100 yards away. The party would shift from one trailer to another, with usually a late afternoon lull as many would lie down to nap (read: pass out) before resuming the party for the evening drunkathon.

You couldn't walk from the end of one road to another without a beckon from a trailer full of inebriated neighbors. Some were retired military personnel. There were puffy-faced women and cackling old hags and one woman who walked like a stork. There were jaundiced men aged beyond their years, and young couples whose idea of a good time always included booze and drunkenness. At the time, I fit right in.

Throughout the years, there have been eccentrics in abundance. There have always been colorful characters, the drunks, the dreamers, the doers and others.

There was one old guy who was a world-class musician in his time, playing with and writing music for the biggest names in the business. But by the 1970s he was an old man who liked to drink. His 50-year-old son looked and acted like the fitness guru Jack LaLanne.

The son left the old man alone at Cantamar during the week and hid all the booze. He and his wife implored the neighbors not to abet his father's addiction. Oh yeah! Sure. Instinctively, drunks like to help other drunks. So as soon as his offspring left, the old man would wander door to door bumming just "one drink." You can figure out the outcome, and his son would get artery-bulging mad. It was probably the worst place in the world to leave the old guy.

And there was Frank Brendel, whose lifetime creating Hollywood special effects resulted in the Oscar for his work on the movie "Earthquake." The glittering Oscar statuette rested on his Cantamar mantel, scratched on one side, "...where I tried to clean it with a Brillo pad," he confessed to me. Frank by the way, is most likely the only Oscar winner to have also earned an Olympic gold medal — as a member of the rowing crew in the 1932 Los Angeles Olympics.

Julio Nieto, who looks 20 years younger than his mid-70s, still strolls the cobbled streets barefoot. Nieto, a direct descendent of the Los Nietos Rancho family of Long Beach, was married to another early California family, one of the Figueroas, producing three beautiful daughters. Two of the girls married other "Cantamar kids," helping to interlink the families of a Mexican beach community rather than those of the California pioneers.

That "Song of the Sea" is a seductive song as other "Cantamar kids" have also met and married. Now it's even a third generation out there, waiting for the sun to drop over Punta Descanso and the ocean to glisten with moonlight, as if darkness somehow might lessen the awkwardness of those teenage years.

ACTION WAS AT THE CANTINA

We called it the cantina, the El Faro (lighthouse) Restaurant and Bar, and it was the most lively place along Baja's Gold Coast. The bar was packed, the piano bar was standing room only, and the dance floor gyrated with body to body steaminess every summer weekend. Guards had to control the crowds.

There were nights some of us couldn't even find our way home from the place, only yards away. One morning I found a character we called Rocket Morton sound asleep in the iceplant just off the parking lot.

While the lighthouse still stands guard over Cantamar, the adjoining El Faro Restaurant is now a sedate grocery store with stacks of Bimbo bread looking out of place on the old hardwood bar.

We had Cantamar parties that turned into fiestas for the entire trailer park. Goats from the Tecate ranch owned by a Cantamar resident were barbecued in Hawaiian-type pits.

The whole area was one of reckless abandon. Nearby campers would often invade our sanctuary and race their dune buggies and three wheelers down our roads. On busy weekends we even had to lay 2x6 planks across the road to slow the intruders down.

Slowly things changed at Cantamar. The palm trees planted by Borja and his son Carlos began to grow, creating an overall tropical impression. To this day, houses must be built around the sacrosanct palms.

Power arrived and with it a new breed of Baja buff. We had to pay to hook up and the steep fees weeded out those unable or unwilling. But

Cantamar never looked back. That was the end of the trailer park and the beginning of the development.

A long list of unforgettable characters, both Mexican and American, helped people with their construction needs as trailers were being pulled out to make way for sturdy, concrete block homes.

A PLACE OF REFUGE

The trailer and cabaña became mine following a 1974 divorce settlement. I thought of selling but by this time was thoroughly inflicted with Baja Fever and found the diversion good therapy. My kids, Steve and Annalies, loved the place and on their weekends we'd swim, surf fish and roast hot dogs on the beach.

It became a great place to take a date and I made the most of that too, introducing several to a relaxing weekend south of the border.

Or I'd invite a group of single friends for a wild, party weekend. Thus, it became three different places, for three different moods. I liked each, fun with the kids, a quiet weekend with a date, and the craziness of a drunken party.

My wife Leila also became enamored with the Song of the Sea village, and in 1979 we chose to marry in nearby Rosarito Beach. The preacher at the last minute decided not to perform the rite on our Cantamar beach.

Leila quickly made many improvements as the years of hard living were tough on the old place. We also bought the lot next door which had just become available, giving us a patio and room for expansion.

While some Baja developments, like the trailer park at Popotla, retarded development by not allowing additions and building, Cantamar encouraged it. And it was a wise decision.

The 24-room hotel was turned into 13 condos and a beachfront row was added in front of the old trailer park for homes to be constructed. Later, all of Cantamar's trailers had to be covered if not removed. Residents were given a couple of years to put walls around their trailers, or otherwise camouflage them. Today, only a few trailers remain and they're hard to spot.

Never ones to sit still, Leila and I bought another trailer on the next street toward the ocean and moved into it, turning the original trailer into a rental for American vacationers. We then bought a third trailer, giving us two small rentals in addition to our new place.

Over time, we had the trailers of both rentals pulled out and solid two-bedroom houses constructed on the sites. As the vacation rental business demanded so much attention, we decided to sell them. We first sold our newer and nicer one (which by then was commanding $75.00 a night) in 1990, and the original place, in 1996.

Over time, the lots on either side of our new home became available so we bought them. We pulled out the trailer and in several major phases over a 16 year period constructed a large, beautiful home with an office and deck looking out over the breaking waves. It's my very favorite place to be.

Only memories of the dusty campo remain. The streets have long been cobbled, lovely homes peek out from swaying palms at the ocean, telephones are in, a delightful new restaurant has been built where the iceplant once provided comfort to Rocket. The Palmira has a gourmet menu, live music outside amid the palms, and has become a beacon for many expatriates along the Gold Coast.

Even the palm-fringed lagoon on the north edge of Cantamar seems more idyllic, and we no longer refer to it as the old slough.

Our adjacent Mexican village of Primo Tápia has grown and is interwoven with Cantamar, in geography and in economy. The Americans at Cantamar provide work and sustenance for the locals. And markets, restaurants, shops, bakeries and video stores are patronized by both.

The lobster village of Puerto Nuevo is only a mile up the road and has become a reference point for the entire area.

The whole Gold Coast is now being developed. High rises, unheard of even in 1990, are in evidence in Rosarito Beach, Calafia, K-38, Las Rocas, and so on down the coast. Even 20th Century Fox has built a movie studio at Popotla and reconstructed the ship Titanic for its first movie "Titanic," which along with earning Academy Awards, became history's number one grossing film.

Development up and down the coast remains far away for me as I relax on the top deck of my Cantamar home. I look past the crashing waves and see dolphins slowly cruising just offshore. I see pelicans patrolling the skies. I watch small birds flit from palm to palm, I feel the sun, and I think, "Thanks, compadre, for introducing me to my own Song of the Sea."

Steve Cuts His Leg

Cantamar — 1971

I was surf fishing out front, wading up to my waist and flipping my line out as far as I could. I was rewarded with a few small barred surf perch. Baiting a sand crab for one last cast (They're all that one last cast), I heard someone yell my name.

It was not a friendly "Hello, Greg," but an abrupt, frantic "Greeeeg" yelled loudly, and then repeated even louder. I knew something was wrong.

A neighbor approached the sea wall, saw me, and hollered to come quickly; something had happened to Steve. Ohmygod! Last I saw, my 9-year-old son Steve had been riding around the area on a mini-bike.

I grabbed my rod and fish bucket and started running toward the house. Halfway there my compadre Bob's van came flying down the road. "Drop that fishing rod and get in," he ordered.

Steve Niemann, a little younger than when he cut his leg.

"My kids'll get your stuff," he added as I jumped in the van.

I first recognized my wife Eileen in the darkened interior. Then I saw Steve, who had crashed on the minibike, lying on the carpeted van floor. His pant leg was ripped, as was the flesh on his shin, sliced back and laid bare exposing cartilage and bone.

Eileen and I both held, comforted and reassured Steve as Bob sped up the toll road north toward Rosarito, where the nearest doctor was in those days.

We tried to control shock and retard the bleeding, of which there was surprisingly little, as the van sped north.

"Damn that minibike," my wife said, seeking an outlet or her anxiety. We'd bought the temperamental little thing through a newspaper ad a couple months previous. It was tiny, had balloon wheels the size of a handtruck's, and a lawnmower engine that powered a link chain. Steve had fallen trying to negotiate a ditch but the engine kept going, digging the chain into his leg.

While it was probably the fastest time we'd ever made the 12 miles to Rosarito Beach, it seemed the longest. Steve was proud and stoic and took the pain well. We adults were not as calm.

Bob knew Rosarito well and pulled up in front of a Dr. Fragoso's office, a small, nondescript pastel building on the ocean side of the main street. We carried Steve in and the doctor attended to him right away.

Dr. Fragoso scraped the wound clean and sewed Steve's leg with a number of sutures. We waited. The surgical procedure took well over an hour and soon a groggy son with a big white bandage was gently laid back in the van.

Back in Los Angeles the next day Eileen wanted Steve's leg to be looked at by our regular doctor. Our doctor cut aside the bandaging, examined the wound and sutures and whistled. "Whoever did this job really knew what they were doing. It's a real masterful piece of surgery," he admitted in respect.

Eileen and I were not only relieved but impressed that a country doctor practicing in a rural community like Rosarito Beach could be so professional.

Our next visit south we stopped at Dr. Fragoso's office to pay him the remainder of his minimal fee and thank him again for such a dexterous job. I noted on the wall that he received his medical training at the University of México in México City. Obviously he could have established a much more lucrative big-city practice if he so desired. We're testimony that the community of Rosarito Beach is well served by his presence.

We did something else on that next visit. We sold that nasty old minibike!

Fighting Fowls and Bickering Birds

Dutifully, we guys were headed back to Cantamar when we got distracted. Our waiting spouses would be furious at our late arrival, now to be extended to several hours.

Robert, James, Ron and I didn't mean to be so distracted but the diversion smacked of illicit intrigue and delicious excitement and we just lost track of time.

We had been out to Ron's ranch near Tecate and were heading back to the highway, bouncing down the dusty old dirt road when we saw a Baja oddity. Instead of pickup trucks and old sedans, several late-model luxury cars were roaring up a similar nearby dirt road across a small valley, kicking up clouds of grit and dust to settle across the barren hills.

The first car was followed by two or three more. After yet another sedan bounded up the road and went around a hill, we were curious. So Ron turned left at the next crossroads to follow.

He'd bought his cozy little ranch, snuggled amid hillside boulders, rich clumps of cactus and gnarled oak trees the year before. His wife preferred Cantamar where they owned the trailer and cabaña across the street from me and Eileen.

James and Robert were L.A. friends of mine who had often visited Cantamar and also got friendly with Ron. They too had been afflicted with Baja Fever for many years. All together, we'd made several excursions to the idyllic little ranch which bespoke a simpler, rural era. I loved the ranch and envied Ron his providence.

The ranch had a modest main house and a bunkhouse across the dirt courtyard. There were a few simple gardens of peppers, tomatoes, corn and cactus, a well, a water trough which you could swim in, and a rocky hillside that overlooked a broad valley to the American side of the border. His caretakers, Lupe and his prodigious family, squatted in a pastel stucco box of a house near the drive-in entry from the olive-tree lined community road. They fed his few farm animals, a couple of pigs, three horses, and a few goats.

Each summer we'd go and butcher a young kid and bring it back to Cantamar. There we'd wrap it with palm fronds and prepare in a pit Hawaiian-imu style for a weekend feast that all Cantamar enjoyed.

Several times with our wives we spent the weekend out at the ranch, but the girls preferred the beach at Cantamar. This trip just we guys picked up some animal feed in Tijuana to drop off at the ranch and were headed back to Cantamar in the early afternoon.

Then our curiosity had us eating the dust from a new Cadillac winding around this seldom-used road. We wondered what was going on.

We didn't have to wait long. Around a bend we came across scores of cars parked in makeshift rows across a grassy field. Their drivers were headed to a nearby corral which had a partial wooden roof cover, giving it the appearance of a house without walls.

Rows of makeshift spectator bleachers, three or four seats high, filled the area where the walls would have been. In the center of all this was a circular fenced-in ring, maybe 20 feet in diameter and about two feet high.

Quickly and excitedly gathering around were the spectators, many rural campesinos with broad cowboy hats, well-worn jeans and cowboy boots. But an equal number were their better-dressed city counterparts, those whose fancy cars had lured us to this place.

It didn't take us long to discover what was going on. Several of the men held small roosters, constantly stroking them and running their fingers lovingly down their smooth feathers.

An illegal cock fight

We had stumbled upon an illegal cock fight. As gringos, even through my partners were Mexican-Americans, we picked up a few stares.

A couple of well-dressed young guys who were fluent in English approached. While teaching us the fighting rules and the betting etiquette, they also assured themselves that our presence was not threatening to their nefarious activities.

I really didn't understand why cock fighting was illegal — until I saw a couple of fights.

The cock handlers, or owners or groomers, gave mixed signals to their animals. They showered them with attention, stroking, whispering to them, even kissing their beaks. Then they plopped them down on the dirt where they were expected to fight to the finish, like Roman gladiators where only victory can prevent a brutal death.

The handlers reminded me of pimps who shower their hookers with lots of attention and a pseudo-love to convince them to give their bodies, their money and their self-respect until there is nothing more to give.

Before each fight the owners entered the ring, stroking their roosters' feathers, occasionally thrusting one forward to crow at the opponent. They did whatever it took to build up aggression.

The aggression was not wasted on the crowd. Aside from certain trainers' notoriety, a rooster's size and a bettor's hunch, it is pre-fight aggression that is often the prevailing factor for placing one's bets.

WAGERING WAS SIMPLE

We learned that cock fight wagering is simple. The roosters wore different colored bands. You don't bet with the house. You bet with each other. The guy next to you might holler, "I'll take ten on the green one."

You might answer, "I've got five of that," and that's all it takes for you to root for the rooster with the other colored band to peck the life out of the rooster with the green band. You settle up in a gentlemanly manner after each bout.

The roosters were goaded into action by their trainers. The men held their claws and circled their fighting birds closer and closer, round and round, occasionally thrusting the bird up to face its opponent beak to beak.

When the cocks were sufficiently agitated, the men let go and stood back. The crowd roared as the small animals went at each other. They circled like prize fighters, waiting for that opening, then attacked the vulnerable neck and head of their fighting prey.

Some fights were quick. Just a few pecks and the wounded rooster would flop over, endure a few spasms and die. Others lasted a long time with both birds suffering irreversible damage, even the victor bloodied never to fight again.

I was pleased to see that several times an owner would stop the fight and award what boxing would call a "Technical Knockout" to the opponent, thus saving his bird from certain death and allowing it to fight again.

The cock fight was fascinating, but I would never go again. I failed to see the need for the planned destruction of animals in the name of spectator sport. I've never attended a bullfight, nor do I ever intend to. I don't hunt. I fish but I eat or release what I catch.

Even though much of the cock fight activity repulsed me, all of us got caught up in the wagering. Soon the afternoon shadows grew long over the corral and the sunlight faded to a flat sky that soon began to darken.

It was night when we finally arrived at Cantamar. We were late and didn't call, so we expected the wives to be upset but they were irrationally irate. It seems that one of the more insecure wives kept getting madder and madder at her husband as we kept getting later and later. Next thing you know, especially since it was called to the other wives' attention all afternoon, they were all upset and angry.

These birds were bickering so badly when we arrived, I was tempted to return to the roosters on the hill. At least the fighting cocks weren't the wrathful hens we faced at Cantamar.

Ron was divorced shortly thereafter and I followed suit a year later. Yet I understand that the most insecure spouse that day is supposedly still driving her husband mad. Later, living in Orange County, I ran into Ron one day. "Haven't seen you in ages," I said, "You still have the ranch?"

"That was all I got out of the divorce, but I love being up there," he replied.

We reminisced a while about the good old, wild days down in Baja. "Hey, remember that cock fight we saw that time," I recalled.

He laughed and said, "I also remember how pissed our wives were when we got back. Ain't it great not having to worry about that kind of crap."

I chuckled. It was the day of the fighting fowl and the bickering birds.

Driving home after my encounter with Ron, I reflected on the experience. The rooster handlers gave mixed signals to their animals, expressing affection but demanding destruction.

The practice is as old as life itself. We all give mixed signals, especially in the area of domestic relations, saying, "No honey, I don't mind" when we really do mind.

Saying, "Have a good time on the ranch," but meaning "When those guys get together, they'll be up to no good." Saying, "See you in a couple of hours," when we really mean "See you when I see you."

Mixed signals among spouses can lead to frayed relationships, mistrust, bickering and divorce. To a haughty animal like a fighting rooster, those mixed signals may be the final ones they receive.

Contamar
Capers

Sunset at Cantamar. Photo by Leila Niemann

"If you enter Mexico without preconceived prejudices, if you can throw away the key to the clock and forget the calendar in this land of little hurry or worry, if you can embrace the Baja Californian for what he is, a pioneer in a poncho not very different from our own Western past... then you will love Baja, perhaps even as much as we do."
— *Tom Miller and Elmar Baxter, "The Baja Book," 1974*

Leila and Greg Niemann in 1996. Photographed by Debra Bergman.

A BAJA WEDDING

CANTAMAR — 1979

My bride answered the rapid Spanish with a bold "Sí," and smiled. The Mexican mayor then turned to me and read the same passage. Neither of us really understood what we were saying "sí" to, but we knew. After I said "sí," the mayor motioned to us that we were now man and wife.

Leila and I kissed to seal our union on that April day in 1979 while our dozen or so friends who were crammed into the Rosarito Beach City Hall cheered their approval.

First we thought about getting married in the cliffside gazebo in Laguna Beach, but made the decision to do it in México. We wanted to get married on the beach at Cantamar but we couldn't find a preacher willing to make the trek south. Even getting someone from Rosarito Beach proved difficult and exorbitant.

So Rosarito Beach it was, right in the city hall on a Saturday afternoon.

We invited some close friends along with my kids Steve and Annalies, Leila's son Ken and a couple of her Oregon friends. Rounding out the entourage, we added a few Cantamar associates giving them additional reason for weekend revelry.

Our new Orange County home was in escrow, and we planned a large reception there later.

When our post-nuptial reception announcements went out my dad called, seemingly hurt that he was not included in the actual wedding. But I was convinced his disdain for non-religious secular ceremonies would have invoked negative comments. I knew he approved of Leila and that pleased me. His approval shouldn't have mattered that much to me, but it did.

Leila and I arranged for the Mexican wedding several weeks earlier and arrived early the day before to take care of all the necessary paperwork.

Years ago when U.S. laws were more formidable, people crossed the border at Tijuana for quicky weddings. There, in small offices under blinking neon signs Americans sealed their vows for princely sums of about $20.00 or $30.00. What people actually got in those days were official-looking wedding applications that had to be recorded by the principals before anything legal would commence.

To do it proper in México was neither simple nor quick. In fact, as most Mexicans are Catholic they usually have two weddings, one the official civil ceremony which is binding by law, and the other the grandiose church wedding which forms the religious bond. Leila and I opted for just the civil ceremony.

The day before the wedding, we ran headlong into that debilitating, energy-sapping bureaucracy so prevalent in Latin countries.

"Ah, no problem, señor. First you take two copies each of your tourist cards and..."

"Wait a minute. We don't have tourist cards. We understand they're not needed in this area of México," I answered.

"Jass, but you need it to get married," the civil servant officiously replied. He went on to explain that we could get the tourist cards at the Immigration Office back at the border. We looked at our watches.

"Than joo haf to go to Cruz Roja for a physical. And than joo come back and I will issue the papers.

Great. So Leila and I sped to the border to pick up tourist cards. Stamp, stamp here, and a few signatures there and we were out of there. We still had to get to the Cruz Roja (Red Cross) for the physical, buy Leila's wedding dress, return to the city hall with all the completed documents and get back to Cantamar to greet our arriving guests.

The physical was daunting. Crammed into a side street clinic with the sick and infirm local citizenry, we waited, watching the minute hands on our watches spin around. The check-up was minimal, but they needed blood tests. For that, they sent us to a medical clinic a few blocks away, in a second floor office directly above a rowdy local bar.

With the blood report in hand we returned to the Cruz Roja where the report was assembled with our growing paperwork.

We dragged the whole file back to city hall. The same civil servant tried hard to find something else wrong but failed. We were issued the license and had our wedding time confirmed for the next afternoon.

Fortunately Leila had not only a good idea of the dress she wanted, but also a good idea where she could find it.

She chose a simple, but elegant and distinctively Mexican dress. It was a long white ankle-length gown with a broad band of colorful flowers around the hem. I would wear my charcoal gray suit, white shirt and tie.

We arrived back at Cantamar exhausted but exhilarated from overcoming the bureaucracy and with the knowledge that all was now in readiness.

Our friends dribbled in throughout the evening and we partied and partied, drinking and laughing until the wee hours of the morning. A hangover is not the best way to start one's wedding day, but that's what I did.

Midday we gathered out on the dirt road in front of the Cantamar house, Leila in her long white dress and me in my suit. Neighbors passed and made comment, most seeing me in shoes for the first time not to mention a charcoal gray suit and tie.

We caravanned up the old road to our date with the altar. But the Municipal Building had no pretense of an altar. As Policia and other emergency vehicles jockeyed for position in the minuscule parking lot outside the official stucco building, we parked on the dusty side street.

After a brief wait, we were led to an inner sanctum, the office of someone obviously important. As Rosarito Beach was not yet a city, it was the head of the Municipal Delegation, often referred to as the mayor.

Young for such an important position, the mayor also spoke English. Looking dignified in his gabardine leisure suit, he motioned us into his chambers. My friends gathered round and the ceremony began without delay.

The vows were written in Spanish and that's how the ceremony was conducted. The group stood there listening to us say "si" when directed, with their hands folded and looking as solemn as possible. Our kiss broke the tension and all knew that a wedding had just taken place, whether anyone understood it or not.

Cops exiting patrol cars and tourists strolling down the main street were equally amazed to see a small group of dressed-up gringos come out of the city hall throwing rice and acting silly. We didn't care. We were married.

The group went on to Cantamar and Leila and I stopped for a drink at the Popotla bar where we looked out to see waves crashing on the rocky shore. I needed a drink, to lessen the pain of the hangover and to quell my jittery nerves over the major step just taken.

Back at the house, we continued the revelry. The late afternoon soon became night and everyone wanted to go down to La Fonda's for some music and dancing.

By this time I was in no condition to do anything. I'd had plenty to drink and the seriousness of my actions weighed heavily upon me. I was in love with Leila and knew that my party times would diminish if I assumed the responsibilities of marriage as seriously as I knew I would. I just hadn't really planned to be a party-pooper quite so soon.

I rebuked the appeals and pleas for me to go. I really needed to sleep and Leila decided to stay back with me. I told her to go too, that I'd be asleep in five minutes anyway. Plus her friends were just here for a couple of nights, whereas she and I would have many nights together.

"Go, go, have fun," I implored. "See you all later," I mumbled, stumbling towards my bed. So the entire entourage, including Leila, all went to La Fonda's while I slept. How's that for a romantic wedding night?

The original trailer.

Running a Vacation Rental

Most of my Baja experiences are positive, but one episode became such a source of frustration I have to share it. The frustration was not so much Baja-induced, but nurtured by those decidedly American qualities of ambition, drive, hard work and entrepreneurship.

I recently met a new Cantamar neighbor who said he was looking to buy a second Baja house.

"We'd love to have a rental here too," he said, as his pretty wife nodded assent.

I winced. "It's a lot of work," I countered diplomatically, "We had a rental here for years and when it sold last summer the relief was enormous."

Some people however, cannot be dissuaded from what they think will be a fun and profitable enterprise. Leila and I told them it was rarely profitable, and the fun wears off real quickly. We tried to convince them, but I heard through the Cantamar grapevine that they just made an offer on a place down the street from me.

I've actually had a rental at Cantamar since 1971 as my ex-wife and I sometimes rented out our original trailer and cabaña. In those days it meant us having a big cabinet at the rear of the cabaña where we could lock up a few of our personal things every time we left.

As rustic as the place was, we were only able to charge $15.00 a night. Even at that, we had people complain who imagined they would be getting Marriott-type amenities. That unrealistic-expectation mentality never ceased.

Then when Leila and I married, we spiffed the place up with a new roof, paint, carpet, new furniture, drapes etc. After we moved a block away, we dedicated that original dwelling into a rental. We started charging $25.00 a night and filled the place up each summer.

But the trailer was old and small. The tiny bathroom was in the center with minuscule bedrooms on either side. The cinder-block cabaña was one long room: living, dining and kitchen. That was it.

The trailer was so old, the bathroom floor was like a trampoline and we were afraid that some day, especially with a heavy person, the commode would fall through to the dirt, astonished renter and all. The shower was rusted so bad that no matter how many times I painted it, it was still a bucket of rust.

So we had the trailer pulled out and donated to the Rosarito Beach Charros Association. Years earlier I had purchased the lot next door, so onto the solid cabaña we built an adjoining two solid bedrooms, a hallway, and a tile bathroom. The cabaña was strengthened and remodeled with new kitchen sink making for a total real cute house of about 900 square feet. Out front a wall and gate enclosed a concrete patio and cobbled off-street parking.

The new house became all-electric and we purchased an electric stove, electric water heater and built a pila (water reservoir) with an electric pump.

We put two single beds in the front bedroom and a double in the rear one. The couch in the living room was a hide-a-bed, so we advertised it as a six-sleeper.

Now we were charging $50.00 a night, with a two night minimum. We advertised primarily in the *Baja Times* because we had nothing but problems with people who had never been to México. About 50 percent of our business soon came from repeat renters and/or their referrals.

Interested parties would call our Orange County home. Leila would then go into the spiel, describing the area, the house, the furnishings, etc., which took considerable time. Sometimes snooty people hung up when they learned the $50.00 furnished house was not ocean-front, but about 100 yards away. Pity. . . .

We tried to screen prospects by refusing to rent to groups of young single people. The youngest had to be 25. We also insisted on a maximum of six people including kids. We had to ask them how many people, because if you told them the limit was six they would always say six or fewer. Unfortunately, we found the majority of people would lie to us and bring carloads.

If the callers were interested, we would send a brochure which answered almost any question they could have, directions, what's provided, a check list for departing, insurance and shopping information.

We'd ask them to mail two checks, one for the agreed amount, and a

$50.00 security deposit. Later, we would return the security check when they returned the key. We usually did all this by mail, unless time prevented it and other arrangements had to be made. When we received the money, we'd send the key.

INHERENT PROBLEMS

Of course, cleaning became a problem. We asked renters to leave the place as they found it. Some did. Some even cleaned it better. Many did not, leaving sandy floors, dirty bathroom and kitchen, articles of clothing and trash strewn about.

Our rental arrangement was always noon to noon, leaving no doubts as to when occupancy should occur. If people arrived early they had to hang out unless it was vacated earlier. Sometimes departing people would load their car and stay at the beach longer. Even so, there were a few problems with the transition too.

When people left and others arrived on the same day, it was difficult if not impossible to check the premises for clutter and cleanliness between each tenant. I had hired cleaning ladies and asked them to check for me and clean when needed. But that was difficult to do given slim time frames, which usually occurred on a weekend. I often made special trips just to make sure it was clean. Of course, undoubtedly the one we missed would turn out to be the problem.

When we still had the trailer, two butane tanks provided stove fuel. When one tank emptied, you just switched the other one on. I constantly had to make sure there was plenty of butane.

No matter how many notes and explanations I made, people could never figure out how to change the butane tanks. Most often they'd switch tanks and not indicate that they had done so by moving the sign from one to the other. The next people would of course run out. You needed the sign because it was hard to tell by lifting the tanks for weight.

Butane stoves usually need matches to light them and even with box matches in a holder and a handy nearby sign, people would complain that the stove didn't work. Even when we got the electric stove, they would forget to flip the switch on, not reading the instructions.

Aside from butane and general cleaning, I spent most of my "relaxing" time in Baja getting five-gallon bottles of drinking water from the store and resupplying the toilet paper.

I had a bottle dispenser for drinking water and kept a spare alongside. A water truck comes almost daily and for a few cents, the driver will even put the bottle on the dispenser for you. I urged people to replace the water, yet in all those years only one person did buy water to leave for the next person.

Most often both bottles would be empty and I would have to load them up, drive to the store and wrestle full water bottles to the house. I replaced water and toilet paper almost every trip to Baja. Once I broke a full bottle in my Jeep making quite a mess. Worse, once I broke an empty bottle on my toe necessitating three stitches.

Our renters went through large packages of toilet paper rolls faster than I could imagine possible. I was buying and restocking every other week. Of course, most of these were those nice folks who assured us of only six people when they meant six carloads.

If you've ever slept on a hide-a-bed, you'll know what I'm talking about. After about two months even a new one seems to break down and all you feel is this bar across your back. We bought several hide-a-beds, and were amazed at how quick it was before people started complaining about them. I would check and concur that the floor was more comfortable. We could not find a moderate priced hide-a-bed that was comfortable and eventually substituted a couch, essentially converting a six-sleeper house to a four-sleeper.

Other inherent problems were trying to keep a barbecue clean. Only two people in all those 15-plus years bothered to clean the barbecue. I even provided two barbecues so I had a longer time between my cleanings.

Weeds also grew between the cobbles and around the side of the house. I had to find a local worker to pull them for me, or more often just did it myself.

Bugs, insects, mosquitoes and cobwebs seem to thrive in the damp ocean environment, especially in the summer. If there was considerable time between rentals, I would have to spray for insects and knock down cobwebs.

Problems with tenants

The biggest problem with a weekend rental in México was the party-time mentality of the visitors. Neighbors, some of whom lived there full time, complained.

We rarely told people that our own home was but a block away and that we would also be in the area. We would show up at our house to find carloads of people over at the rental. We found that well over 50 percent of our tenants lied to us, and that's just the ones we discovered.

Once while cleaning we found the remnants of marijuana, and México is very strict about that. I've even seem them confiscate one trailer where drugs were used. The next year those same people wanted to rent again and we kept putting them off. Finally after they tried having different members of their party call, we had to tell them they were not welcome.

Or we'd tell people please not to bring their dog.

They'd say no problem, then bring Fido anyway. Of course, Fido would go out in the flea-infested street and invariably bring fleas into the house to irritate the hell out of the next people.

Breakages were not too troublesome but from time to time we'd have to add more cups and glasses. Once, two girls broke the overhead light having a pillow fight. But the mother informed us, was apologetic, and asked me to take it out of the deposit.

My favorite story involving damage to the rental was when some young people slipped through our screening process. We arrived a couple of days later to discover the door to the bedroom was missing. A neighbor said he saw our tenants carrying a door to the beach. There, on the beach, we found the remnants of a huge bonfire that I'm sure kept them warm. In the middle of the ashes was my doorknob!

When we withheld their deposit to buy a new door, they threatened to sue us. Leila said, "Go ahead, make my day," or something to that effect. They never did, however.

We were sued a couple of times. One party wanted their money back because they bought sour milk at the store and saw policemen carrying automatic weapons. So they beat a nervous and early retreat back to the comfortable U.S. Another moved to a motel because they were scared when a cat got on the roof. (Those are among the many reasons we quit renting to people who've never been to México.)

The only lawsuit we lost was when Leila had just bought a new space heater. At that time only one working heater was in the house, so Leila offered to drive the new one to the renters before they left. They said don't bother, and then sued when it got so cold that Thanksgiving weekend they went to a hotel. They chose the most expensive hotel in San Diego, so here again it seemed obvious we rented to people who never should have crossed the border.

Our instructions asked people to flick on all the electric switches by the rear door upon arrival, and turn them off upon departing. Still, people would reach in the refrigerator and turn that setting off too. The next people would then complain about the refrigerator not working. We had to duct tape the knob where it should be. Or tenants would "be helpful" and unplug things to the consternation of the next folks.

Cantamar Capers

Or they'd be real nice and leave a vase of flowers in the center of the table. Isn't that pretty? But two weeks later when the next person would arrive, the messy pedals and the odor of the stale water was gross.

Sometimes nice people would turn off the water coming into the house. Then, of course, no water is replacing that in my pila. And when the pila goes dry, the motor would stop and the house would have no water. Nobody could ever figure how to turn it back on.

A LOSING PROPOSITION

We had been paying space rent to Cantamar for the rental and it was going up each year. In addition I had to provide insurance, pay a maintenance fee, taxes and electricity. Then to discourage weekend rentals, Cantamar began to assess a 20 percent fee on gross rental income.

We needed to gross over $300.00 each month just to break even, losing money each of the last two years. We made money in the summer and lost it in the winter.

In the winter I was mad because some months there would be zero income. It would rent a few days around Christmas and New Years, maybe a couple of weekends in February and then maybe Easter week.

In the summer the income was better but the work was incredible. About mid-April the phone would start ringing. All summer, up to September we would get two or three calls every day. The problem was each call took time. If the messages were on the answering machine, it was costly calling all over California (and beyond) to answer each call.

Then they all wanted the same weekends, either Memorial Day, 4th of July, or Labor Day. We would get 50 or 60 calls for each of those three weekends and yet might have it sit vacant the weekend before or the weekend after.

People even called us at midnight Friday and as early as 6 a.m. Saturday on those holiday weekends hoping it might be available. Drove us crazy.

Like an albatross over our heads, we had to keep it rented to recover some of the costs. Like a mistress, it demanded attention and we could never relax while it needed it.

When we first started renting, there were only a couple hotels in the Rosarito-Gold Coast area and very few houses were available. Competition arrived in the area seemingly overnight in the late 1980s and Baja visitors soon had innumerable choices. Our income plummeted for several years, and by that time we were running two vacation rentals.

Can you imagine having two such rentals for several years? You can almost double the aggravation I've outlined here about just the one. We sold the newer one in 1990 and also decided to sell the original at that time. But we only tried halfheartedly.

Finally we got serious and kept dropping the price until we had a buyer. As it turns out we received a little more than it cost us to buy and build it. And we sold for cash, too.

As I told my new neighbors, "The relief is enormous." Cantamar for me has changed from a perpetual job-site to a relaxing place. Maybe I should let them read this before they commit any further.

There's a lot to be said about the simple life so typical of the Bajacalifornio. The need to get ahead, to ambitiously embark on an economic enterprise seems more of an American pursuit. I learned the hard way, "Simple is better."

WEALTH AND AN OLD MAN

CANTAMAR — 1986

My mother always loved to travel. Since she and my father divorced, she's been happiest spending time with her brood, visiting first one kid and then another. And if they were to head off on a trip somewhere, so much the better. At the slightest opportunity she'd be ready to go. Sometimes she'd remind me of an eager puppy and would usually be the first one in the car.

On a visit to Cantamar she and I strolled the cobbled streets, reminiscing about our large and varied family. We talked and walked. I was showing her about the area since it had been a while since her last visit.

I also talked about my job, my Cantamar house, how we were fixing it, and other things that were important to me at the time. We talked about the Baja of my youth and how she and Papa discovered the simple life on their many camping trips on Mexican beaches. She mentioned how such fine homes and fancy restaurants in the area were a far cry from the rustic lifestyle of generations past.

While walking about, we approached Santos, an old man with a broad-brimmed hat who toiled daily at keeping the streets clean. This day Santos was meticulously picking weeds from between the cobbles with a small tool.

Other times, he'd rake leaves and detritus accumulated from the afternoon winds into a homemade dust pan common in México. Made from a square gas can, one side is cut off at a diagonal and nailed to a broom handle, so that the broad, flat part of the can scoops the litter.

Or sometimes he'd pick up fallen palm fronds and haul them to dry out so that they might be used for roofing material.

Whatever the task, Santos always performed it in the same slow steady fashion.

Whenever I would pass and say "Buenos Dias" or otherwise greet him, his face would break into a big, broad smile and he would make slight condescending bowing motions which made me uncomfortable.

When I introduced Santos to my mother, I realized I'd never really known him before. His dramatic and emotional reaction startled me. He jumped up, hugged her, hugged me, all the while muttering to me that I was so "rico" (rich). "Que rico," he repeated while moisture came to his eyes.

What was going on, I wondered, and what was leading this man into thinking I specifically might be rich? I was proud of my successes in life and what I had been able to accumulate, but had this guy seen my profit and loss statement or something? Or did he assume all Americans were rich, which by the standards of a Mexican laborer we are.

Then it dawned on me. I was associating rich with money and material goods.

To Santos and thousands like him all over Baja, all over México, rich had a different meaning. He said his mother had died years ago and that he still felt her loss. He went on to say how lucky I was to have my mother. That I had the wealth of family.

He gave me another big abrazo (hug) and confided, "You are a rich man to have your mother. Family is the most important thing in the world."

I walked away shaken, but stimulated. That day I learned some values I have never forgotten. Whenever I get caught up in the day-to-day American accumulation of toys and status and property, I often think about the simple caretaker named Santos.

Santos knows that the secret to wealth is measured by the number of family members and friends. His knowledge and acceptance of that simple truism makes him one of the richest men I know.

His wealth can never be taken away.

Author's mother, Gladys "Moma" Niemann, inspired caretaker to reminisce on the wealth of family.

Cantamar Capers

A SMASHING BIRTHDAY PARTY

CANTAMAR — 1990

It wasn't quite as grand as her 40th, but Leila's 45th birthday party was a smashing success. In more ways than one.

Leila doesn't drink much, just a little Kahlua on social occasions. And she rarely has more than a couple of those. So you can imagine my surprise when I saw her staggering across the dance floor, laughing and taking long sips direct from a whiskey bottle. I was stone sober as I had quit drinking about 10 years earlier.

"Uh oh," I thought. I really hadn't noticed how much she'd been drinking and immediately thought about how to get her out of there. This would certainly have been a first.

Just then she flung the bottle against the door and it shattered, creating a sudden and shocking silence in Cantamar's palapa bar. The crowd was as dumbfounded as I was. Leila laughed. Then Paul, who was nearby, abruptly produced a beer bottle and bashed it over his friend Vince's head.

Ohmygod, what had this party deteriorated into? A few more bottles and more shattering. All our neighbors and friends were speechless, except Leila, Paul and Vince, who were laughing with the knowledge of an inside joke.

I should have realized earlier that something was up when we'd invited Paul, an old friend who worked at a Hollywood studio and was a die-hard practical joker. That should have been a clue when the bottle smashing commenced at the party.

We had invited a few friends down to help Leila and a couple other neighbors celebrate their August birthdays. We put Paul and his buddy Vince in one of our guest rooms, other friends Lorna and Jodie in another and others in our nearby rental.

Several times that afternoon I'd caught Paul, Vince and Leila in hushed conversation but they would change the subject when anyone else approached.

The pool-side palapa bar was the place to be that night and we Cantamar dwellers held proprietary claim to it.

It was a circular room, with tables and chairs placed around the edges, leaving room for dancing in the middle. The narrow bar jutted out behind the round palapa, overlooking the pool. We had several parties there of late and similarly we set up tables by the door for a pot-luck dinner.

It was a warm summer evening and many people representing a cross-section of Cantamar age groups were in attendance to celebrate the three birthdays. The food was wholesome and plentiful, the music too loud, and the dancing a frolicsome diversion. Altogether it was a fun night — until the shattering bottles created an instant somber hush.

Finally the laughing perpetrators let the others in on the joke. Paul bashed a bottle over my head. Nothing. I mean it was soft; I hardly felt it. He picked up pieces of the broken bottles which I now noticed were too small to be glass shards. "Sugar," he laughed. "They're breakaway bottles from the studio."

We all breathed a sigh of relief when we learned that this destructive rampage was a rehearsed choreographic stunt designed to shock the unwary. It worked. I'd give it a 9.9 for shock value. With the excitement from the diversion over, we all returned to enjoying the party.

But I saw a couple of tables on the far wall where some of our older residents sat, still looking on in consternation. I don't think the news that the incident was a planned shocker had reached them and they continued looking at us with a mixture of bewilderment and disapproving resolution.

I mentioned this to Leila and suggested she go enlighten them lest they think she went bonkers and became a violent drunk overnight. This she did and all the old folks were soon laughing with the rest of us as Leila left their tables.

And I guess displaying a unique sense of humor didn't hurt Paul's chances with romance that night. After the bottle hurling settled down, he began to dance with Lorna. It took a few years, but they finally wed and Leila was matron of honor.

At weddings, people invariably ask whether you are friends of the bride or groom. At this wedding I enjoyed answering, "Both, you see one night we had this party."

The View from The Deck

My home is smack dab in the middle of the Cantamar development, about 100 yards back from the ocean. Sometimes people ask why I did not strive to be on the water's edge, thus socially confirming my standing and personally affirming my status.

It's a long story, but I'm quite content where I am and enjoy a killer view from my deck not enjoyed by those limited to the singular attraction of the pounding surf.

Leila and I originally leased our homesite when it was a large triple lot with a trailer anchoring one end. Over a period of almost 20 years we purchased the lot outright and built the home in several phases, now and then earmarking funds for the project. We ultimately ended up with a much larger home than any on the oceanfront, and with a second floor, not allowed on front row lots.

Unknown by many, a few caveats imperil those in front. Most days there is an unrelenting and constant afternoon offshore breeze, which blows sand particles off the beach onto the front row patios. It chases sunbathers indoors. But those just inland behind the first row of houses rarely notice it.

Another tradeoff for a front row house is a lack of privacy. Friends, strangers, beachwalkers, lookyloos and vendors constantly ply the beach, even stealing the concentration needed to read a book.

But the worst problem is when a winter storm strikes during the extreme tidal fluctuations. In December and January high tides can be seven feet above normal and if a storm hits, especially one with high winds during those times, you've got flooding. In 25 years, I've seen the front row flooded on three separate occasions. One couple was frightened but not hurt as they were washed through their house with the door-smashing ocean.

My favorite room

When I show people my home I save the best for last. I love my second floor sanctuary, a combination office/library/family room with view windows, but the second floor has a more important function; it supports the third level deck. The deck is my favorite room and the crowning highlight of my home tour.

It's not that large, perhaps 25 x 15 feet, and along with a few plants and knickknacks, has a table with four chairs, two padded lounge chairs and two padded swivel chairs. We sometimes enjoy our morning coffee at the table or play cards with guests there, listening to the sounds of the surf.

I love to lay in the afternoon sun and read, occasionally glancing about to notice something I've never seen before. The view is omnidirectional and as I move about the deck, the vantage point affords an entirely new vista every few feet.

A broad swath of ocean dominates the western view, bright blue out to the horizon. Sometimes I'll see white caps on the waves form and begin to chop the ocean, knowing about a half hour later the afternoon winds will begin to ruffle the palms.

I can see waves breaking around the rock, El Pilon, that juts in the center of Descanso Bay. Occasionally I see schools of dolphin playing as they work their way north and south just outside the breakers. I've never seen a whale from the deck, but I have from the shore at Descanso Point. They rarely come inside El Pilon anymore. But someday, I'll see one who will decide to venture closer.

I can see small fishing pangas usually dashing to and from the kelp beds along the coast. Tankers and cruise ships can appear large upon the horizon, pushing on at a steady clip. The popular Carnival cruise ship from Los Angeles to Ensenada makes its appearance at regular weekend intervals.

I can see waves crashing and surfers riding the fine beach break out front and people on horseback bouncing down the beach. Sometimes pelicans will skim the surface like large ungainly airplanes, tilting their wings like bombers in their search of prey.

Seagulls, cormorants, terns and other birds of the ocean ply the sky, gracefully swooping and gently flapping their wings to soar like gliders on the thermals created by the collision of cool ocean gusts with the warm air above the land. Small birds anxiously flit from one palm tree to another.

The ocean view to the west is climaxed each evening with a sunset so brilliant that Kodak loves my wife, so often does she photograph it. Unfortunately, during the summer the sunset is diffused as it drops onto a marine layer far offshore. But in winter it is magnificent and colorful. From the green flash at the moment of setting, the sky changes from coral to tangerine to a bright orange. Sometimes clouds provide a backlighting thus intensifying the drama and creating a more lingering warmth.

So far those with a front row seat to the ongoing ocean pageant can match or top my view. But the rest is mine.

Fields, mountains and hills

To the east is a valley with farms, ranches, fields and mountains and golden hills on all sides.

El Coronel, a high peak seen from as far away as San Diego, dominates the landscape, adjoined by a volcanic-looking dome and a rocky spur on its eastern and southern flanks.

Cattle and horses graze the slopes and fields while the deeper greens of the valleys signify crops of tomatoes, chiles, nopales cactus, peppers, cilantro and squash, much of it destined for American markets.

Just inland is a nursery and a greenhouse next to fields that in spring sometimes come alive with multicolored flowers. Farther up the valley are olive trees, sycamores and a few large eucalyptus trees.

The view east means sunrise, and the rolling hills bask in the salmon glow of a new day as the sun begins to kiss this area of coastline.

Bisecting my view of the valley and hills is the highway. The old road and the toll road to Ensenada run parallel here. I can see traffic entering and exiting the Cantamar toll gate. Cars are whisking excited tourists to weekend getaways while shared taxis full of local residents stop to squeeze in just one more person.

Busses and trucks can be heard as well as seen. Large tractor-trailers downshift for the Cantamar hill, sounding like motorboats without mufflers, or the mouth of a balloon being held snug while the air escapes, creating a different symphony with each gear.

I can see the old road bridge over the lagoon, which because of its narrowing has been the site of numerous crashes over the years.

Twice a year, in April and September, when I am not participating I can watch the thousands of lycra-clad cyclists in the Rosarito-Ensenada 50 Mile Bike Ride from the comfort of my own deck.

I can see two villages from my deck. The Ejido Primo Tapia, which sprawls across the barren hillside to the south, is home to many of the area merchants and construction workers. Many times I have driven its steep streets to take a worker home.

Farther to the north is the brickmaking village of El Pescador, where brick kilns sit beside almost every house. El Pescador bricks help fuel a continuous building boom along the Gold Coast of Baja.

At the end of my street to the immediate north is the Cantamar Lagoon. We used to call it the slough, but now that we're gentrified, lagoon sounds better. I can see ducks swimming its calm waters. I can see the palm- and reed-lined shore where a Mexican movie company once shot a scene depicting a boat arriving in the jungle for the movie "Maria Metalla."

To the north where the point of land comes down to the ocean is the Punta Descanso, an important landmark in the development of Baja California. I can see the Calafia restaurant and the tower beyond it.

My view south spotlights the Palmira restaurant, where I can glimpse people dining outside. Nestled amid large feather date palms which provide a roof for the summertime band, the Palmira is a favorite for expatriates along the coast.

The Cantamar entrance next to the restaurant has been enhanced with a waterfall and fountain, adding to the tropical flavor of the area.

A dominant feature of the Cantamar landscape has been the lighthouse, built in 1969. While inside it looks abandoned, stairs rusting from non-use, from a distance the sparkling white tower still evokes a commanding presence over its domain.

AROUND AND ABOUT CANTAMAR

The most interesting views are not north, south, east or west, but around and about. I can see a good many of the 100 or so Cantamar homes. I can see tile roofs, rounded domed turrets, brick fireplaces, graceful stairwells, satellite dishes and patios. The jumbled architecture runs the gamut from hastily thrown-together small wood dwellings to elegant and beautiful homes.

I see people preparing barbecues and relaxing on their decks. Other sunbathers are as zealous as I am in spending time just laying out on their decks.

There are always workers. On weekends it's the Americans, making improvements, or repairing roofs, or painting gates. During the week it's usually locals hammering or sawing, having been contracted to build or remodel yet another house.

The palm-trimmers are most interesting to watch. They shimmy up the 40-50 foot palms, cutting dead fronds as they go. When the winds come up, they undulate back and forth like circus acrobats, still cutting as they sway.

The Cantamar developer planted many Washingtonia fan palm trees several decades ago and continues to raise them by the lagoon. Cantamar palms now grace most of the developments along the Gold Coast. One of the few rules regarding construction at Cantamar is that palms are sacrosanct. You may not cut one down, and many houses have been built around the graceful trees that signify Cantamar.

Along with the fan palms are the plants. Gardens of all varieties of succulents, ice plant and cactus dot the area, each blooming at different times of year. Banana trees and bird of paradise plants aid the palms in providing tropical splendor. Splashes of brilliant bougainvillea, some orange, but most the shocking lavender or pink drip over walls onto the cobbled streets, like spilled paint on an unfinished canvas.

Sturdy geraniums from white to red to bright hot pink combine with apricot-hued hibiscus plants to add to the palette seen from my deck.

Another view is up, into the bright baby-blue sky, that following its colorful metamorphosis into night provides yet another spectacle. Here, far from a city, the sky blackens, forming a canopy to allow thousands of stars to shine and glisten and force your acceptance of their existence.

The view from my deck is a splendid view. Once in a while I'll enhance the details with binoculars, but most often the visual overload suffices without them.

I have it all, and while I'm not quite right on the sand, it's but a short walk away. Excuse me. I've got to go. Right now I see a kid on horseback leading some cows up to a higher pasture. Think I'll watch those cows going up that steep hill.

Along the Gold Coast

ALONG THE GOLD COAST

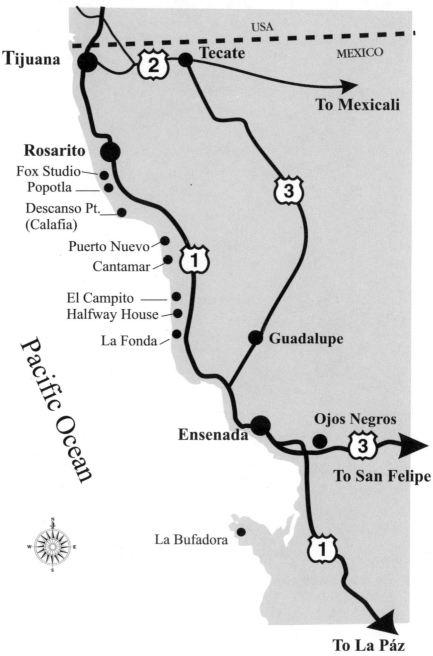

Tijuana

USA

Tecate

MEXICO

To Mexicali

Rosarito
Fox Studio
Popotla
Descanso Pt.
(Calafia)

Puerto Nuevo
Cantamar

El Campito
Halfway House
La Fonda

Guadalupe

Pacific Ocean

Ojos Negros

Ensenada

To San Felipe

La Bufadora

To La Páz

"It (Baja) is an enigma, a paradox and a challenge. If you have the will to survive in its waterless wasteland, you are on a par with the courageous, friendly people who call it home. If you have not, you had better stay close to the border or fly down to one of its splendid resorts."

—Choral Pepper
"Baja California: Vanished Missions,"
"Lost Treasures, Strange Stories Tall and True." 1973

Don Lund with a yellowtail and a grin.

Typical panga used at Puerto Nuevo. Leila Niemann photo

Baja Fever

Searching for Albacore

Ensenada, 1989

The abundance of bottom fish salvaged a two-day long-range fishing trip out of Ensenada and allowed everyone to go home with an ice box full of fresh filets.

We were among 19 anglers who left the port of Ensenada aboard the venerable "Ensenada Clipper," the starship of the Ensenada Clipper fleet in search of albacore, which had just started appearing in Baja waters the preceding week.

While we found a few "albies," most were caught trolling and we were unable to lure a school to the boat. In addition to about 15 albacore, also brought to gaff our first day out were a dozen dorado and 17 yellowtail.

But it was that second day, primarily devoted to bottom fishing, that filled everyone's gunny sack.

It was a long range two-day trip to the area of San Martín island in search of albacore that lured me, my Cantamar neighbor Don and my Orange County neighbor Kent.

We boarded early

Our excitement led us to board hours before the 5 p.m. Tuesday departure. We'd drawn pillows and blankets and had our pick of bunks.

We were pleased to hear there would only be 19 aboard, instead of a full boat of 29 anglers. Nobody would get in each other's way — or would they?

We introduced ourselves to our fellow anglers. There was Jim, a man in his late 60s from Ventura, California, and his two sons. There was a curly-headed character who looked like a holdover from the flower children days of Haight-Ashbury. Looks were deceiving; far from being mel-

93

low, he constantly bragged about other fishing ventures. We enjoyed an energetic young black man named George who really got enthusiastic (He yelled "hook up" the loudest, and filled his sack with the most game fish). Rounding out the group were 11 members of a Los Angeles-based fishing and hunting club.

The club members were the movie stereotypes of fishermen: mostly men in their 50s and 60s (or older), red faced, heavy drinkers, heavy smokers, presumably with their cholesterol levels as high as their weights, most well over 200. While their group did include a few younger blue-collar workers along with the retired executives, it was fishing and hunting that provided their bond.

THE FOOD WAS EXCELLENT

The food aboard the 85-foot vessel was excellent, plenty of it and delicious. It was a combination of Mexican and American cuisine, with one meal consisting of carne asada and tortillas and the next of roast beef and bolillos.

The boat features 36 bunks, a sun deck, a 33 seat galley, three GMC engines, a shower, video player (We saw portions of "Return of the Jedi" four times), four radios and three bait tanks.

Skipper Oscar Susarrey, a veteran long-range specialist, is well respected by his crew and fishermen alike. Pedro Moreno, second in command, speaks English and proved invaluable to the venture. The relationship he established with the anglers became the key to a successful time. Moreno constantly walked that line between crew and guests and did it with aplomb.

There were a cook, galley helper and deck hands as well. They all knew their jobs and went out of their way to help the fishermen, especially when they needed it the most. When the fishing was hot, they were right there, advising, helping newer anglers cast or reel, readying bait, even baiting hooks — more than one would expect "up north."

A NIGHT OF HEAVY ROLLING SEAS

After a night of enduring heavy rolling seas, we were all up early in anticipation. We were about 100 miles south of Ensenada and 50 miles west of San Martín island which is offshore from San Quintín. No land could be seen and low clouds provided a chill over the deep blue sea.

Four teams of five were selected to troll brightly colored feathers for an hour each. If and when there was a hook-up, the rest of us would hastily cast live anchovies to swim around the boat toward a school of albacore brought in by judicious chumming. That was the theory.

They weren't anchovies, but sardines. And they were dying faster than we could bait them. While we did catch fish off the bait, there was not enough live bait for chum to attract any substantial school, if there was such a school in the area.

In practice, it was the third hour before a hook-up. It was my team and Kent's only hook-up all day; he lost the fish. A little later Don broke the ice with a nice yellowtail. I caught the first dorado, a gilded fighter with acrobatic leaps whose bright color typically fades after a short time on deck.

The game fishing was rated fair to good as each angler averaged about 2-4 fish. I caught two dorado and a blue shark; Don had two yellowtail and an albacore.

I LOST A DORADO

I lost a dorado due to interference of one of the "clubbies." Trolling, I hooked a nice one and was trying to maneuver it to gaff in and around the crowd now furiously casting over and around me. One of the guys I was trying to get around got a hook-up. With my line and fish almost straight down, the sharp pull of his line from a large fish way out snapped my line. And my dorado and $30 feather were inches from the gaff. I never saw either, again.

If we thought the first night was a roller, the second night we bounced around even more as the skipper made his way back north to a spot off Punta San José. It was about 4:30 a.m. and still dark when I stumbled on deck. I noticed lights from the boat shining into the water.

A SCHOOL OF GIANT SQUID

A school of giant squid (about 24-30 inches) were attracted by the lights and had rewarded the earliest risers. Rubbing my eyes, I sidled up to Kent whom I then spotted at the rail and told him about the squid that people were catching. He said nothing, but pointed to his sack. I looked. He had started the day even before I got my line wet with two giant squid and a white fish. It was to be his day as before it was over his 15-pound ling cod would win the daily jackpot.

The bottom fishing was excellent, with many white fish, bass, a sheepshead or two, rock cod and ling cod. All were of good size. We caught

Along the Gold Coast

plenty of large mackerel, some of us switching to rock cod rigs for them. The mackerel provided most of the bait for that second day.

We continued the hot fishing by bouncing baited lures off the bottom, just offshore from Punta Santo Tomás. Looking ashore I could just make out the houses built by the gregarious Mr. Gomez, a character immortalized by the popular Los Angeles writer Jack Smith.

By the time we rounded Punta Banda and headed for the Ensenada harbor, the roiling seas had calmed; the sun beat brightly and we could stand or sit without securing ourselves.

Crossing the wide Bahia Todos Santos we could see that the wide sandy beaches south of Ensenada were now dotted with homes, for vacationing Americans and Mexican workers alike. We glided close to the sand dunes and beach of my youth. It was where my struggling parents brought their growing family for two weeks of refuge, solace and togetherness each summer. It was in those sand dunes that I first became afflicted with Baja Fever.

Stepping onto the dock, I reflected that it was a fun trip, and even though there was a bait problem, I'd go again and with the same crew, too.

The biggest fish caught on the trip was a 34 pound albacore (trolling on the first day); winning the first day's jackpot was a 20 pound yellowtail; Don's 16 pounder was second.

The next weekend I visited my daughter in Kona, Hawaii, and she'd tried fishing that same week, catching what she said was a small ono (wahoo). Apparently others on the boat had caught larger fish in those warm waters around the Big Island.

Imagine my chagrin when I asked her how small and she apologized, "Oh, it was only 35 pounds!"

Let's Go Bottom Fishing!

Descanso Bay, B.C. México — 1993

"Let's go fishing, Frank."

A wide grin expanded his craggy 79-year-old face into a countenance of expectation. "When?"

"How about tomorrow? Want to take a local panga out or do you think the 'Yellows' are running at Ensenada?"

"Let's try Ensenada. There's always a chance."

So three of us, Cantamar pal Frank, his brother-in-law, and I took the Delfin Azul out of Ensenada, but after two hours of plying the waters with live anchovies and dead lures looking for game fish that just were not there that day in June, we dropped the sinkers and pulled up scores of those denizens of the deep, those omnipresent bottom fish.

We were happy to catch enough to fill our gunny sacks with some tasty fish, but there's something about the fight of the game fish that's as exciting to an angler as the perfect wave is to a surfer.

June proved to be too early that year for the migratory yellowtail which put Ensenada on the map and earned the lovely port city the title "Yellowtail Capital of the World."

Put fish on the table

One thing about Baja — whether you're fishing for yellowtail, bonito or barracuda in the north, or dorado, tuna or wahoo in warmer waters — if you want to put fish on the table, ask the skipper to stop trolling and find some bottom fish.

There are good spots all around Baja, including the Sea of Cortez, that abound with an abundance of good eating bottom fish. These are the many different bass varieties, plus rock cod, ling cod, red snapper, white fish, sculpin, sheepshead, cabrilla, croaker, halibut, corbina, perch and more.

All the local Mexican fishermen know where the good spots are, seamounts, rocky points, islands, etc., and usually a sinker, two hooks and plenty of bait is all you need. The bait need not be live as when top fishing for game fish. Frozen squid (calamar), anchovies, mussels (choros), clams or cut fish all work well.

On the Pacific, the broad, wide Descanso Bay (From Calafia to La Mision has many such spots. Local fishermen will take anglers out in their 16 to 22 foot pangas for negotiable rates (usually about $20-$25 per person, plus an additional cleaning fee).

I've gone many times from several fishing villages and have never been skunked, almost always bringing in a dozen fish or more (can't say that about Dana Point or Newport Beach).

You can engage such a boat at Puerto Popotla (about 3-4 miles south of Rosarito), Puerto Campito (3 miles south of Cantamar) and Campo Lopez (4 miles south of Cantamar) among others.

This type of fishing is not for everyone. The old boats often leak a little (you help bail); I've rarely seen life jackets; the engines sometimes quit working or run out of gas; you may stop and check lobster traps on your way in or out; you should speak a smattering of Spanish; you usually get your feet wet getting in the boat; you usually have to help them push the boat into and out of the water using logs as rollers, and most exciting is the waiting for a gap between the waves and "shooting it," heading straight out to crest a breaking wave.

But to those who do it regularly, it's fun, it's exciting, and you catch fish.

Puerto Campito

In July, Cantamar neighbor Don Lund and I went on such a trip out of Puerto Campito. This place has an added thrill: the skipper has to skillfully negotiate a dog-eared rocky channel with oars, switch to the engine at precisely the right time, and then goose it to get the boat out over the waves.

The fishing that morning was typically great. After only about three hours though, the wind started and began to turn the glassy-calm ocean into a white-topped frenzy. Our sacks were full, and we opted to head back before the wind got worse. Most of the skippers will always head back in when the ocean starts getting bad.

Bottom fishing out of a panga, Baja-style, has its rewards — they're called fish.

It won't be long before either Frank or Don approaches me with an eager, wistful expression. I know that look, and I know they're going to hook me too when they say, "Hey Greg, let's go fishing!"

Fishermen's boats crowd into the small village of Puerto Popotla.

Fishing Pangas used at El Campito. Leila Niemann photo.

Welcoming arch at entrance of Puerto Nuevo

Along the Gold Coast

Where Lobster is King

It's just a mile up the road from us. And we've watched it grow into a real tourist destination for those seeking a great meal.

It's not the place for steak, nor chicken, nor ribs, nor quiche. It's a lobster village, and lobster is king. Virtually unknown just two decades ago, now Baja's Puerto Nuevo (New Port) is more popular than the surrounding communities.

Approximately 35 restaurants line four block-long streets on an ocean bluff about 11 miles south of Rosarito Beach. A trail drops down from modest fishermen's dwellings between the restaurants and the sparkling sea to a tiny cove where the town got its start.

This cove allows fishermen to penetrate the surf with shallow pangas and fish the area. About 50 years ago several families of fishermen from Lake Chapala in Jalisco relocated there and began a modest fishing enterprise.

The plentiful succulent California spiny lobster in the area lured the fishermen to set traps.

Aside from supplying local restaurants and markets with their catch, the fishermen would sell lobster and fish directly to tourists and locals alike.

In the mid-fifties the first modest restaurant opened.

By 1970 several of the families had set up tables in their living rooms and the term "Puerto Nuevo Style" was born. "Papa" passed the freshly severed lobster halves through the kitchen window to be cooked while guests gathered round to watch.

In those early days, the customers actually felt like members of an extended family. We would just go in the kitchen and grab our own sodas or beers out of the family refrigerator. Before we left, the owners would

100

just tally up the number of empty bottles on the table, a practice many restaurants still employ.

Even today the basic meal is almost the same in each restaurant: two halves of "Langosta" fried in lard (now also boiled or grilled), mouth-watering hot, home-made flour tortillas, beans, rice, butter, salsa, chips and limes, all served family style.

Mariachi music wafts through the now-cobbled streets as musicians stroll from restaurant to restaurant along with purveyors of freshly cut flowers and trinkets made of seashells.

Leila and I will never forget that summer weekend day in 1985 when we went to the village to hire a mariachi group. We were throwing a party in Cantamar about two weeks hence.

Several groups of musicians lounged in the shade of a tree near the end of the main road, down about where a market is today. We were introduced to the leader of a group who would be willing to come to Cantamar on that date. We began negotiating how many hours they'd play, how much per hour, etc.

As we were closing in on a deal, they proudly offered to let us hear them. We agreed. So Leila and I stood, our arms around each other, in the middle of the dusty, dirt road, while this mariachi group serenaded us in the hot August sun. Quickly a crowd gathered out in the road while these guys just kept playing and playing.

Their enthusiasm won us over. That we felt special amid a large group of gringos didn't hurt either.

Puerto Nuevo is now well identified with a welcoming arch, neon signs, modern buildings, hundreds of cars and tourists and numerous curio shops, yet for decades the place was hard to find.

Even giving directions was cryptic. We used to tell people, "About a quarter mile south of El Pescador restaurant, you'll see an old white building with a 7-Up bottle painted on it; turn down the dirt road next to that building. Stop at the first house on the left and knock on the door; it's really a restaurant. If they're out of lobster or busy, go to the second house."

By the late '70s demand outpaced the supply. Long lines formed at restaurants not "sold out." Many people were turned away, no lobster to be had. Now the village imports most of its lobster from villages and towns farther south.

Today the restaurants run the gamut from a few tables in a modest house to beautiful marble and tile three story extravaganzas. The meals are fairly consistent, with many places also offering mixed drinks in addition to beer and sodas, and broader menus which now even include steak.

Along the Gold Coast

Most of the village is related. Brothers, sisters, cousins and in-laws may all own restaurants on the same street. The Ortega family (Juan and Petra and their 10 children) was one of the first to offer home serving in the mid-'50s and now boasts five Puerto Nuevo restaurants and two in Rosarito Beach, further spreading the "Puerto Nuevo Style" fame.

Prices have risen at all of the restaurants over the years but still remain about half of most stateside prices. You can get a chica "small" lobster (2 halves) from $7.50 to $10, and mediums from $10 to $15. For two people it's often better to buy a "Grande" for $16 to $20 and split it.

Once Leila, Ken and a teenage buddy split a large $25.00 lobster three ways. There was still some left so we bundled the remainder up and took it home. The next morning it became a delicious lobster omelet that fed all four of us.

Smaller places on the side streets usually have the best buys and the quality is the same or better.

Most of us who live in the area have our favorite places even though the offered fare is similar. I've eaten in at least half the places and keep gravitating back to one on the last street. I've gotten to know the family and watched the younger ones grow up, get married and have children of their own. The owner is most gracious and always whips up a special treat for his friends.

Busloads of tourists now make Puerto Nuevo their México destination, and on busy weekends it's hard to find parking. Today Puerto Nuevo is a far cry from when we used to give directions to it based on a well-placed 7-Up sign.

Take free (libre) road 11 miles south from Rosarito Beach. From toll road, there is a marked "Puerto Nuevo" turn-off about 10 miles. Or you can take "Cantamar" turn-off and go north on old road one mile.

Puerto Nuevo is more than eating a dinner out. It can be a complete Baja experience: the succulent food, strolling mariachis, vendors and purveyors of trinkets and curios, a bustling village, and killer sunsets over the sparkling blue Pacific.

Many who have succumbed to Baja Fever received their first bite at the village of Puerto Nuevo.

Behind the Intriguing Arch

Puerto Popotla — 1996

Tourists occasionally walk its lone, rocky street in search of fresh morsels from the sea, but Puerto Popotla is anything but a tourist destination.

If you are the type of Baja visitor seeking the rustic charm of earlier decades, with neither T-shirt shops, inflated prices, nor fancy restaurants, yet don't want to drive hundreds of miles farther to the south, the simple fishing village of Puerto Popotla is for you.

Only about four miles south of Rosarito Beach, off the old road, Puerto Popotla is hardly visible from the highway. Just north of the Popotla Trailer Park and Restaurant, it is an incongruous next-door neighbor to the modern 20th Century Fox movie studio. The village can be reached via a short (300 yard) dirt road next to the studio's south wall which begins under a distinctive double white arch.

Back in 1971 I watched the construction of this intriguing arch which was to highlight a planned subdivision. The subdivision never got off the ground and the arch greeted an empty field for 25 years, attracting curious stares from passersby.

In 1996 the Fox movie studio opened on the lot next door to the north, and the surrounding area has boomed leaving the quaint fishing village in its midst.

Unlike the ill-fated subdivision, the fishing village did get off the ground and its primitiveness is its charm. The sheltered Popotla cove has long harbored a simple fish camp, where hardy "pescadores" would push out daily in their wooden pangas to either bottom fish off the nearby kelp beds or race off on an hour's journey to Los Coronados islands.

Fresh fish "right off the boat"

Returning mid-day and early afternoon with their catches of bass, sheeps-head, halibut, cabrilla, white fish, sculpin, rock cod, ling cod and other species, locals and gringos in the know would greet the returning fisher-men to bargain for the fresh catch. The fresh seafood "right off the boat" is still the biggest attraction in the village.

As time went on, more and more people met the returning boats and a few little stands were constructed to sell "super fresh" fish tacos to waiting customers and other weary men of the sea.

Haphazard stands and restaurants

In the late 1980s the idea caught on and a village was born and has since exploded in growth. Haphazard stands and restaurants of all descrip-tions began appearing around the cove and out over the rocky promon-tory that shelters it. Last summer the cacophony of hammers and saws added to the gentle sounds of the waves, gulls and sizzling fish tacos as the town doubled in size.

Restaurant sign at Puerto Nuevo.
Will Puerto Popotla become
another Puerto Nuevo?

Now over two dozen "restaurants" are based in Puerto Popotla. Mariscos (sea food) are the order of the day at such places as Elancla Mariscos, Mariscos Pancho, Mariscos Delma, Mariscos La Ola Marina, Mariscos Miramar #1, El Pulpo, Las Gaviotas, Punta Blanca, Mariscos Popotla and others.

EXTREMELY RUSTIC, BUT WHAT A VIEW!

Most restaurants are extremely rustic, with perhaps an old car seat for seating and a large wooden wire spool for a table. Many of the floors are dirt or sand. Many are open sided with tremendous views of pelicans splashing into the ocean and waves crashing on the rocks all the way to Calafia at Descanso Point about a kilometer to the south.

In addition to the restaurants, fishermen often approach tourists with a fresh selection of live fish, crabs and lobsters right from the boat.

If you want to fish, several of the fishermen will take you out with them. I've been out several times with an American fisherman whose Mexican wife runs one of the restaurants. A couple of the Mexican fishermen also speak English. I usually go there the day before and ask around; I've always been able to find someone to take me out.

While there is activity in the village every day, on Sundays Puerto Popotla really "comes alive." Cars, mostly those of locals, line the dusty entrance road. "Norteña" music from radios beckons from the shanties. Sometimes strolling mariachis compete with the boom boxes to lend a decidedly Latin air to a definitely Mexican fishing village.

Will continued growth diminish the charm? Possibly, although the tight space around the cove will inhibit dreams of grandeur.

Most Baja regulars are still amazed at the prolific construction of high rises in Rosarito so the growth of a small village comes as no surprise. Oldtimers know it was just two decades ago the famous village of Puerto Nuevo farther south served lobster out of living rooms.

What will the future bring to Puerto Popotla? Who knows. But for now, it is the most charming of the accessible fishing villages — if you don't mind sitting on a beat up old car seat while pigging out on fresh fish tacos.

Hollywood Comes to Baja

Fox Studios, Popotla — 1996

It started with rumors. It seems there are always rumors among colonies of expatriates. Huddled together, insulated from the world around them in protective cocoons, these minority groups thrive on gossip, hearsay, innuendo and rumors.

Few can read or interpret the local newspapers. Most of their "knowledge" is gained over a martini or a cocktail, or in the case of those in Baja — a margarita or a beer.

As a journalist, I find it difficult to succumb to stories not documented by several sources and immediately discard most rumors. I ignored the hubbub about a new casino going in next door, and also the excitement that a marina was to be built in the Cantamar lagoon, and hundreds of other stories, each of which never came to fruition.

So I was obviously skeptical when I heard the one about a major motion picture studio going in up the road. Yeah, sure!

Imagine my chagrin when scanning the local newspaper *Ecos* during a haircut, the headline with the word "Fox" jumped out at me. There it was! 20th Century Fox was planning to build a major movie studio south of Rosarito.

During the ensuing weeks, other media expanded on the story and soon the entire Gold Coast was going giddy with excitement. Hollywood was coming to Baja!

Next thing we knew, bulldozers and heavy equipment began grading a wind-blown dusty bluff a few miles south of Rosarito, just adjacent to the Popotla arch. The 33-acre site that was being prepared for the new 20th Century Fox Baja Studio stretches from the Old Road (Libre) to the pounding ocean cliffs.

Construction began on June 1, 1996 and wasting no time, preparation for the studio's first movie began right away. It was the movie "Titanic" and, along with the new studio, a detailed life-size replica of the Titanic which would dominate the landscape for months was being constructed.

The original Titanic ship, renowned for its ill-fated maiden voyage from England to New York in 1912, cost $10 million to build. This movie "Titanic," filmed in Baja California by 20th Century Fox, was expected to be the most expensive movie ever made, with estimates around $200 million, or 20 times what that original ship cost.

Huge replica of "Titanic" was reconstructed on set of
Fox Baja Studio for filming of the blockbuster movie.

Curious, I accompanied friend Paul Holehouse, a veteran motion picture consultant, for a facility visit in October 1996. Holehouse, who spent time on the "Waterworld" atoll set in Hawaii, was astonished at the progress in just a few months on the Popotla bluff. "This already has the potential to be larger than the Fox studio in Century City," he marveled.

Twentieth Century Fox originally planned to build the studio for the one production, but once underway, decided to construct a studio that will long endure.

James Cameron, known for such successes as "Terminator" and "True Lies," was to direct "Titanic." Starring is Leonardo DiCaprio; also appearing is Billy Zane, who starred in "The Phantom," and Kate Winslet, a lead actress in "Sense and Sensibility."

Along the Gold Coast

World search ends in Baja

I learned the Baja site was not selected lightly. The search literally took them all over the world, from Malta, to the Czech Republic, Australia, the United Kingdom, Italy and California. When they saw Popotla, officials said, they stopped looking. Fox Film Entertainment chief financial officer Simon Bax said, "It had everything we needed. And the great thing is, it's so close to Los Angeles."

Filming on the "Titanic" started on September 16, using finished parts of the studio while the remainder was still being constructed.

Fox sent down its top facility executive, Fernando Carrillo, Director of Studio Operations, to get the studio job done while keeping the production team on schedule. No stranger to Baja, he and his wife Lilia have owned a vacation home at La Paloma for nine years.

"It would have been ideal to have the studio completed before Production took over," said Carrillo, "but we're making the best of it and we're staying ahead of them."

The studio contracted out about 700 workers, most of them Mexican citizens, to build the tanks, pumps, roads and buildings. More than half were bussed in from Rosarito, Ensenada and Tijuana.

According to contractor Howard Hargrove, the benefits of building the studio and making the movie in México are great. "If this was being done in the states, it would cost five times more and take 10 times longer. At this point, we'd probably still be getting permits in the states," he said.

Production had about 500 people building, preparing and painting sets, producing scenic art, filming and making sure the movie "Titanic" gets finished.

Everything I saw on my two visits impressed me. The Titanic was in pieces, all over the lot. We walked past fiberglass anchors and smoke stacks. Pulleys, vents and portholes were all being constructed for their eventual day of glory in front of the cameras.

In Stage 4 shooting was going on. Extras in wetsuits covered with life jackets bobbed in a pool-size tank amid debris and crates and began pleading to be rescued once the cameras started rolling. Outside the stage, hot tubs whirred at 105 degrees to thaw out the durable cast.

Workshops, paint shops, set design shops, carpenter shops, all hummed with activity. Names of the "Titanic" characters were painted on the dressing room doors.

Up to 1,000 extras

Scores of the 1,000 extras were checking in, going through make-up and being matched up with the costumes and wigs that would fit their characters. Hundreds of photos of such temporary cast members lined the walls.

The Southampton docks had been completed, the windows smoked and siding aged for effect. As we walked by, I grabbed a warehouse drain spout for support, but the real-looking plastic bent with my touch.

The bow of the Titanic had been constructed on a large hinge above a pit. The bow would raise, dropping stunt people into the airbag-filled pit. I noticed stunt people, secured by rock-climbing straps, going through the choreography of who would bounce off which boom or obstacle, which side they would carom off, and the sequencing of who would land in the air bag first. The average movie-goer could hardly suspect the depth of the planning, only seeing in the final film a few seconds which would appear spontaneous and tragic.

The world's largest water tank

The main thing the Popotla site offered was the unobstructed ocean view.

The world's largest water tank, covering eight total acres, was dug and concreted for the reconstruction of the Titanic. Called Stage 1, the entire irregular-shaped eight-acre tank can be flooded to its 3'8" depth. The ship was constructed in two deeper pools in the center of the shallow one.

A weir, or waterfall, on the ocean side of the eight acres can render the visual effect of a ship at sea, as the cameras look out over the tank to the open ocean.

The entire tank holds 17 million gallons of water.

They scraped a channel out of the rocks below the bluff to pump and release sea water into the tanks.

Stage 2 is the world's largest covered tank at 100x200 feet. Elaborate sets constructed down in the bowels of this tank were flooded during filming. I was impressed at the detail of what was to be washed away. Entire rooms of the Titanic were duplicated in all their original splendor. Ornate ceiling designs were being gilt trimmed, and beautiful, thick, flowered carpets tacked in place.

Stately curved wooden bannisters and fully furnished staterooms were all built to be destroyed. It appeared wasteful to those not in the entertainment business, but a more discerning moviegoing audience demands such attention to detail.

The "Titanic" sets were built to be taken down, but the studio buildings remain, along with the world's largest water tanks. Anyone who saw the old pirate movies of the 1950s, where miniature tall ships bobbed in bathtub-sized tanks will appreciate the difference.

MORE MOVIES FOR BAJA

The Baja experiment has already made the movie industry sit up and take notice. "We're getting a lot of interest in our studio," said Carrillo.

Next to be filmed at the Fox Baja Studio is "Terminator III" with Arnold Schwarzenegger, and following that, Sylvester Stallone is slated to make an action movie there.

Baja Norte Tourism Director Juan Tintos Funcke said, "Hopefully, this will put Baja California on the map as a major location for film-making."

It's certainly been alluring to the residents along Baja's Gold Coast. I recognized one American expatriate in costume headed for the lunch tent. He proudly hollered at me, "Hey this is really a hoot! I'm actually in a movie as an extra!"

Several Cantamar neighbors and fellow Baja writers joined the excitement, donning period costumes and enduring long days, not only for the extra income, but also to share in the excitement and participate in the magic of Hollywood, Baja-Hollywood, that is.

And when it comes to rumors along Baja's Gold Coast, I now listen more carefully — sometimes they come true!

Note: This was written before the movie's release. Who would have guessed that the movie "Titanic" would eclipse all box office records and earn numerous Academy Awards including best director and best picture? Most of us who visited the set had never heard of Leonardo DiCáprio at that time. He could have sat near us at lunch and we would not have known it.

DIVING FOR SEA URCHINS

EL CAMPITO, B. C., — 1996

When the vital motor sputtered to a halt, I was sure he was in trouble. Luis had been walking along the ocean floor, at a depth of 25 meters (80 feet) and the motor had been pumping his lungs with air.

His 17-year-old son Daniel kept trying to restart the temperamental old motor. Pull and sputter. Nothing. Pull again. Nothing. The boy was calm, going about his business with incredible maturity, knowing his father trusted him with his life. He kept trying.

While I was watching the son, the skipper Pedrin had given the air line a couple of strong jerks. The motor had obviously stalled before. The jerks meant "you had better start your steady slow ascent to the surface because shortly you'll be totally out of air."

About a minute later Luis surfaced. The little air in the hose gave him the time he needed.

In a way, I was surprised it didn't happen on the first dive. The rusty old Briggs & Stratton 8 hp motor was held together by an old wire hanger and some duct tape. It leaked gas and belched noxious smoke all day. It was bolted to a 2x12, which was tied by rope around the front seat of the shallow 18-foot outboard panga. Luis' air tank occupied the small bow seat.

Luis was down deep, gathering "erizos," or sea urchins, which would end up in Tokyo sushi bars. The mature urchins are about the size of a baseball, covered with spines.

We were off the coast of Baja, about a mile off shore from Campo Lopez, just south of the Halfway House. The Halfway House restaurant was once a landmark located about halfway between Tijuana and Ensenada. It is now overshadowed by newer and more modern developments that better cater to the growing legions of American tourists.

The diving for sea urchins offshore is not a world for the fussy gringos however. It is a business that only few brave men experience. It is extremely dangerous, requires a great amount of skill and daring and pays very little. Work days are limited by weather and storms; there are no paid holidays nor even medical, much less hazard insurance.

I PLANNED TO GO FISHING

I kind of stumbled onto this expedition. A fisherman, Jorge, who was supposed to meet me at the small fishing village of El Campito at 7 a.m. to take me out, never showed (ran out of gas, he said later).

I waited on the El Campito bluff now dotted with fishing shacks and small, rustic family restaurants, and watched the waves crash onto the rocks.

It was a gray September morning and the ocean was much more unsettled than the day before. We were due to receive big surf whipped up from a hurricane that had earlier struck Baja's tip. The overcast sky itself should clear about noon, if at all, and the sun would make El Campito more vibrant and picturesque. But the ocean would still dance to the beat of the faraway storm, rising and falling like the lungs of a sleeping dog.

Two sleepy-looking guys exited a fishing shack, stretched and spat to welcome the day, and went right to work. They carried their heavy outboard motor down the cliff, hooked it up, loaded their fuel and gear and pushed their panga out into the heaving and frothy ocean to check their lobster traps. It was 7:30 a.m. No Jorge.

A short, light haired man with a broad smile, about 35-40 years old, emerged from another shack behind me. "Quien espera?" he asked, wondering who I was waiting for. After I told him, he said that if Jorge didn't show, maybe I could go out with him. It was now 7:40. I'll wait a little longer. I thought about how, in Spanish the word "to wait" is the same as "to hope," both "esperar." Must be a reason.

An old, rusty white van arrived and backed down the treacherous slope. It was full of gear which the light haired man and a couple of others loaded onto one of the weatherbeaten wooden pangas that had been roped to the base of the cliff. I walked down the steep, rocky slope that served as a ramp to watch.

They'd hooked up the Mariner 70 hp outboard and had most of the gear loaded. They were divers. The man I'd talked to, who identified himself as Luis, was fiddling with the other motor, a Briggs & Stratton, which would provide him his precious air. Pedrin, about 35, was fiddling with the Mariner.

An older man, the van driver, handed nets, air hoses and a box with a rubber wetsuit to the youngest man, Daniel, and then left.

Luis pointed to a narrow wooden shelf next to the outboard and again said I was welcome to come along and sit there. It was almost 8 a.m. and I agreed. I knew fishing would literally take a back seat to their diving, but it sounded like an adventure I couldn't pass up.

THROUGH THE ROCKS IN CRASHING SURF

There's a sandy break in the rocks just wide enough for one of these small pangas to get through. The break, however, does not go straight out. It makes a sharp left turn and then a right. All this amid crashing waves pounding the rocks. The tide was just starting to come in when we departed. We four, Luis, Daniel, Pedrin and I pushed and shoved the panga each time water from a wave swirled around it. After about the eighth or ninth hefty push, it broke free from the sand and floated. We jumped in, wet from the waist down.

Pedrin quickly rowed left, then as the small craft was positioned for the open ocean, started the outboard and carefully watched the large waves. Between wave sets, we made a quick dash to a comfort zone outside the breakers.

Smiles all around. Just the commute to get to work is dangerous.

It was worse coming in at high tide. You couldn't see the rocks; you had to "know" them. And the waves were much larger, forcing us to ride up and crest several large waves a split second before they broke just to stay outside and wait for a smaller set.

We headed south, keeping the panga in troughs. A huge kelp bed rests offshore from Campo Lopez. We glided to a stop over it. Soon, Luis and Daniel began tearing and collecting seaweed, grabbing the newest, softest, cleanest ends. "Shampu," laughed Luis. But I still didn't understand.

As Pedrin aimed us toward the "erizo" area nearby, Luis filled a net with the gathered seaweed. He then started stomping on it, making a gooey mess that looked like soap suds or shampoo.

HE GREASED HIS BODY WITH GOO

It made sense as he made his initial preparations. He coated his body with the goo, and easily slid on a thin body wetsuit. He zipped it up and coated it too with goo. This facilitated his pulling a thicker suit over the top of it. Pretty ingenuous, I thought.

Along the Gold Coast

The black wet suit, like the Briggs & Stratton motor, had seen better days. There were scratches all over it and it had a couple of rips that had been patched with pieces of rubber cut from an innertube.

Luis then put goo on his head and slipped on a thick black rubber hood. He pulled worn old gloves, with holes visible on most of the fingertips, over his gnarled hands, knobby from the venom in the spines of so many sea urchins.

He put the air hose up under his crotch and over his shoulder and secured it with his weight belt. A mouthpiece was at the end of the hose. He attached a long three-pronged spear to his air line, grabbing distance away. He secured a sharp knife around his wrist with a strip of rubber. Then he grabbed a makeshift tool that would pry the erizos loose. It was about 18 inches long, with two metal bent prongs at the end.

He slid over the side.

I tried fishing every time he was down there, but my heart was not in it. I was too interested in what was going on. I got my line tangled several times around kelp, and once around the air hose. Fishing was discouraging and all day I only caught one decent rock cod and a larger male sheepshead (red bottom fish).

He came up gasping

Luis would be down on the bottom about a half hour each time. After his first dive, he came up gasping, spitting and complaining. Apparently oil had gotten into his air line, and it tasted bad and was giving him a headache. He even handed me the mouthpiece to try it. It was awful; how he could breathe that foul air was beyond me. I thought they'd abort the dives after that problem, but no, he made four more dives, including the one when the motor conked out.

His first dive, however, was successful. His big net was full of sea urchins and the smaller net with a slatted top had two sheepshead he had speared. Not bad for a half hour. After five dives, he filled a large bucket he knew would contain four kilos of the succulent urchins. He had also speared two more fish.

There are several classes of sea urchins, and Luis was gathering the finest, with a bright yellow meat. Some of the darker brown and black meats are of lesser quality and command no market.

Ninety percent of the west coast's harvest is exported to Japan. In one recent year, in California alone, over 30 million pounds were pulled off the ocean floor.

The sea urchin industry has grown in México as well as California to help fill the sushi restaurant demand. The urchin's bright yellow or orange colored sex organs, incorrectly, but delicately called "roe" by people in the industry, are sold as "uni."

We broke one open and the yellow meat did look like fish roe. Pedrin loved the stuff and was slurping it raw out of the shell. I tried some at their suggestion. They laughed and implied that it did good things for a man's virility. I thought it tasted a bit like caviar, a little salty, but good.

When Luis was down below, the other two were busy. Pedrin had to stand all the while and row the boat, keeping Luis' air line free. It constantly got tangled in kelp, and Pedrin used the tip of his oar to bring it in. Daniel then whacked the offending seaweed away from the lifeline with his machete. I grimaced more than once, seeing how close those machete's swings were to the line.

Daniel also fed out the line to his dad, and was responsible for keeping the untrustworthy air motor running.

Pedrin is also a diver and he and Luis have dived all over the Pacific Coast, from the vast sea urchin beds around El Rosario, about 200 miles south, to California. Luis has been diving about 18-20 years.

While neither complained about shark or other animal attacks, both agree ascending too rapidly is the greatest hazard. There only two decompression tanks in the entire area, one at the aforementioned El Rosario, and the other at San Diego, about 60 miles north.

30 HOURS IN DECOMPRESSION

Pedrin once narrowly escaped with his life down in El Rosario, and spent 30 hours in the decompression chamber. Luis escaped once with air pockets blotching his skin, and had many close calls where his lung power helped him survive.

Luis' buyer, who eventually gets the sea urchins to Japan, pays him $18 U.S. per kilo. His four kilos for about five hours of hard work for the three of them netted $72. Probably another $5 for selling the fish, and then what I gave him. Less than $100 total for three men for the day.

For this he was sucking bad air all day that gave him a headache. In a flimsy suit he exposed himself to about 50 pounds per square inch (psi) air pressure, or well over triple that of sea level. Then there was the one near disaster where he had to come up quickly because his air was shut off. And then the high waves created a difficulty just to get back in to shore. "But I need to work," he laughed. "I've got seven kids."

Along the Gold Coast

In typical Mexican fashion, he started bragging about his brood: Daniel here, one kid married, no, no grandkids yet, and one just finished high school. He was real happy about his kids getting an education. Maybe they would not have to risk their lives daily on the ocean floor.

Conservationists are divided as to the future ramifications of vast urchin harvests. Most agree there should be some regulations. Northern California already recognizes a potential problem. The warmer waters of Southern California and Baja California have more kelp beds and the urchin colonies should be better able to withstand more indiscriminate harvesting.

Some contend that fewer kelp-munching urchins could mean new and bigger kelp beds, which encourage greater numbers of other species, including abalone.

The conservation question is one far removed from divers like Luis and Pedrin. The urchins are there; they work hard to get them; they get paid.

From the panga we could see cars on the coast road on their way to Ensenada. Little did the people in those cars realize the dramas played out daily by these hardy men offshore. They couldn't expect to know. Nor could Japanese patrons in sushi bars half a world away.

An urchin diver's panga equipped with air compressor.

Taco and the Mountain Man

Agua Caliente Rancho — 1997

The weekend scene at Cantamar was getting to me. Various groups of Americans get together, socialize, eat American food, speak English, drink, laugh, and tell tall tales about their frequent excursions into this exotic foreign country and the timidity of their acquaintances who may dare to visit.

The farthest into backwoods Baja most of these experts have ventured is a day's outing to La Bufadora, that over-developed waterspout in the cliffs just south of Ensenada.

But they find comfort with each other. They have commonality, not all of it adverse. They seek each other's company and can spend an entire weekend without seeing a Mexican peso, using a word of Spanish, or really identifying with their host country.

Perhaps I'm perverse, but I'm much the opposite. The socializing is fine, but there is so much more to Baja.

Even crossing the highway from Cantamar and walking up the local arroyo one discovers a Baja far removed from any American settlement. I can walk past the farms and nod and wave at the field hands and stop and talk to ranchers.

After the weekend I was ready. I was alone on this escape into the back country. Leila was out of town visiting family and I only had a couple of days for exploring. Poring over my Baja books and maps, I thought I'd just go up and camp at Laguna Hansen, that small pine-rimmed lake high in the Sierra Juarez and only a couple hours east of Ensenada.

I had several objectives. I also wanted to explore a little-known canyon out of Guadalupe that was part of the old gold-miners' overland trail from the border to Real del Castillo and the goldfields. I had read about this

117

route in my great-grandfather's 1889 book, "The Gold Fields of Lower California." I knew there was no current road through that area and wondered what it was like.

From Guadalupe I planned to go north on Highway 3 to the Tecate area and approach Laguna Hansen from the north, a route I had not yet taken.

Then leaving Laguna Hansen the next day, I planned to find the village of Real del Castillo itself, which now can be reached from the south by dirt road from Ojos Negros, about 30 miles east of Ensenada.

MY DOG TACO REBELLED

As my Baja trips go, this was not a major undertaking. But my dog Taco had other ideas.

Taco and I left Cantamar at 8 a.m. that Monday morning. I couldn't coax the dog, an aging, almost 13-year-old German Shepherd mutt Leila found as a pup in Cantamar, into doing all of her personal business before we left. She just peed, so I figured I'd stop later. It was sooner, however.

Taco

I was on the old Tijuana-Ensenada road winding up the "killer hill" that is the scourge of the bicyclists, just south of La Mision, when Taco starts acting skittish.

I'm concentrating hard and winding up the steep cliffside road. Then I smell something. A quick look back confirms the worst. Taco has pooped all over the back of my Ford Explorer. She's trying to move up in front of the mess, but the car is winding with the curvy road. No turnoffs. I have to keep going, keep winding up. The uphill motion of the car keeps Taco sliding back into her mess. Nothing I could do but endure and finally pull over at the top of the hill.

I had the seat down and fortunately had set her on a tan tarp and a blanket. But during the sliding around she got the mess on both garments and herself. So I start cleaning, finally rolling up both the blanket and tarp to wash thoroughly when I got back.

Meanwhile Taco is wandering all over the adjacent field. She wouldn't respond when I'd call, even yell. I know she's almost deaf, but I'm sure she chose to ignore me. I had to get her leash and chase her down. "This will never do," I muttered to myself.

I still had a large blue plastic shade tarp in the car which I folded a couple of times and placed on the Explorer floor for Taco to sit on before we left. Later, I was glad I did too.

I turned off the pavement onto the all-weather dirt road to the Guadalupe Valley. This is a pretty part of Baja, beautiful green fields, olive trees, lots of vineyards and acres of brightly-colored flowers.

A WELL-TRAVELED ROUTE

The last of the Baja missions was established here, and only ruins remain. A Russian religious sect settled here in 1905 but nothing remains of their settlement.

During the 1889 gold rush, the main road from San Diego to Ensenada passed through Guadalupe. From Tijuana it went inland paralleling the Tecate road and then cut south at Carrizo into the Valle de las Palmas. At Guadalupe it followed the left fork of a canyon up into Real del Castillo, once a booming town and the capital of Baja California's northern district from 1872–82.

I wanted to find that trail if possible. One book mentioned some caves and another some hot springs at Agua Caliente, up a canyon east from Guadalupe that was probably part of the old road. The maps show two roads so first I took the shorter one to eliminate it.

The dirt roads joined about a mile up the valley floor near the La Cetta Winery, so I just came back down one and went up the other one. But as the left fork road got narrower and rockier, Taco again showed her displeasure.

This time she barfed — all over the place. I looked back and the entire surface of the blue canvass tarp, as well as the dog, was covered. I stopped and got Taco out, this time leashing her to the bumper. Then I pulled out the blue plastic and used about a liter of valuable water to wash it down. With a towel I wiped Taco off as well as I could.

While the blue tarp dried rapidly in the hot May sun, I looked around with binoculars. Pine trees dotted the top of the nearby mountain to the south, probably Cerro Ensenada and I could see a pass that might have been the one used over a century ago.

Cleaned up, we set off again. By this time, I knew then I was going to abort my camping plans and somehow shorten my trip. With Taco it was too ambitious of an undertaking.

Along the Gold Coast

After the vineyards and a couple of ranchos the road narrowed. I stopped to open one gate made out of barbed wire and tree limbs, drove through and walked back to close it. These gates are typical in rural Baja and people using the roads are expected to close them when they pass.

The road crossed the stream and it was no problem for the Explorer. One guide book indicated that most cars would need to park at the next stream crossing and travelers should proceed from there on foot. I found that second crossing also doable and carefully rolled down the sandy bank and drove across.

A SADDLED HORSE AT THE RANCHO

In less than a mile the road reached a tidy rancho which stretched across the narrow canyon. A barbed wire gate enclosed some animal pens. Beyond them were rows of fig trees, olive trees and grape vines. The ranch house sat on high ground nearby. A saddled horse was parked at the front door, reminding me of an old western movie.

I parked a prudent distance, got out and waited. The door opened and a tall, gangling cowboy emerged. Behind him were his smiling wife and one older child.

Upon approach, I could see this cowboy was no kid. Under his 10-gallon hat was a thick head of hair, salt and pepper gray. He wore a full gray beard, the ends of which had turned white. His creased, well-worn face was dominated by his eyes. They sparkled with friendliness and earthiness, with a hint of worldliness. It was hard to guess his age knowing how hard living can age these mountain people quickly. It turned out Federico was 69 and although close-up his face looked it, his physique was that of a man much younger.

When I started speaking Spanish, he seemed to take a liking to me. I asked about the caves that were in the area and the hot springs. He said I would need a full day to explore the caves, but the "agua caliente" was just a couple of kilometers up the canyon after the road ended. He told me it was $5 or 20 Pesos to enter the property. "You do have pesos, don't you," he seemed to implore with a big grin. We both knew that his quoted rate in pesos was about half the $5 gringo fee. I quickly whipped out the pesos.

Federico walked ahead of me and opened gates on either side of his enclosed corral and I drove through. He said that the hot springs were past a waterfall on the right.

I drove the remaining kilometer past his ranch over decent road, fording the sandy, cobble-strewn stream once. When there was no more road I parked. The day was beginning to warm up so I put more than a liter of water in my day pack along with other emergency items.

Taco and I were boulder hopping up the riverbed when Federico came upon us on horseback, two camp dogs following along. He pointed out the better trail on the left side of the stream as he headed up the canyon. On it, Taco and I made our way to the waterfalls.

At the waterfalls, a small but consistent amount of water drops from a hanging side canyon off a dramatic 40 foot cliff into a sandy pool. Thick trees, the calm pool, sandy beach and shade from the cliff make this alone an attractive and rewarding hikers' destination.

I didn't know where the hot springs were, but by now the sun was hot and we rested in the shade, me wading in the cool water while Taco enjoyed lounging on the damp sand.

HE CAME OVER FOR A CHAT

Shortly, Federico came clip-clopping down the canyon, leading a cow and two calves. He let the dogs and cattle go on ahead and came over to my shady respite for a chat. He tied his horse to a branch and sat on a cool rock.

He knew a few words of English, and used them occasionally, but I was pleased the conversation was in Spanish. An American has a hard time practicing his Spanish in any of Baja's tourist areas.

This is because English to the Spanish-speaking Bajacalifornio is about 100 times more important than Spanish is for the tourist. In our case it's a matter of convenience. To them it's more a matter of economic survival.

Mexicans know they can make more money, a lot more, by speaking good English. This dictum is ingrained; they hear it all their lives.

So when you order a meal in a border area restaurant in Spanish, and the waiter reverts to English, it's not bad manners — it's just that he needs to practice English a lot more than you do Spanish.

Often when speaking with a Spanish-speaking person whose English is good, or even marginal, we tend to go the easy way and speak English. They prefer it anyway and keep showing you they understand English.

My problem is I have to visualize my Spanish words and sometimes people speak so fast all the words run together. It usually takes me a few seconds to break the words down and let my brain translate. So I'll often ask them to repeat. When they repeat, if they know English they invariably say it in English the second time to help me. But if they don't know English and repeat it in Spanish, 95 percent of the time I will understand the slower, second version.

Along the Gold Coast

Finally we tend to give up trying to practice Spanish with those who also speak English. Pity, because we then lose an opportunity to practice.

However in backwoods Baja, by necessity my Spanish improves drastically each day. To me a good Baja visit is one in which I rarely utter an English word.

WE TALKED ABOUT EVERYTHING

The conversation with Federico was a pleasure. We talked and talked while his horse stood half in the sun and half out and Taco lazed on the wet sand.

This spry old guy has seven kids, only the youngest still at home. Three of his kids are teachers and he had reason to be equally proud of all of them.

We talked about Baja California. He said the old stage coach trail went up this canyon to Real del Castillo. He said that farther up the canyon was the remains of an old puesto (station) used by the pioneers.

He knew all of Baja. He mentioned places near and far, including El Barril and San Francisquito, remote places about 400 miles away on the other side of the peninsula. I said I'd been there several years previous and met an American gringa living at San Francisquito.

His twinkling eyes lit up in recognition, "Deborah," he offered.

"Si. Deborah Lucero," I answered. I was impressed. He even knew her name.

We discussed other remote places of Baja. We concurred that the Bahia road was the worst road to take to San Borja. He said he had family in that area too. I looked harder at this old guy. He was taller than average and had a prominent nose, a Roman Emperor type nose. Old-time mountain men like him descended from only a handful of old Baja families. His unique characteristics are typical of one clan that comes from those remote mountain regions of central Baja that he's familiar with. He's probably related to...

I stabbed at it. "Federico. What is your last name? Could it be Villavicencia?"

If I was shocked at his acquaintance of Deborah Lucero, he was dumbfounded. Thunderstruck. He jumped up laughing and holding his nose. "Is it my nose," he queried.

"Yes, partly, and your height, and how prominent that family is in that part of Baja," I said.

Villavicencia was his father's family, but his last name was different he admitted, still surprised.

His knowledge was worldly

Not only was his knowledge of Baja vast and far-reaching, but he knew a lot about the world beyond. This I found rare as most Baja mountain men's geographic knowledge consists of the closest large town.

We talked about China, Japan and Europe. It was his turn to surprise me. He asked me if my ancestors came from Germany or England. "Both," I answered laughing, with Norway on my mother's side.

Sitting under the modest falls, I mentioned the large dramatic Iguazu Falls which border Brazil and Argentina in South America. Upon query, I drew a map on the sand. He pointed to the sand, "And this country. Is it Bolivia or Paraguay."

"Paraguay," I answered, "with Bolivia next to it."

"Tell me. Is Paraguay the country they speak two languages? What is that other language?," he asked.

"Guarani," I answered, something I hadn't known previous to visiting that landlocked country, and totally shocked at this simple mountain man's vast knowledge and thirst for more. He repeated the word several times, undoubtedly committing it to memory.

We could have talked all day, but I wanted to get to the hot springs and then just head straight back to Cantamar. Forget the camping idea.

Federico mounted his horse and took off down canyon while Taco and I continued up. Taco kept balking and plopping down on the hot sand. I had her on a leash and prodded her along. She really didn't want any part of this enterprise.

I finally found a small, hot bubbling pool off to the right of the stream, the agua caliente! I stripped naked and immersed myself, feeling the approximate 105 degree water soothe my muscles and dusty body. Taco was content to lay on the damp bank.

Refreshed, my body dried in seconds. Instead of putting my shoes back on, I just slapped on my thongs and put the shoes in my pack.

Heading down canyon Taco was getting worse, just balking, sitting down and refusing to move. Then I saw she was protecting her paws. I removed my thongs to feel the hot sand burn my feet.

Poor dog, she's an inside dog and her feet are not tough like the ranch dogs.

I coaxed her up and we made a beeline for the stream.

We walked the entire way out of that canyon wading in the sandy stream or boulder hopping. Only once did we have to make a quick fast dash around some willows.

Along the Gold Coast

Taco loved the stream so much, several times she just sat in the water refusing to budge. At 65 pounds, she was be too heavy for me to lift and carry.

The sun beat down on us. I was drinking my water and getting tired of the ordeal. I knew my car was just around a bend or two, the ranch not far beyond that, and water at my feet which I could drink in an emergency, yet I had one of the most helpless feelings I've ever had in the wilds.

Finally I coaxed Taco back to the car. We drove out of there without incident and headed straight back to Cantamar. I think Taco in her twilight years knew going camping was a bad idea. She certainly let me know her displeasure in enough ways. I think she just likes the more civilized, social atmosphere at Cantamar. I know she doesn't give a hang for a hot mountain canyon.

For me, I'll never forget that canyon. I felt I was visiting history, trodding over the same land as did those hearty gold-miners, many lured there by my own great grandfather.

Did those men, while chasing dreams of riches, perhaps pause and relax in the hot springs? Or did they hurry on, anxious to find their wealth? They probably kept moving.

I learned wealth is measured differently south of the border. To the gringo, it usually means gold or money. To the Bajacalifornio, like the mountain man Federico, it's family, friendship, and the freedom of a simple lifestyle.

Road
to the south

Typical rancho on Highway 1

Sometimes the roads are washed out.

Baja Fever

*"As we resumed our drive southward on "The Road,"
we talked about that wonderful feeling we had — a
high that no chemicals could ever produce, and we
decided to call it "The Baja Feeling."*
— Ben Hunter, "The Baja Feeling," 1978

HIS NAME WAS HANSEN

SAN QUINTÍN — 1948

The pavement of Highway 1 ended in the late 1940's not many miles south of Ensenada. It just stopped, to be replaced by a hard-packed rocky dirt road which loomed out over the plain and eventually ran down the spine of the Baja peninsula.

We were just south of Colonet where the pavement ended. Now the current highway continues from there for miles as straight as undiluted bathtub gin as it enters the fertile San Quintín Valley.

My dad eased the old 1936 Oldsmobile off the pavement onto the dirt and soon we were rolling and bouncing alongside the naked red earth, kicking up enough ochre dust that our progress could be monitored by anyone miles away.

A tire was a car's most vulnerable part, especially so in those early days before steel-belted tires became an off-roader's best friend. The frames and structures of those pre-World War II cars were much stronger, but the rubber weaker. Fenders were so solid you could get mad at your beast and kick it hard, yielding little damage but a sore toe. But we who drove those older cars learned how to change those older tires. Because it was inevitable that we would.

So it was with us on this rocky road. Pow! A tire blew and we wobbled to the side.

As soon as the fine, graphite-like dust had settled like drizzling rain all over the car and upon the neighboring countryside, Papa, Mama and all us kids piled out of the car.

Shortly after we had stopped, another car approached from behind us, through the dissipating cloud of billowing dust. The car pulled off the road and the Mexican driver got out to render assistance. I've never forgotten that simple friendly gesture through all these years. In the States a person who has been eating dust for miles would be more than happy to take advantage of the situation and zoom past, possibly even giving a finger salute as well.

But not in Baja.

His newer car looked out of place on that windblown field. And the man was too well-dressed to be a local campesino. He sported long city-type pants and was wearing a suit jacket. His shoes were polished. We all thought he looked quite dapper.

He pitched right in to help my dad change that tire.

We kids stood by the roadside with Mama and watched. Then the man bent down and his jacket opened. It revealed a leather holster strapped to his shoulder. And a pistol, a real gun, was inside the holster!

I quickly nudged my brother Fritz and gulped, "Look."

"I see it," he stammered.

My older sister Camilla joined us and saw what had our attention. "Maybe he's a robber," she whispered.

Now we three were scared. We couldn't tell Papa because the man was with him. And Mama was keeping the younger kids out of the way of the car and the road. We stood back, unsure of what to do, and strained for that occasional glimpse of that frightful but tantalizing, for-real pistol.

We were whispering some brave ideas like, "If he tries anything, you hit him with this rock and I'll jump on him and try to get his gun." But deep down we knew we wouldn't do anything.

The strange dapper man and Papa finished the hot, dusty chore, stretched, laughed, and slapped their hands clean. "This calls for a nice cold martini," the stranger said.

"Don't we wish," my father laughed.

"Come over here," the man said, walking to his car. He opened his car trunk to reveal a custom-made mini-bar. A dozen or so bottles were snugly secured into the contraption along with glasses, mixing spoons and even an ice container.

So there, on the side of the dusty Baja road, the two men saluted their handiwork with a chilled martini, much to the surprise and delight of my father.

"My name is Hansen," the stranger said. "I'm the owner of Hansen's bar in Ensenada."

As the two men forged a friendship that would endure for decades, we kids slowly realized that just because Hansen packed a pistol didn't make him a threat. Our earlier bravado quickly and thankfully turned to relief.

Later that day Hansen joined us as we stood on the old pier in San Quintín's inner bay. Today the only remains are a few rotting wood pilings that rise above the surface of the bay. In its memory, the name "Old Pier" graces a small motel/restaurant on a hill above.

But then as we walked out on the pier a school of small fish swam below us. Hansen chuckled and said to us kids, "Watch this." He produced a few firecrackers that looked to be the size and shape of dynamite. He lit one and dropped it into the water.

KERPLOW went the charge underwater and little fish came flying up out of the water landing at our feet dazed and shocked by the explosive. It was quite a demonstration and impressive to us awe-struck kids who saw another feat of magic performed by this guy Hansen.

Once he left, we continued south to camp on the beach, about where the La Pinta Hotel is now, on the north shore of the broad, sweeping Santa Maria beach. During the week, we caught and cooked lobster, fish and large pismo clams. It was an idyllic respite in what was then a very remote beach.

We had ventured well beyond the end of the paved road and had found a virtual paradise. While it would be years before I would explore the area south of that point, after that trip I constantly thought of doing so.

On maps and even on world globes, I noticed the Baja peninsula loomed large, yet the San Quintín area was still far to the north. There was that much more land to the south. By an early age I was hooked. I knew that some day I would explore south of San Quintín.

I would not necessarily find the "land of sunshine and silver, of fruits and flowers, of grain and gold, of gems and jewels, of the walnut and wine, of the olive and the orange, of banana and tobacco, of fish and fowl..." as promulgated by my great-grandfather Bascom Stephens, but I did find sunshine and warmth, as evidenced by the people of the peninsula, like the mysterious, helpful and fun-loving Hansen.

The Lifeline of the Peninsula

Along Highway 1

Americans often ask those afflicted with Baja Fever about the safety of travel in Baja California, México. They usually don't say it outright, lest they offend you, but they're concerned about terrorism, bandidos, crime, debilitating diseases inflicted by bad water or food, or troublesome animals from mosquitoes to snakes.

The biggest hazard facing the Baja traveler is none of these — it's the safety, or more specifically, the lack of safety on the roads. Traffic accidents claim the lives of the vast majority of Americans who die abroad, and this is true in Baja as well.

Old well-worn foot and animal trails once linked the missions of the Baja peninsula. These mission trails fanned out from Loreto south to La Paz and the cape region, east to the mission villages in the mountains and stretched north all the way to the present state of California.

Eventually roads were constructed in and around the populous regions at the extreme northern and southern tips of Baja. Until 1973, the best way to reach the south was to drive down the Mexican mainland and take the ferry across the gulf. The center of the peninsula was a stark, scarcely-populated desert with little water, and the old mission trail was but a rocky, rough meandering track that challenged the sturdiest off-road vehicles.

By late 1973 road crews from the north and south, after working, long hours in their race to complete the transpensinsular highway, met just south of the boulder-strewn Cataviña area. Like the U.S. railroad completion at Utah's Promontory point, this achievement was historic and it assured economic development. Just a year later, the southern territory achieved Mexican statehood.

THE CHARMS OF CENTRAL BAJA

Named Highway 1, the transpeninsular road opened up convenient access to some of the world's most pristine areas, broad deserts, virgin mountains, secluded coves, great fishing and camping. Americans began to trickle in and 25 years later are still enamored by the unadorned charms of central Baja.

My great-grandfather Bascom A. Stephens was wrong when he felt the discovery of gold or the settling of a few areas would open up Baja. It was the completion of the highway that finally made it accessible.

Americans soon found that the 1,059 mile paved road from Tijuana to Cabo San Lucas was not a high speed freeway. The length of it is paved and that's where any similarity to a U.S. type highway ends.

It is extremely narrow, especially in central Baja, and there are usually only inches to spare when a truck, bus or motor home passes you going the opposite direction. Upon approach, you must place your right tires as close to the shoulder as you dare. Then you concentrate hard, hold the steering wheel tight, and breathe the tense sigh of relief only after the vehicle has passed.

There are no road shoulders either, should your wheels drift too far to the right. The immediate drop-off is often 18 inches or more in some locations, creating an extreme hazard if your wheels go off it.

In many places there are few if any turnouts and if a large truck is "breathing hard" on your tail it might take a while to stop and let it get by.

In the States most roads are banked on curves to help control vehicles. Not so on Highway 1. Most of the road has a high crown in the center, even on curves, so concentration is required to keep from veering off to the right.

It wasn't long after the road's completion that another problem surfaced, literally. The asphalt surface is not the thickest nor the strongest, and after winter rains potholes appear like wildflowers. I've seen potholes over a foot deep, and I've seen them so thick that dodging the biggest ones you cannot escape the other smaller ones, and the axle-jarring, teeth-rattling holes sometimes force you to slow almost to a standstill.

Mexican crews are constantly repairing the road, even resurfacing in some areas. But I've never driven Highway 1 without bouncing over some potholes.

Along with the potholes taking potshots in attempts to destroy the road, floods have also wreaked havoc on it, especially during the early years.

Arroyos swollen with winter rains wiped out entire sections of the highway. On many occasions I had to slowly and carefully ford a river where a road used to be.

The washed-out areas along arroyo bottoms have mostly been replaced with concrete, but even some of those have been flooded. The hurricane of late-summer 1996 had hundreds of travelers stranded overnight about 100 miles north of La Paz where they waited for waters to subside.

I once forded a deep river gully with my low-slung MGB. The next day the electric fuel pump, which we learned later is mounted too low exposing it to water, caused the car to just stop running. With the delayed effect none of us, including the young Mexican who stopped to help, could figure out at first what went wrong.

ANIMALS CONSTANTLY CROSS THE ROAD

There are still more hazards. Animals are not fenced and cattle and other livestock constantly cross the road, or even just lie down on the pavement for warmth, especially at night. Most of us who've driven the road have had to stop to let animals cross. You can imagine the effects of high speed driving when you round a curve and find animals in the road right in front of you.

Road blockages can also come in the form of vehicles, too. With no room to pull over, sometimes truck drivers will just park in the road and spend hours working on their trucks. If on hills or curves they'll often set a few rocks out, or Tecate beer cans, which are real shiny, to let you know there's a problem.

Of course the biggest hazard on any road becomes the other drivers. Sometimes snowbird Americans with their big RV's take up more than their share of the narrow road. It is one reason I rarely drive Highway 1 between Christmas and Easter.

Then there are the Mexican drivers. You will discover there are usually only two speeds driven by Baja drivers: too fast and too slow. Two speeds: 18 or 80. That's it.

Old, rusty hulks laden with large families, kept patched together with incredible Baja ingenuity, baling wire and faith, clog many Mexican roads. In the farming areas around San Quintín and Ciudad Constitution, combines and pickups laden with workers will putt-putt along a mile or so of the highway to that next farm road, forcing you to almost come to a complete stop.

Another extreme in Baja can be young male drivers displaying machismo at any cost, who tempt fate daily by speeding over the marginal road under marginal conditions.

I've talked to young Mexican truck drivers after they've climbed up ditches where their semi tractor-trailers lay upside down. Most of them feel that dumping a load or two goes with the job. They can be excellent and polite drivers but remember they're young, they're daring, and they're fatalistic.

While I have taken many Mexican busses, especially in urban areas, keep in mind that marginal vehicular safety checks on busses, ignorant or daring drivers and poor roads hugging dangerous precipices, might be reason to question getting on inter-city busses.

Animals cross the roads.

NEVER DRIVE AT NIGHT

People ask me what driving Highway 1 is like and I try to be as candid as possible, so that those who shouldn't be driving in Baja, don't. I always advise people never, but never drive at night in Baja.

Even though the hazards above aren't as prevalent in the populated border areas, one overriding factor makes the border region even more dangerous: alcohol.

There's a party-time mentality among many tourists especially on weekends. Young Americans not accustomed to strong drinks are out there behind the wheel. In addition, many Mexicans themselves put away a goodly amount of alcohol.

I have personally known over a half dozen people who have lost their lives on the Baja highways as well as many others who have been seriously maimed. I am aware of scores more, having witnessed or heard of numerous wrecks. As you'll discover in the next chapter, I personally had several close calls in my drinking days.

I always advise people to purchase Mexican auto insurance. We buy it by the year from the company that insures our Cantamar house. It is true that most American insurance companies will cover damages inflicted in México, but that does not protect you on the scene. Mexican law is different and they assume guilt unless you have cash to pay all damages or a policy from a Mexican insurance company. Just buy it. There are several companies in San Ysidro before you cross into México.

It didn't take long for Highway 1 to be littered with the carcasses of old cars and trucks that didn't make it. You could see several splattered along the hillsides below especially dangerous spots. And every so often the rusting carcasses are scooped off and hauled away for scrap. Once I noted hundreds of such carcasses rusting in the sun. I came by six months later and they were all gone. Six months after that I was amazed at the number of new wrecks that had taken their places.

Out of gas

Another problem is fuel, or lack of it. Pemex (The government controlled gas company) has stations strategically placed throughout Highway 1. There are two grades of gasoline with the green pump marked Magna Sin (without lead) replacing the old Extra premium grade. The other, Nova, is inferior and often makes American cars ping as its octane rating is only 80.

But there are sections along Highway 1 where the stations are almost 100 miles apart. And there have been many occasions when a station runs out of Magna Sin, or totally out of all gas.

The driver must make a concerted effort to keep the tank full, never counting on the next station to be open or having any fuel. In the central part of Baja it's good practice to fill up when you can.

Once when there was no gas at the Bahia de los Angeles junction I calculated I could not make the 65 uphill miles to Cataviña, but probably could make the 40 downhill miles to the Bahia. So I made an unnecessary out-of-the-way 80 mile round trip rather than sleep in the station or chance running out.

Lines form at gas pumps, here at Catavina, motorist had to wait until 9 a.m. to get gas.

Even in December, 1996, Cataviña had run out of gas and there was a long line at the pumps when the gas truck arrived about 9 a.m. I even waited to top off, lest chancing another Pemex station down the road running out.

If you do have a problem, carry a gas STP-type additive and put the Nova in along with the additive. It'll cut down on the pinging. Many Baja stations sell the additives.

Also if you don't keep the gas tank topped off and you have to refuel at some out-of-the-way places, remember that it often comes out of barrels and the chance of receiving gasoline with water or other impurities is greater. Carry a straining cloth or chamois in case you have to get gas out of a barrel. I developed impure gas problems with both my Jeep and my van and taking a little more care could have saved me the money to correct these problems.

MORE THAN A LINK

Like the gas stations, the hotels, campgrounds and other traveler services are strategically located throughout the peninsula along Highway 1.

Highway 1 does more than link north to south. From it, roads spin off in all directions, to timeless villages and missions, to mines and lagoons, to coves and beaches. It provides the setting for further exploration.

True, one can fly to Loreto, La Páz or Los Cabos. Those who fly miss the difficulty or adventure of traveling for over two days on the infamous Highway 1. While I have outlined some of the obstacles on the highway, I only meant to scare off those who want no part of them, and those who don't want their Cabo fishing or golfing time diluted. If you see the highway as a difficulty, it is. If you see it as an adventure, then that's what it is. Those who fly miss seeing the unique cirio trees (only found in the central section of Baja) that resemble a hairy carrot or a stick of asparagus standing on end.

Those who fly miss seeing huge cardon cactus dotting the landscape like sentinels. Or the knarly, stubby elephant trees or eerie fields of giant boulders larger than houses.

Those who fly miss the adventure of being part of Baja. Those who fly miss meeting some of the warmest, friendliest people in the world. Those who fly miss the real Baja.

THE ROAD FROM HUSSONGS

ENSENADA — 1975

Adding veracity to the last chapter, one of my closest calls in Baja California was a foolish, drunken night on the road from Ensenada.

I don't remember leaving Hussongs that night. The night had degenerated into one of those insane alcohol-induced and totally unwise debacles so common that first year following my divorce.

I do remember crashing into the car ahead of me, which seemed to be parked right smack dab in the center of the road. Oblivious to me, the driver had stopped at that first traffic bump on the road out of town.

Anyway, this Mexican driver stopped. I didn't. He and his wife got out and we surveyed the damage. Both were old cars, the dents were marginal and nobody was hurt. The astute driver, however, knew I was in the wrong and knew he could have made big trouble if he so desired. Rather than force us to spend the night, or more, in jail, he decided to cash in on his good fortune. In those carefree days, I carried no Mexican insurance. I was so irresponsible I even let my stateside insurance lapse that year. I was at his mercy.

"Señor, for $60 I will leave and there will be no Policia. Otherwise..." he shrugged and implied an outcome I preferred to avoid, drunk as I was.

Trouble is we'd been drinking all day and were almost broke, just then heading back to my little trailer and cabana 35 miles up the road.

My partners, Kurt and Jim, had already passed out and I had to rouse them to pool our funds. Jim and I scraped up about $40 U.S., including dollar bills and coins. I finally shook Kurt awake. He was lying across the entire front seat where his body slid down once I got out.

He got up, stumbled to the trunk, opened his pack, pulled out a checkbook and, with drunken flair, scribbled out a check for $20. In his devilish or confused state of mind, he signed it "Mickey Mouse" with the flourish of an actor giving an autograph.

Thus, we presented the aggrieved party with all our cash and a check that would stretch all the way to Disneyland. The driver smiled and he and his wife drove away. No one else came by the scene so we departed, back on the road to Cantamar.

A MOST FAMOUS WATERING-HOLE

Hussongs Bar, founded in 1892, has changed little over the years. An old yellowing clapboard building ensconced mid-block on Avenida Ruiz had become Baja's most famous watering hole. In the 1970s, it was usually so crowded a continuous line formed at the door. Inside it was loud and raucous, with boisterous conversation and laughter often punctuated by whoops, chants, yells and screams.

Hussong's, founded in 1892, has changed very little over the years.

Beer was inexpensive and margaritas not only rock-bottom cheap but extremely potent. It was nirvana to drunks like us. I'd been there many times since my divorce.

An artist in the place painted charcoal sketches of customers and I donated mine to grace the wall with many others. They hung my likeness right by the front entrance. It was fun taking unwary dates and guests in there and having them spot me on the wall. It was my kind of place all right.

Road to the South

Once at a stateside wedding, a girl approached and surprised me by reminiscing about us meeting at Hussongs some months before. It seems she was so short I set her up on the mantel where she perched while we carried on our distinctive singles-important conversation. I barely remembered her.

When I quit drinking some years later, I soberly realized that not only was I lucky leaving Hussongs with Kurt and Jim that night, but lucky leaving every time.

Kurt was an old drinking buddy who always brought out the worst in me. Even driving from Cantamar to Ensenada that day he whipped out a flask of Scotch which we passed back and forth. Jim worked for my company and appeared eager to party. He soon learned he was in over his head.

In fact, during our Hussongs revelry, we discovered Jim missing. Not spotting him in the crowd, I went outside. There was someone's van parked in front with the owner standing next to the open door. Inside was Jim, curled up asleep on the floor of the van. I sheepishly approached. The van owner said he was talking to some friends when this guy just plops in and goes to sleep. Fortunately the driver was good natured and I arrived just in time. He was about to re-enter Hussongs to find who belonged to this errant drunk.

I half walked and half dragged Jim to my car and pitched him in the back seat. Then I returned to the din of the popular tavern until Kurt and I stumbled out sometime before midnight.

I wish I could say that the accident on the speed bump that cost us all our loose cash and a Mickey Mouse check sobered me up and that I drove straight back to Cantamar without further incident. Unfortunately I can't.

THE SOUNDS OF A CRASH

Back on the road, the next thing I remember was the sounds of a crash waking me up. I'd fallen asleep (passed out) at the wheel and went off the road.

It was just south of San Miguel near the fish packing plant. There is a median divider in the road there and my car hit the divider at high speed, knocked down some bushes, bounced back into the northbound lane and screeched to a rest on the side of the road, all the while lighting up the night with sparks from metal scraping against the pavement.

This time we were all jostled awake. So were neighbors from blocks around who came to the scene. Cars heading north stopped. We got out and surveyed the damage. The left wheel was bent sideways under the frame. In my drunken state I still tried to drive it. Some Americans advised me to forget it.

Shortly the flashing red lights of the Policia came upon the scene. This second skirmish, though a single-car accident, was far more dramatic, and with the noise, the swelling crowds and the immobile vehicle, I was not going to get away.

Soon there were cops all over the place. Their leader was a heavyset guy with a pencil-thin mustache wearing a full khaki uniform. His captain's cap was tilted at an angle as if he just put it on after emerging from the car. He approached me. One of my greatest gifts is my speaking ability. I've been called "silver tongue" by some colleagues. Others have been amazed at how I've been able to get out of some dicey situations.

I FELT I HAD A CHANCE

Contrite, yet firm, resolute, yet polite, outwardly sober, yet very inebriated, I talked to the officer. I felt I had a chance as there were no others involved in the accident. I told him a not-totally untrue story how I was driving along taking a drunk buddy home. I mentioned how he fell asleep and fell over on me causing me to swerve off the road.

The cop looked at me speculatively and said, "Donde esta el borracho?" (Where is this drunk?).

All right, at least he's listening. Now to show him the sloppy-drunk Kurt. Jim was wide awake now, probably in a state of disbelief, just sitting on the nearby embankment. But we couldn't locate Kurt. Oh no! The whole credibility of my story depended on me producing this drunk guy.

Jim and I looked all over. The cop was about to lose patience, I could tell. There were people lined all over the road and we began asking them. Finally the American owner of a pickup about five or six cars back hollered. "Here he is," he said. The cop and I strolled over to the pickup and looked in back to see Kurt stretched out in the guy's truck bed, sound asleep.

THE CAR WAS IMPOUNDED

The cop said he'd let us go, but he had to impound the car. He gave me the address where the car would be and left. The crowd had dispersed and we were without wheels but alive and safe.

The corner liquor store employees said they'd give us a ride to Cantamar for a few dollars. After they closed for the night we all piled into one car for the ride. Jim had some money back at the house so we could pay them.

We slept most of that next day and then hitched a ride in a friend's van to Orange County. With borrowed cars and currying favors we all got where we were supposed to be by Monday morning.

A few days later I summoned the courage and asked my dad to take me to Ensenada to pick up my car. He was the first person I could think of who could get away mid-week and would go to México. By now retired and divorced, his external demeanor had shifted radically from strict and uncompromising to loose and liberal. Thus, I now found it easier to communicate with this new free spirit.

While our relationship was not a particularly warm one, it was he to whom I turned. His knowledge of Baja was profound, and I suppose so was his influence over me. While he could get ornery over small matters he was always strong and resolute in times of crisis. Thus he didn't berate me but joined me in helping to solve the problem.

When we got to the Mexican junk yard south of town, we discovered the junk yard was where my car belonged. It would take more to repair the axle, wheels and steering column than the beast was worth. Sadly I sold it for peanuts to the junk yard owner.

But I had to pay fines, lest I have a warrant out for me. So Papa helpfully shuttled me back and forth from the Police Station to the Department of Bridges and Roads and every other agency that seemed to be involved. I paid fines and got wads of paperwork initialed, stamped and notarized. I paid for the gouge in the highway and the little bushes I destroyed.

But I could have paid with my life. Just a little farther north of San Miguel the divided road ends and a car leaving the road would have sailed off a thousand foot cliff to crash onto the pounding surf below.

At Alcoholics Anonymous meetings people get up and tell "how it was." These "Drunkalogues" as they're called help reinforce one's decision to quit drinking. I used this true story several times. I can only say just recalling that night certainly helps keep me sober.

Looking for a Fan Belt

The Dodge Dart was now past Cataviña working its way north. A buddy and I had driven it down Baja's Highway 1 to La Paz and Cabo. We then looped the old dirt road through Todos Santos, and were heading home.

The Dart had performed well, even when dropping off the curb-like crown of the three-year-old new highway onto dirt virtually every time we stopped. Except for the streets of La Paz, every road or village frontage, or town, or side road, was dirt.

Even on Highway 1, we'd forded streams and jostled everything in the car loose on some rocky detours, stopped for the ubiquitous animals in the road, and carefully worked our way around some vintage vehicles that had wheezed their last breath right in the middle of the highway.

Jon and I had enjoyed the trip to its fullest, partied hard, drank a lot of beer, and now had less then two days to get back to Southern California.

I'd heard the noise earlier and thought something was wrong. It was a loud WHAP, then thumpa-thumpa-thump, then nothing. But I ignored it. Even though deep down I thought it was a car problem, I willed it to be a rock or something I might have hit.

In those years I figured maybe a problem will go away if I ignored it. Preventive maintenance had never been one of my strong suits. I related easily to many laid-back Mexicans I've come to admire. "If it ain't broke, don't fix it." It's part fatalistic behavior and part a "take it as it comes" attitude. This time it was a problem. A few miles up the road the car began to run hot. I pulled the boxy old Dodge off the pavement, dropped onto a gravel parking lot and bounced over to the entrance of a rancho.

We were at Rancho El Progreso, about 40 miles south of El Rosario, perhaps 80 from San Quintín and about 250 miles to the border. It was the waning part of the afternoon, when the cardon cactus and cirio trees cast long shadows across the hot desert floor. The light of the day was diffused, starting to get flat even though the May sun was still hot.

Steam poured out from under the hood. I opened the hood to let the engine air and the steam clear. Then I diffidently popped open another beer while I waited and pondered my next move. Jon was less mechanically-inclined than me; translation — we were both hopeless.

But as the steam cleared, the problem was quite evident, even to a couple of klutz's like us. There was no fan belt! I reflected, yup, that's what it sounded like, a fan belt breaking: WHAP, thumpa-thumpa-thump.

In those years I hardly carried tools, much less the spare parts I now carry, so we were in a dilemma.

The woman at the rancho said that her husband would be back in the morning; perhaps then he could help us. We decided to try to hitch a ride into El Rosario or San Quintín to seek assistance.

Rancho El Progresso. Where we unrolled our sleeping bags in the driveway

While we waited for a driver to stop, the señora who ran a small cafe out of her kitchen prepared a dinner for us. Then we waited. In those days traffic was rare, and after dark, non-existent.

It got dark so we decided that in the morning one of us would hitch a ride and the other would wait by the car in case help might arrive.

After the rancho lights went out, we dragged our sleeping bags out of the car and stretched them nearby. It was an uncomfortable, restless night. The rancho dogs howled at unseen objects that strained our imagination. And no matter how many rocks I removed from under my bag, there were always others left to jab my ribs.

I was up as soon as the sky began to lighten and the vast panorama of stars began to lose their luster. I was up before the roosters began their chorus to welcome the light of day. The dawn was most welcome but with it came reality. Our predicament became primary. I looked about the harsh desert landscape. Then I noted where we'd set up camp — right in a roadway that led to ranchos in the valley beyond! We were lucky no campesino needed to use the road!

Jon and I were chilled in the high desert dawn. We stretched and packed and waited for the rancho residents to stir so we could buy some coffee and breakfast.

With daylight came activity again on Highway 1. A few trucks rumbled by, and one pulled onto the gravel. The driver was a slender fellow with a large droopy mustache. He looked decidedly older than most of his fellow warriors of the Baja road, perhaps in his mid-to late thirties.

He walked over to us in that bow-legged gait that comes not from riding horses but from a lifetime of squeezing his feet into those narrow, pointy-heeled cowboy boots.

In the Baja outback it is not necessary to ask for help. It is freely offered to strangers and rendered with such sincerity that denizens of big-city America could hardly understand. There is no catch. There is no payback expected. There is just the help rendered as needed.

The truck driver went right into action once he saw the problem. He talked to the rancho people and poked around their salvage pile until he came up with a piece of rope and a small strand of wire.

He cut the rope to the size of the original fan belt, put it on and braided the whole thing with the wire. He squeezed the whole mess tight with pliers and asked us to crank the engine up.

The rope held! The car started right up thanks to that creative Mexican ingenuity so often discovered by gringos in Baja. Refusing a tip, he did let us buy him some coffee before we got on our way.

El Rosario at that time had two small Pemex stations, yet neither had fan belts so we confidently rolled on, the engine kept cooled by jump rope and baling wire.

But neither our luck nor the rope held for too long. The rope snapped on the outskirts of San Quintín and I eased the old car off to the right. I stayed with our crippled transportation while Jon started walking into town.

It wasn't long before I saw an old pickup coming south toward me. The vehicle's alignment was so bad it looked like the rear wheels and axle were trying to get ahead of the front axle. The disjointed pickup pulled off the road (front wheels first) and Jon jumped out.

The driver was a mechanic whom Jon had located after asking around. The fan belt he brought did not fit. So Jon was now to wait while I climbed in the sideways-moving pickup with the mechanic and we roared off towards town.

The mechanic stopped at a week-end swap meet where vendors had their wares spread out on blue canvas mats. The place was crowded with women, children and short, squat native farm workers buying fruit, knick-knacks, toiletries, tools and other necessities at the various stands. He motioned for me to join him.

I thought, "Great. Here's Jon waiting at the car and we're out shopping." Then I realized that there were several vendors with new and used automobile tools and parts. We stopped at each of them and I was delighted to see some fan belts, but we could not find one that would fit the Dart.

We drove another quarter mile to a second swap meet and continued our search. The mechanic suddenly smiled and picked one up. I paid for it and we left. He knew the size from memory and he was not wrong.

It just took a couple of minutes to install. His fee was ridiculously inexpensive so we augmented it with a couple of beers. Pleased, he took off toward town, that bent pickup comically cantered, filling the entire lane.

Like the proverb about a cobbler's shoes, this mechanic's vehicle belied his profession. I'm convinced he could have fixed its bent condition had he been so inclined. But the pickup still ran; it did what he wanted it to do, so why should he bother?

The incident taught me many things. My attitude toward the warm people of Baja and their helpfulness was reinforced. I again saw the mechanical magic performed by the people of rural Baja. While they have the wherewithal to repair vehicles and keep them on the road, it appears they rarely use those skills to perform preventive maintenance or repair something not integral to the running of the vehicle.

I also learned that as I am not a mechanical wizard, I should be more prepared. Since then I always carry a few hoses and belts and other emergency items into the wilds of Baja. And every time I drive past Rancho El Progreso I smile, thinking about that long miserable night spent on that rocky driveway.

A Snake in Camp

Instead of prairie schooners, horses and wagons, our three vans formed the circle around our camp's outer perimeter. Assorted tables and boxes comprised an inner circle. The campfire dominated the center and provided us with fuel for preparing dinner, warmth and a setting for social interaction during the cool, damp nights.

Even in summer the marine layer dominates the fertile San Quintín valley, often billowing in off the Pacific in a thick, moist soup. And when it clears, the wind might howl for three and four days at a time, adding thousands more grains of sand to the sensuous sculpture of broad dunes that line the beaches. Between the extremes are many days of perfection: sunny and warm summer days, cloudless, royal blue skies and soft, comfortable nights.

Cantamar neighbors Don and Marie and Erv and Sally joined me and Leila for the excursion. Our vans formed a caravan from Cantamar to this simple Baja of an earlier era, yet only 120 miles south of Ensenada. The dirt road from Highway 1 to the ocean was a little sandy but only one of our vans got stuck. We were able to quickly tow it out and continue on to the beach.

As we neared the beach, clam shells from many decades littered the dirt road. We found a high, hard-packed area just inland from the big sand dunes which would be perfect for our campsite.

The wide, sandy Santa Maria beach, about two miles south of the La Pinta Hotel at San Quintín was a haven for big perch and Pismo clams. I remembered a week spent in the area when I was a child, the time we met Mr. Hansen. I'd been back several times exploring in my Jeep. Again enamored with the area, I wanted to return to spend more time.

147

As we neared, some Americans passed us, leaving the beach on the dirt road. Bronzed from the sun, they could have passed for locals were it not for their trailer full of motorcycles and other assorted gringo toys. As if changing the guard, we stopped and exchanged greetings. They had figuratively passed the baton on to us as they wearily made for the highway.

After that, we saw no other countrymen all week.

The only visitors that week were a handful of men and women from the village. They would arrive on a mule cart at optimum low tide, even as early as 4:30 a.m., and leave an hour later with gunny sacks bulging with Pismo clams.

Our days were usually spent venturing beyond our makeshift home on that hard-packed earth. We had to constantly wend our way through a pass in the sand dunes to the ocean.

We too joined the locals by going clamming almost daily during the hour of low tide. We waded in ankle deep water and jabbed our pitchforks into the sand. Hitting a hard object was hitting paydirt, for there were no rocks on this beach. In about an hour, we would each unearth about 8-10 large, succulent Pismo clams.

The days were languid. We swam, enjoyed the sun, and wandered the beach searching for marine and crustacean artifacts as well as man-made debris. Singly, in couples or in a group, we hiked the sand dunes and explored the area.

One day I took everyone to the Old English Cemetery where surnames still visible on the weathered wood crosses reveal a decidedly Anglican heritage. These marked the deceased members of the 200 or so English colonists who tried to tame the land about 100 years previous, only to have their dreams dashed by drought.

On previous visits, I'd wandered around the cemetery several times. I chuckled recalling how my old MGB was once stuck in the sand there. Another time I'd seen a rattlesnake slither away from a pitahiya cactus whose spines sprawled across several graves.

My great-grandfather would have been disappointed to see the area he tried to help develop turn arid. But it turned out that he was prophetic. Today, a century later, the vast San Quintín Valley is Baja's most fertile. Large growers regularly supply U.S. markets with truckloads of tomatoes, corn and chiles.

We moved from marker to marker, noting the short lives of some of the colonists, reflecting on the hardships of these adventerous foreigners. It was an interesting and reflective experience.

Back at camp, we fished from the surf, catching the largest barred surf perch I'd ever seen. They were weighing several pounds and were so large Don and I threw back perch larger than anything either of us had ever caught at Cantamar.

In the evenings we made clam dip, clam chowder, fried clam strips and raw clams to supplement the fish. Don was always experimenting, making tasty treats from our bounty direct from the sea. One night he made an outstanding ceviche from some perch.

And at night, under a twinkling canopy of brilliant stars set against a velvet black sky, we'd sit around the fire telling tall tales and ribald jokes.

UNTIL LEILA FOUND THE SNAKE

Until the night Leila found the snake, that is.

Moments after she got up to get something out of our van, a bloodcurdling scream punctuated the serenity of the laid-back campsite.

We all jumped up. In a couple of quick bold hops Leila was back among us, now standing on a camp chair and screaming over and over, "A snake, a snake, a snake is under the van."

Leila's fear of snakes quickly spread. Marie also jumped on the same chair, sharing Leila's space. They held each other, both now jumping up and down.

Erv, Don and I grabbed flashlights and sought the cause of this upheaval. Yup, there he was right under my back bumper, just attempting to slither away.

Knowing Leila would not sleep thinking this "snake in the grass" was still lurking about just outside the van, we decided to assuage her concerns and make sure he would not return. So Erv got his machete and did the dirty deed, flinging the body of the poor serpent out into the bushes.

The night finally got back to normal, the girls came down from the chairs, and the fire dwindled to a few charred logs.

While lying in the van waiting for sleep to overtake us, Leila said, "You're sure that snake's dead, aren't you?"

"Yes, I'm sure."

"Maybe there's more out there. Maybe he's got brothers and sisters."

"Maybe."

"Can they climb up van tires and get in?"

I sat up, realizing she was serious. I comforted her.

"Honey, there's no way they can get in here. We're safe in here."

Nervously she fell asleep and we never saw another snake.

The next year a couple more people joined our group of six for another San Quintín trip. But the same narrow dirt road to those sand dunes was now surprisingly an improved road that took us to a built-up area. A large cyclone fence surrounded a wide area behind the dunes, including our old hard-packed campsite. A new sign now indicated that this was Honey's Trailer Park and Campground, complete with concrete slabs and showers and people.

It was a huge disappointment for us as we wanted to recapture that blissful summer week sans civilization and we all knew Honey's wouldn't cut it for us.

My Jeep reconnoitering of earlier years paid off. I'd remembered another dirt road which we then followed behind the dunes for about a mile until we found a large flat spot where we again pulled our vans into a social circle.

While we were denied our same idyllic campsite, we continued to catch record perch and fill our sacks with delicious clams. And we never saw another snake.

The English Cemetery

Going to
the Gulf

Going to the Gulf

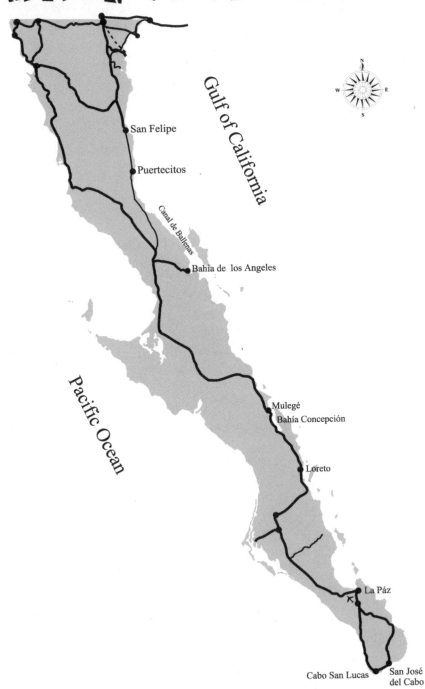

Gulf of California

San Felipe

Puertecitos

Canal de Ballenas

Bahía de los Angeles

Pacific Ocean

Mulegé

Bahía Concepción

Loreto

La Páz

Cabo San Lucas

San José del Cabo

"Since no two humans are alike, trying to find the unique qualities of a whole population is not easy, but below the border towns of Baja California there are some striking differences in human behavior. With few exceptions, the people are honest, opposed to violence, generous, affectionate, and very happy. They are not as aggressively ambitious, nor as industrious, and not as competitive as the people of the U.S. ...

— Ray Cannon,
"The Sea of Cortéz," 1966

Going to the Gulf

The Sea of Cortéz

Baja Fever

CLAMS FOR DINNER

EL REQUESÓN, BAHIA CONCEPTION — 1978

"Here's one," Leila said, "Left foot."

So I dove down, felt her left foot and pulled the small clam out of the sand beneath her toes. The water was only waist deep or so and the little sandy bay was filled with succulent butter clams.

We'd only been at it about 15 minutes and already the plastic sack was getting full. We just waded, wiggled our toes until we felt something hard and reached down to extract a clam. These were not the big Pismo clams that we often found along the broad sandy beaches on the Pacific, but enough of these small ones would make for just as tasty a meal, never the less

We were on the Bay of Conception (Bahia Concepción) a beautiful arm of the Sea of Cortéz between Mulege and Loreto. Traveling south most visitors stop at Santispac, the first campsite as you approach the bay. Santispac also has the most amenities for RVs, and sometimes in the winter it's hard to see the water for all the rolling boxes of aluminum at bayside.

El Coyote, farther south, is perhaps the prettiest cove reached by car along this side of the sparkling clear bay. But once when I was there at dusk, I found the troublesome no-see-ums (gnats) so thick you could-see-um. They were so numerous they looked like a dark menacing cloud as they massed for attack. Result: No-see-ums, 1, Me, zero. I left.

That's how I originally, on an earlier trip, discovered El Requesón farther south, by default. It is just a sand spit separating a very shallow cove on the left with a larger one on the right. The spit goes on out to a small, sandy island, but for most people, the sand spit is the destination.

A half dozen palapas sit at water's edge on each cove, perhaps a dozen in all. On the sand spit there is nothing else, no vegetation to attract the insects, just sand and sun.

Leila and I were traveling north, on the final days of our first trip together. It had been a fun trip, with all those little adventures that Baja travelers enjoy. Sometimes we camped and some nights we stayed in hotels, but most important, we got to see each other in times of stress and adversity as well as times of fun and frivolity.

The author and Leila drove this MGB the entire lengh of the Baja peninsula.

We'd been stuck in the sand, been lost, had car trouble and sometimes were hot, tired and irritable. How we weathered these minor crises was definitely noticed by the other, and from that character-awareness trip, romance blossomed.

So heading north, we were almost totally out of food and planned to spend a little time in the water at El Requesón and then head up the road to the store and either camp at Santispac or get a motel in Mulege.

Then we started finding the clams. After a while, we'd filled the plastic bag. Back at the little MGB, Leila rummaged through our meager provisions.

"We've got some crackers," she said. "And some hot sauce and some limes. Why don't we cook up those clams and just camp right here."

It was this type of response that told me I was traveling with a winner, not a whiner. She was definitely stroking up points in the "keeper" department. I knew she could fit in beautifully in social occasions. Now in a manner of speaking, she was being "Baja-tested" and winning the battle of Baja.

That may sound cold or heartless, but that's what courtship is, a period to determine compatibility. All individuals going through courtship look long and hard at the other's actions and reactions. Then they assess the virtues and faults and make an educated judgment. At least they should.

My actions were being scrutinized as well. Leila mentioned later that she was impressed when we were stuck in the sand earlier in the trip at San Quintín. I didn't throw a tantrum, just calmly and methodically went about taking care of the problem.

The palapa and sand pit at El Requeson.

So we set up camp under the palapa, throwing our sleeping bags on the shady sand. We let the clams soak to get as much grit out as possible, changing the water several times.

We found an old tin grate and I set about making a small fire. The bottom of our bucket quickly turned black with soot, but the clams steamed open as we watched and prepared our plates with crackers and limes.

Darkness was falling and the full moon became a bright white beacon as we sat on the sand with our legs crossed under us, holding our platters of clams and crackers. There were no tablecloths, not even a table. There were no fancy implements, nor even condiments. There were no candles, but the fire below our feet still sparkled. It was the most romantic dinner I ever had.

SANTA AND THE CLAM MAN

"Clam Man here. I'm the Clam Man. Wanna buy some clams? My clams make you horny," the bearded old man chanted. San Felipe's resident character dragged an old gunny sack through our campground. While selling clams was his business, the camaraderie and banter with visiting Americans was what really motivated the Clam Man.

Santa and the Clam Man.

The gunny sack befit his attire: loose, baggy pants held up by a rope, a wool watch cap and a thick, worn overcoat to thwart the wintry chill.

This was the first time I met this living legend, but over the next decade I'd see him many, many times. He came to our camp site as my buddies and I were setting up that day, sat down and began to extol the merits of eating clams, always implying that they did wonders for a person's sex drive.

Jon and Ray and I marveled at this old man's vitality and lust for life. After he left, we decided that when we approached his age we wanted his youthful outlook.

We were both in our early thirties, divorced and single guys who found the family-oriented Christmas holidays uncomfortable and fled the warmth of suburban Orange County on December 24.

Without really giving it much thought I was falling into a pattern my dad went through when he and my mom divorced a few years previous. After nine kids and over 30 years invested in their marriage, they called it quits.

My dad's change was radical, almost overnight forsaking all his conventional behavior for that of a more Bohemian demeanor, including growing long hair and becoming one of Laguna Beach's beach-strolling eccentrics.

He loved chasing women of all ages and having a good time. He traveled, usually solo but sometimes with a date, as the whims suited him. He would often go to México for sustained visits, sometimes driving the Baja peninsula, taking the ferry to the Mexican mainland and camping out on beaches all the way to Guatemala.

We kids started noticing a pattern; his long trips usually began around the time of his December birthday and never ended until way after the first of the year.

That year I didn't think about him or his pattern as we crossed into México. I just found that the adventure of a new and different place, especially an exotic foreign one, would overshadow any pangs of regret or self-pity in missing the comfort of typical Yuletide togetherness.

WE PITCHED OUR TENT

We three arrived in town and pitched our tent in the San Felipe Trailer Park right in town behind the pool hall. In addition to its close-in location, it had the amenities of electric power and hot showers.

After wishing the Clam Man a Merry Christmas, we walked the few blocks to downtown.

Near the main intersection ahead a crowd was gathering. Curious we approached the small mob of about 10–15 kids and a few adults. The object of their attention was an older man. From his back we could see his long white hair and a large, full white beard visible from both sides of his neck.

The children crowded around him giggling, "Santa Claus, Santa Claus," even though his uniform consisted of blue jeans and a checkered wool shirt rather than a furry red suit.

He turned, saw me, and bellowed, "Gregory. What are you doing here?"

He was surprised but I was shocked. "Papa," I said, "I didn't know you were coming to México."

"I didn't tell anyone. You know me, I just come and go when I please,"

Going to the Gulf

he roared in that authoritative voice that still tempted to set me to trembling. "Who are these guys?" he demanded of my partners in his typical blunt style.

While he looked like Santa Claus and many of the kids around him probably thought the jolly old man had actually arrived, in a Honda pickup yet, I knew my father as a much more complex being.

"Papa, this is Jon and this guy's Ray. They're neighbors in that MacArthur Village apartment complex I live in.... And Jon, Ray, this is my dad, Gus."

Now it was my buddies' turn to be surprised. "I told you guys he travels all over México by himself, so I shouldn't be too surprised that I'd bump into him some time," I explained.

Old truck pulls panga out to water in San Felipe. Leila Niemann photo.

"I remember telling you both how I ran into one of his girl friends that time down in La Paz. She still comes up and spends a few weeks with him now and then," I continued.

"LITTLE BRATS KEEP BUGGING ME"

Now I'd actually caught my dad playing and bantering with the kids. With we adults around now, he didn't want his friendly side revealed. He'd always tried to preserve what he considered a macho image. While the kids still crowded around calling "Santa Claus," he barked to us, "Little brats keep bugging me. I shouldn'ta come down here at Christmas."

I thought my dad was going to whack 'em to let them know the fun was over, but he just growled at them and they scattered. They weren't going to get more joviality out of this guy. Believe me, that growl made the Army sergeants in Basic Training sound welcome.

"Where're you guys staying," he asked.

"We just set up camp down there," I answered, pointing to the trailer park. "How about you?"

"I just got here. I usually go down around the point and camp in the sand dunes, but I'll come by your place and check it out," he said.

After our stroll through town, we headed toward our camp and my dad followed in his car.

He pulled up to our tent, got out, and immediately proceeded to berate us. "A pay campground. What's wrong with you guys. There's miles and miles of places to camp, and you wimps pay to camp right in town. I thought I raised you better, Gregory."

The guys laughed, not knowing whether he was serious or not. I laughed too, probably because the years had softened my reaction to his bellowings. After all, I'd been living on my own since I was a teenager, spent two years in the army, was married for 12 years and divorced since I'd cowed to his opinions.

"We wanted to be close to town so we could check out the night life," I answered. That he understood as he loved flirting and bantering with women. Later we all went to town.

That night was so slow and quiet I think we were the only would-be revelers out. After all it was Christmas Eve, Nochebuena, and a religious time for the Catholic Mexicans. When we four finally stumbled back to camp my dad again called us wimps for using a tent.

He unrolled his sleeping bag on the sand just below the sea wall, and snorted himself to sleep amid the brilliant display of stars, and a few twinkling lights from town.

One day he took us for a walk that stretched for miles through arroyos and dry stream beds and up and down sand dunes. The other guys were moaning "Uncle," and started lagging behind, but we all kept going. I just kept going and kept my mouth shut lest I be called a wimp again.

We were later lounging around camp when the Clam Man returned. His eyes lit up when he saw my dad. He smiled seeing this fellow old crony, "Gus, como está?"

My dad affectionately returned the greeting, called him "Pasquale," and they began to compare notes since they last saw each other.

Jon and Ray and I looked askance. "Guess I don't need to introduce them," I quipped.

"I think they've met," said Ray.

"Hey guys, meet Pasquale, the Clam Man," my dad finally offered. "He's got more kids than I do (I am one of 9 children)."

Going to the Gulf

Papa continued, "I once asked him how many kids he has and he couldn't remember, saying 'Señor, down here we don't have television, we go to bed early, and I eat a lot of clams.'"

So that was their mutual admiration, aside from their long hair and beards (one white, one dark) — they both had a lot of kids.

I realized it was more than just that. Their bragadoccio was limited. They both liked to pretend they were not affectionate with kids, but when you caught them one-on-one, you realized they could be.

Jon said, "Greg, your old man's cool. He's got a tough bark, but I like him. He's got that youthful outlook we talked about."

That he did. And it sure was fun that Christmas in San Felipe, when we were able to see Santa and the Clam Man compare notes. Little did I realize when we drove into México that I would be spending that Christmas with family.

The Pied Piper of Baja

San Felipe, B.C. — 1977

The kids pushed and shoved each other, giggling and chattering. They each had the same objective — to get his attention. They tapped on his leg and pulled on his sweater, "Señor Grande, por favor. Mi, mi."

The tall man with a camera was caught in a crowd of children who buzzed about him like a small school of fish. They were all fascinated by this large stranger in their midst. The stranger looked from face to face as the Mexican kids waved their hands in excitement.

He crouched to their level and focused his camera on a shy brown face whose dark eyes lit up with the honor. The others jumped around and tried to crowd into the photo behind the selected child, even making "V's" with their fingers behind his head.

For a week it was like that. The children of San Felipe followed his every move, even when he didn't have the camera out. In restaurants we'd look up from our machaca and huevos to see at least four or five little noses pressed against the window.

Along the beach, they'd run ahead picking up sand dollars which they'd present to him, seeking his favor.

Kids

163

Three kids even followed us around town piled astride a single rickety bicycle, yelling and waving when they'd pass.

Jon and I were both overwhelmed. All his life people have noticed him because of his 6' 8" frame. But he admitted he'd never seen anything quite like these kids!

Climbing the steps to the shrine of Our Lady of Guadalupe we discussed the conundrum of his being awarded celebrity status among the children here. At the shrine, the wind whipped his curly blond hair as we took in the panorama of this quaint Baja fishing village on the Sea of Cortez.

THE TOWN STRETCHED OUT

The town stretched out to the south from the cliff-top shrine. Below, the empty fishing boats created a spooky formation as they rested on the glistening sand at low tide. Pelicans gathered at the base of the cliff to occasionally depart on dive-bombing missions over schools of fish.

At the bottom of the steps about 10-20 children waited. They passed the time chasing each other and playing hide and seek behind the ice house.

We wondered why none had followed Jon to the shrine. Was it respect for the shrine, or respect for Jon, giving him some personal time. Or were all those steps the deterrent?

While honored by his new-found status, the tall man with the boyish face sat on the top step to ponder the enigma. He'd been with kids before, many times. His photography studio specialized in capturing them for loving and doting parents. He's learned to relate with kids, but this was still different.

His size? He'd always stood out in a crowd, even in the states where many are taller. In México he towered above the average person. I learned that tall people are constantly besieged by the curious, many offering inane comments. Just that day alone he'd answered "Dos metros" several times to fishermen who were astonished that anyone could be two meters in length.

Whatever the reason, we found in San Felipe even greater attention than what we'd noticed all over Baja California. There were always kids brave enough to approach and follow. They followed us at Rosarito and Cantamar and Puerto Nuevo on the Pacific side, and in small villages and towns all over the rugged peninsula.

These kids crowded around the bottom step as we descended. Jon knew he was in for an interesting afternoon. I thought that sooner or later, the kids were going to tire of this.

Kids adopt him

But I was wrong. For days, they showered us with attention until the day we headed across the desert and home to California. On this trip to Baja, it was the kids adopting an adult.

That afternoon our entourage paused to watch a fisherman and his teen-age son repair their nets. Down by the old town square they had tied the ends to the trees and with dexterous fingers nimbly removed and repaired the broken strands.

The frivolous children got in the way and one boy tripped over a portion of net creating a new rip. As the little ones scampered to the fisherman's threats, Jon suddenly felt a sense of responsibility to his volunteer charges. The kids were fun but we hoped an incident like this wouldn't happen again.

Nearby was a concrete slab, the village's basketball court. A few kids were playing. Soon the court swarmed with children. Appearances are deceiving. I knew Jon had never played basketball and was not really athletic, but to the kids his size suggested that he was a natural. They handed him the ball and looked at him expectantly. He looked to me. I shrugged. He took a little time, aimed, and shot once from near the top of the key. Swish! The kids roared their approval. He wisely refused to do it again. Jon and I were the only ones there who knew luck when we saw it.

Friendly neighborhood kids of Baja.

The town was ours. Wherever we walked people looked at us, the tall man, a large group of kids and me. We were noticed everywhere. A woman sweeping her doorway quickly vanished inside to return moments later with the rest of her family.

We walked up the dusty hill to where the town settles on a plateau. We walked past the police station and the fire station to a little plaza with trees and a place to rest on a bench.

LITHE AND PETITE TEENAGERS

We saw two older girls turn the corner by the fire station and start to cross the plaza. They each held one end of a shopping bag and were heading in our direction. They were lithe and petite teenagers, similarly dressed in white blouses and colorful skirts. They giggled as they passed and stole a glance at Jon.

The kids were jabbering excitedly with a couple newcomers to the group. Just then one of the group ran toward the girls and dropped something in the shopping bag.

The girls screamed and dropped the bag. As soon as it hit the ground the bag started jumping around to what sounded like a machine gun. Rat-a-tat-tat. The bag fell over on its side and the girls jumped a few feet away. Rat-a-tat-tat. Firecrackers! The mischievous kids had scattered in all directions. Soon the noise from the pack of firecrackers subsided.

We walked over to the girls and helped them pick up the bag. Aside from a bag of frijoles which had burst and a couple of jangled nerves, there was no damage.

One of the lithe, petite young teenage girls, however, became an enraged woman as she started to chase the laughing "chicos" around the plaza. We were able to understand a few of the choice words she hurled at them and they seemed a paradox coming from such a dainty person.

Jon approached her and put a comforting hand on her shoulder, smiled, and she was quickly transformed to our original vision of loveliness. Calmed, the girls continued on their way.

Jon slumped on the bench as the grinning perpetrators returned one by one. This is it, he thought. I'm going to have to do something. We gathered them around. Jon's grin was replaced by a scowl. They noticed and fidgeted uneasily as he scolded them. They didn't need to understand the English words to know he was upset. They were quiet and orderly on the return walk to San Felipe's main street, Calle Baja California.

ROSA AT THE TORTA STAND

The main street was full of pedestrians enjoying the warm, late afternoon. We were hungry and headed for our favorite food stand in the middle of town. With our entourage now reduced to fewer than a dozen boys, we walked past the curio shops, panaderias and licor stores to the popular taco stand. We had become enamored with their steak asada tortas (steak sandwiches on rolls) and Jon had also become enamored with Rosa who prepared them.

She greeted us and Jon was fascinated by her as she prepared our food. Dark hair toppled over her shoulders. She had a full mouth and sparkling white teeth. A nice figure. But those eyes. They were captivating. Dark, dancing brown eyes that invited, enticed. Jon, at a loss, turned away to face me and the kids.

"Look at him," she seemed to think as she placed the thin slices of steak on the hot griddle. "He has the whole town in an uproar."

As she sliced the large rolls, it appeared she too was considering the reasons for his popularity.

"He's tall — nobody in all of San Felipe could miss him. But there's more." She pulled the heated roll off the griddle and flipped the steak, spicing it appropriately.

"He's blond, that in itself contrasts with everyone here." Lettuce, tomato and sauce were added to the heated roll and she began slicing an avocado. She stole another quick glance at him.

"He's good looking. In a youthful sort of way. Maybe that's it. He looks just like a giant kid. Look at that grin. It's mesmerizing. That's it. To these kids he's just another one of them. Just a giant kid." Onions and cheese were added to Rosa's creations and she wrapped them in wax paper.

We paid and sat on the little wooden bench eating them. When we finished and started down the street, Rosa watched us. I got the feeling she was envious of the kids; she liked him too but was tempered by the restraints of culture and adulthood.

Jon took one more look into those dark eyes, shrugged, and we turned down the street with the kids behind us.

"Damn," he said, "She's beautiful. But what can I do? We can't communicate too well and we'll be gone the day after tomorrow. I suppose she'll marry a fisherman here and they'll have lots of bambinos. Oh well."

The group of kids had thinned out a bit by the time we walked back to camp. The sun had dropped below the mountains to the west and the sky was ablaze in a fiery sunset as we arrived at our tent.

Jon looked around and counted the remaining boys. "Siete," he said and he reached into the tent for a bag of cookies. He passed them around to the delighted kids and told them that they should be heading home. They agreed to leave but grinned and said, "Hasta mañana, Señor Grande."

A neighbor camper watched the kids leave and laughingly called out, "Hey Seenyor Grande. For a while there I thought you were the Pied Piper."

I knew the attention had gone to his head when Jon answered, "Maybe I am. Yes, maybe I am."

Going to the Gulf

Hot Sand, Cold Shops

It became a passage of summer, our annual treks to San Felipe. We usually went in late June just after school was out. Those weeks in San Felipe were perhaps the laziest, most restful times I'd ever spent.

Leila, young Ken and I would load the camping gear at Cantamar and head over Highway 3 out of Ensenada to the hot sands of the upper gulf.

North of town we bypassed all of the campgrounds that appeared like individual retreats at the end of long, straight, dusty dirt roads spinning off from the highway. In our initial camping forays together we didn't want to be too isolated, lest boredom develop from ennui.

The San Felipe Campground and Trailer Park right in town became our regular destination. I'd stayed there previously with friends and we liked the amenities: flush toilets, hot showers, picnic tables and palapas with electric light and power outlets.

The electric power allowed us to dispense with gas lanterns and other time-consuming camping chores. And after the first year we learned to bring a large electric box fan which cooled us as we slept.

The campground was just two blocks south of the town's main intersection and right behind a pool hall. The same proprietors owned both and we would pay our space rent and buy ice from the same guy who monitored the billiard balls, cue sticks and beer.

About 40 spaces constituted the campground, four rows of about 10 each. Even though the front, or beach row, cost a little more, it was well worth it. And if it was filled when we arrived, we would sit around and wait or move at the first opportunity.

The reason was the heat. Summers in San Felipe are oppressive, with almost every day topping the thermometer's 100 degree mark. August would be the worst, because the humidity that accompanies a monsoon condition accompanies the heat.

Even June was very hot, but a drier heat. The main solace was an afternoon breeze that would waft in from the bright blue Sea of Cortéz. This most welcome breeze could not be felt inland, even from the second row back from the water.

The most spectacular phenomenon in the San Felipe area is the tide, which fluctuates some 20 to 22 feet. Outside Canada's Bay of Fundy, the upper Sea of Cortéz has the world's most dramatic tidal swing.

San Felipe, 1976. Author's children, Steve and Annalies overlooking the town.

Water comes surging up the narrow sea filling the sandy shore so fast we often would just sit and watch it come in. It's quite startling the first time you see it. You can arrive in the evening, set up camp and see the shore line a long way away. Then you're startled awake by the sound of lapping waves, discovering the shoreline but a few feet beyond the sea wall.

At low tides we'd walk way out, a quarter mile or more, and look for the critters of the littoral. Sea snails, sand dollars and crustaceans of every sort made tracks across the sandy bottom.

San Felipe, before tourism became its number one industry, was primarily a fishing and shrimping village. Boats being repaired in dry dock seemed a long way from the water's edge, especially at low tide. But the periodic lunar high tides come up so high it is not that difficult to get the boats back in the water.

The waters of the shallow upper gulf around San Felipe are not only tepid, but quite warm during the summer months. Surf-side water temperatures run in the high eighties and into the low nineties. While just cooler than a Jacuzzi, it feels refreshingly cool because of the furnace-like surrounding air.

We campers would all continually trek over the hot sand to cool off in the inviting water. It's one of the few places in Baja where local Mexicans join the tourists by cooling off in the water.

On a typical day we'd hit the water at least four or five different times, while the kids seemed to live in it. Even when the tide would be at its lowest people hiked out to swim. As the incline was steep most often the water's edge would be less than 100 yards away.

The problem was getting to it. As the summer days wore on, the sand would get so hot it could and did blister feet. Usually we'd wear rubber thongs (or flip flops, or sandals, or zorris, or whatever your culture calls them) to avoid burning feet. But sometimes in the cool mornings we'd hit the water barefoot and get so comfortable with the small waves lapping over us, we'd forget the sand was heating up to its unmerciful stew and have to make a mad dash to the shade.

If the sand was hot and the sun unrelenting, the opposite was true of the shops in town. We would usually go for a midday stroll around town, stepping into the souvenir shops and paleterias (popsicle shops). The store's, air conditioning in contrast to the outside temperatures to which we had become used to, felt like stepping into a freezer, so cold were they. The blast of frigid air would hit you at the doorway instantly giving you a headache. I preferred the stores that used more restraint in their settings, or those that used only fans to temper the pervading heat.

Usually at least one day each summer I would engage a panga and go fishing. It was nice having town so handy then. Leila and Ken weren't so isolated with the shops and stores so handy.

We made friendships that evoked correspondence for years. Neighboring campers would return about the same time year after year for several summers. They provided fishing partners for me and a social outlet for all of us, including playmates for Kenny.

I've been to San Felipe several times before those bucolic days of the early eighties and many times since. I've stayed in four or five different hotels yet almost always take time to at least drive through the old campground.

It's spruced up more now than it was then. It seems cleaner, neater and even more civilized. A large hotel now graces the former empty lot next door. More restaurants are along the street out front. In effect, it seems even more downtown.

I miss the old campground. Maybe what I miss is the old me. My life then was simpler, less complex. I remember really relaxing then, napping midday, rising to lounge and swim in the balmy water, returning to read a little while the heat dried my trunks in minutes, sitting in the evening breeze to marvel at the acrobatic pelicans, and the tide, and the jumping fish, and... loving those simple pleasures that Baja seems to bestow on you.

Van in the Sand

Puertecitos, B.C. — 1983

Leila and I drove south from San Felipe for a day visit to the community of Puertecitos before we had to return to Cantamar. I had bounced down the 50-mile road to Puertecitos before but Leila had not.

In our Ford van, we took the old, inland dirt road that folks used to travel before the coastal road was graded, much less paved like it is today.

The inland road was sandy but good and straight, only occasionally dropping through rocky arroyos which slowed our progress as we negotiated amid the boulders.

The road finally entered some barren hills and passed the remains of an old sulfur mine. The hills were splashed with brilliant yellow streaks looking like mounds of dessert. The odor of sulfur jolted us back to reality from our visual fantasy of lemon frosting.

The road joined the coast and the less-used coastal route just north of Arroyo Matomi. We passed a few American campo-style developments before descending a hill and onto the cove that protects the village of Puertecitos.

Puertecitos has always had an American presence, with seasonal homes dotting the tree-less hills around the small bay. There was one Pemex station which was closed most of the time, and one modest cafe where one could rent a sleeping room.

Ours was to be a day trip and we set about walking around town, past the boat ramp and onto the rocks at the point where hot springs bubbled into a natural pool at low tide. The hot springs have been a Puertecitos attraction for years. Nowadays you have to pay to get out there.

SANDIER COASTAL ROAD

Our adventure occurred on the way back to San Felipe. We opted for the sandier, slower coastal road. We figured we'd camp back in the San Felipe area and then head for Cantamar in the morning.

The sparkling blue Sea of Cortéz looked inviting that hot and humid August afternoon as we drove north. There were several blufftop areas where homes were being built. Short roads took off every so often leading right to the blufftop.

We drove down one road where on the ocean bluff empty thatch palapas enticed us to stop and spend some time cooling off in the tepid gulf water.

Alone on the beach, the afternoon was one of those "Baja Fever" times that keep Baja aficionados returning to the hemisphere's longest peninsula. There was no other person in sight and we spent a languorous, carefree time in the water and on the sand.

Back at the van, we noticed the afternoon was waning and we were about an hour from San Felipe, so we decided to press on. But the soft sand around that inviting palapa served as a seductive web for an unsuspecting vehicle.

Within seconds I was dug in so deep that even the back bumper was buried in the sand while the front of the van was high and dry. Our supplies and camping gear, earlier packed so fastidiously, slid down toward the rear door.

We tried to extricate the van to no avail. I started digging under the wheels. I crammed the area's little available brush under the wheels and tried again. Nothing. We just made it worse.

We decided to seek assistance.

I remembered seeing a shack about a half mile back where we turned off the coastal road. We began walking down the road. It was obvious the makeshift tar paper shack was still used as living quarters but its occupants were nowhere in sight. There was the usual stockpile of detritus normally found around desert cabins. There were old rusting vehicles in varying stages of usefulness; there were piles of parts and junk and debris. But the people were gone.

We disturbed nothing and walked back to the van.

Darkness was settling in so we prepared to spend the night. We would seek help in the morning.

A MOST UNCOMFORTABLE NIGHT

So we re-arranged gear and moved boxes around in the van. Then we set up our sleeping bag on the van floor, with our heads at the high end; all night long we were sliding down onto the van's back door.

Years later, we both still remember the night as one of the most uncomfortable we had ever spent.

The incredibly high humidity that accompanies the occasional August monsoon condition kept us both drenched with perspiration all night long. Pesky mosquitoes accompanied the dampness in the van and seemed to have invaded us at will.

The gear kept poking us in elbows, ribs, thighs and backs and seemed to worsen with each change of position. And of course, the canter to which our bodies were subjected had us almost standing all night.

I suggested sleeping outside, but Leila was sure the place was crawling with snakes. The power of suggestion even had me wondering about them. I should have taken the time earlier and set up the tent, but you know what they say about hindsight.

Up to this point Leila had not camped out much in the wilds of Baja, and she was concerned. It seemed that every little sound of the desert was magnified into a threatening beast. On a couple of occasions headlights bounded down the coastal road, but none turned off our way.

We awakened early, that is if we ever did sleep. The first hint of light was welcome and soon the rising sun created a warm glow over the blufftop.

I thought one of those cars during the night stopped out by our turnoff, but I could not be sure.

We decided to check the shack to see if its occupants had returned. They had.

AN OLD MAN WAVED US IN

As we approached, an old man waved us in. He was sitting on a box in his patio, such as it was. The patio was a hard-packed dirt area by the back door covered by a primitive palapa made of the skeletons of dried cactus and mesquite trees holding up pieces of cardboard to provide shade in this desolate palm-less setting.

The old man's well-creased face wore a broad smile which displayed a large gap where a couple of teeth should have been. His well-worn blue jeans were almost brown from the ground-in dirt of the desert. His cowboy hat had holes at the creases, looking like perhaps a bird had at one time poked a nest in it.

His appearance and his dwelling shouted poverty, but the continual broad smile and affable hospitality gave us a different message, one of genuine friendliness.

Another man came out of the shack. He was younger but it was really hard to tell how old these desert dwellers were. Just the chores of daily survival were hard on them and aged them quickly. The younger man's smile and intense interest in our predicament was no less than the older man's.

It turned out they were son and father-in-law. The women and children were visiting relatives in Mexicali, and these two went with some friends to San Felipe for the evening.

We would first socialize and talk, and then we would worry about my problem. This is the way of the rural Bajacalifornio. As a middle-manager in a large corporation I had to force myself to unwind my anxieties to their pace. Once unwound, I realized that the slower lifestyle was one of the big draws of Baja, but my background often fought the change.

"How about some coffee," the younger man suggested.

The older man found another box and a rusty card table chair and soon we were all seated. The kitchen was the bottom half of a 50 gallon drum, placed strategically in the center of the dirt patio. They added twigs to the fire and put a piece of tin across the opening. They set a pan of water on the tin to boil and found four cups and a jar of instant coffee.

OUR PROBLEM WAS THEIR PROBLEM

Our Spanish at the time was very poor and we had to augment our limited vocabulary with a lot of hand signals. It didn't matter. These guys understood. We got the feeling that no matter what they had planned for the day, our predicament was most pressing. And if they had nothing planned, it gave them something to do.

After coffee, the younger guy went to one of the rusting vehicles, a large pickup with a winch in its bed, but the tires were flat. He started up its engine and to our surprise it turned over, loud and spewing smoke, but the engine actually worked.

His plan was then to figure a way to pump up the tires and then we would go down and pull the van out of the sand. They finally found an old manual tire pump in one of the old piles of debris, but the cord had a hole in it. So now they're looking for duct tape, to repair the pump, to pump the tires, to get their pickup running, to go to my van and to pull it out of the sand. This succession of events seemed puzzling and tedious to us, but it is a quite typical, logical solution in Baja, and if a simple task takes all day, so be it.

We were saved from the long day and the possible addition of more chores in the succession by the arrival of their friends who had dropped them off last night. An old Ford pickup pulled up just as I started walking the one-mile round trip to my van to find duct tape. The two additional Baja denizens were apprised of the situation and we all jumped in the pickup bed and roared off toward our van.

With six people and the pickup pulling, we were quickly jerked out of the soft sand. Smiles all around. This time I was the host, handing out refreshments.

None of the four would accept any money for doing what their up-bringing and their culture had ingrained in them. I solved the matter by giving the newcomers the remaining gas out of my extra five gallon can. That they graciously accepted.

Leila and I found a jar of coffee and several cans of food that our earlier hosts bashfully accepted. I gave them my new roll of duct tape, too. I knew they'd get some use out of that, even if it would be just to help the next gringos stupid enough to get stuck.

I have often used this story to illustrate the friendliness of those I have found to be the world's most friendly people. The people of Baja are a people of caring, of an empathy that transcends cultural barriers to help whoever needs help at the time.

The rural Bajacalifornio may not have the most comfortable bed in the world, but he will never have a problem going to sleep at night.

No Boat in the Bahia

Rounding a bend in the road, I could see the majestic Sea of Cortéz appear dramatically before me. The grand Isla Angel de la Guarda loomed far across the deep blue Canal de Ballenas, enclosing the natural bay named Bahia de los Angeles. Other dramatic rocky islands broke the calm beauty of the bay, helping enclose the memorable scene by jutting skyward with proprietary pride.

The islands sing, and the beckoning sirens from the craggy headlands and rocky shores that call out to passing mariners and sportsmen are not the nubile nymphs of antiquity, but fish, plenty of fish, enough fish in the warm turquoise waters of this midriff region to excite the most jaded fisherman.

Fishing spawned this village which seems impervious to growth even though the road from Highway 1 was paved at the same time the transpeninsular highway was completed. For years fishermen have also flown in, landing on the air strip which became the center of this little town.

The town was developed by Antero Diaz, proprietor of the Casa Diaz, a rustic resort at the southern end of the landing strip. Papa and Mama Diaz became Baja legends offering rooms, hospitality and family-style dinners served by request.

I'd been here many times, camping out under the stars or renting a room at Casa Diaz. On my previous report for a magazine I even stayed at the new Villa Vita Hotel. It had been five years since that article and little had changed since. This is what I wrote about the town then:

"The 26 rustic rooms of the Casa Diaz, built of rough-hewn stone, are scattered and either face the runway or the bay. The rooms have shower baths, single and double beds, electricity from 6 a.m. until 8:30 p.m. and have hot water 'solar heated' by above-ground pipes warmed by the sun by day, turning cool by night. Breakfast and dinner are served family style by Cruz 'Mama' de Diaz and her daughters. A good many of the villagers are related to the Diaz family.

"Inland from the Casa Diaz there is a small tire shop (llanteras), a couple of very small grocery stores, and the villagers' houses seemingly scattered at random on the rocky hillside facing the bay. Aside from a Pemex station (Nova only), a curio shop, trailer park, a limited-supply liquor store and a very primitive panaderia, there is little else to the town.

"The dirt airstrip, around which the whole village is strewn, is 3,116 feet long and welcomes several small aircraft daily. The strip is the virtual heart of town; a corner of it is used as an outdoor market; and the villagers use it for soccer games or horse races, moving to the side for the occasional plane.

"The strip is also the heart as it brings in fishermen to tackle the warm gulf waters which still teem with abundant fish. The balmy waters are also home to turtles and shellfish, although the lobster fishery is primarily for local use."

To paraphrase the remainder of the earlier article, I noted that Diaz was no longer the only show in town with Guillermo's Trailer Park opening a restaurant and curio shop, the new Villa Vita Hotel developed in 1979 by Señora Vitta Agundez of Tijuana and her Peruvian husband, and the opening of Las Hamacas Restaurant, owned by José and Delia Estrada, in-laws of the Antero Diaz family.

ON MY RETURN — 1987

Now as I return, I see a few other slight signs of change.

A newer restaurant on the hill with a commanding bay view is La Enramada, built by Antonio Ramirez Gobbi and wife Laura. From Rosarito Beach, Laura's family runs the local-popular Vince's Seafood. Good seafood, good service and good English make La Enramada popular with gringos.

The few hotels are rustic and simple, even at Villa Vitta and Casa Diaz. Town generators still go off at night diminishing the little air conditioning to a day-time event.

A couple of smaller places have sprung up, La Posada de Bahia on a back street, and a "Mini Hotel" at Las Hamacas. Las Hamacas has three large sleeping rooms each with a tiled shower and a large shaded porch with a view, a very good deal. (I've stayed here several times and guests often move their beds out to the porch to catch the breeze each evening when the air conditioning goes off).

The town changed slowly. The landmark dirt airstrip around which the village was born got too dangerous with a growing population, so a fenced, paved airstrip was completed just north of town.

Parts of the old airstrip are now covered with R.V. camping spots and ramadas for camping. Townspeople still play soccer on one corner of it, and the rest, uncared for, has rapidly returned to wild desert shrubbery.

YELLOWTAIL FEVER

Fishermen lured to the area have not been disappointed. The offshore islands of the midriff provide coves and shelters from which many species of fish abound, including schools of yellowtail, bonita and pez gallo (roosterfish).

On one visit, we chartered a panga and headed for nearby Smith Island (Also called Coronado Island). Our skipper took us to the northwest corner where we seduced yellowtail to strike by the yo-yo technique (dropping lures down and winding straight up real fast).

On another trip I noted the whole town had seemingly caught "jurel" (yellowtail) fever. Large schools of good-sized yellowtail occasionally congregate in a deep hole on the back side of Smith Island, near the northern tip.

When that happens, storekeepers lock their shops, mechanics drop their wrenches, and the soccer ball gets put away as townspeople hastily prepare their fishing gear and speed out over the glassy gulf to the yellowtail hole. That day, there were over a dozen boats bobbing above the hole and we were catching 15–20 pounders all day.

For this hole we were using heavy lead weights about the size of a lemon and dropping them with baited hooks to the bottom. It was a wonderful frenzy, made even more notable by the camaraderie and banter of the townspeople.

One lone female, and an attractive one at that, was skillfully pulling in yellowtail, one after another. Of course this elicited a number of comments from the others. My skipper told me she was the daughter of Sammy Diaz, granddaughter of Antero and one heck of a fisherman.

Her friendly antagonists, if not cousins or brothers, had grown up with this determined and gritty girl. Their chiding was indeed a sincere form of flattery.

Pangas and small boats can be launched almost anywhere in the gentle surf. Those without skiffs can rent or charter space, for one to four people, from either Guillermo's, Sammy Diaz, or even a small fish camp north of town at Punta Gringa.

Most who arrive at the Bahia de los Angeles bring their own boats. There's an excellent boat launch in front of the Villa Vitta Hotel.

I'm often amazed at the immense size of some boat rigs negotiating the narrow, winding Highway 1 some 300 miles south of Ensenada and then the final 40 miles over hills and a dry lake bed before dropping down into this sleepy idyllic village of Bahia de los Angeles.

My Jeep pulled no boat

My Jeep pulled no such craft — in fact no boat at all. On this trip I was to camp and surf fish a few days before heading into the mountains to explore some remote missions.

The dusty town was lazy and quiet in the hot, late afternoon sun as I arrived for a few staples. Even the dog laying across the tienda's doorway merely opened one eye and sluggishly made a feeble attempt to give its tail a half a wag as I stepped over it.

Punta Gringa, about seven miles of good dirt road north of town, is a large, curving sand spit forming a sheltered bay. There were a handful of campers there, either along the sandy bayshore or nestled in the rocks to the north.

It was dark by the time I set up camp where the sand bar hugs the rocks, so fishing would wait until the morning.

Even before the dramatic gulf sunrise bathed the Sea of Cortéz in saffron and vermilion, I had anxiously baited up. I was rewarded on my first cast. Within minutes I had a strong strike and hookup. I then reeled in a feisty medium-sized halibut from the surf. All right! Who needs a boat, anyhow?

While that was my only halibut, over the next couple of days I had pulled in many nice fish from all along the shore at Punta Gringa — without the benefit of a boat. When the bass hit at dusk that night, I caught about six of them within 40 minutes.

I caught a sting ray (looks like a skate), even though the locals called it a manta raya. It seems to me they call anything similar to a ray a manta raya. I caught large perch and cabrilla and some bright and beautiful, thick-skinned triggerfish.

I caught a number of unusual fish called bullseye puffers. They have teeth like a parrotfish, loose skin and croak like a frog. I'd caught several before one puffed up and displayed the reason for that loose skin. It blew up to a round ball. Good judgment told me these scale-less fish were not to be eaten. I consulted Tom Miller's Baja Book II which confirmed that they were poisonous. Locals call them botetas and contend that it's their liver that is quite poisonous to eat.

The fishing at Punta Gringa was relaxing and fun. I feasted on halibut and bass cooked over open flames. One day I wandered over to a neighbor camper to see if he wanted to share the expenses of a boat with me.

He had his line in the water and a large bucket of fish at his feet. Just then he got a solid strike and reeled in the largest bass either of us had yet caught from the shore.

"No thanks," he said, "You don't need boats around here!"

My camp at Punta Gringa, North of the Bay of Los Angeles.

Going to the Gulf

182

San Ignacio mission.

The ruins of Mission San Fernando Velicata.

Sign in front of ruins.

Baja Fever

The Baja of
Yesteryear

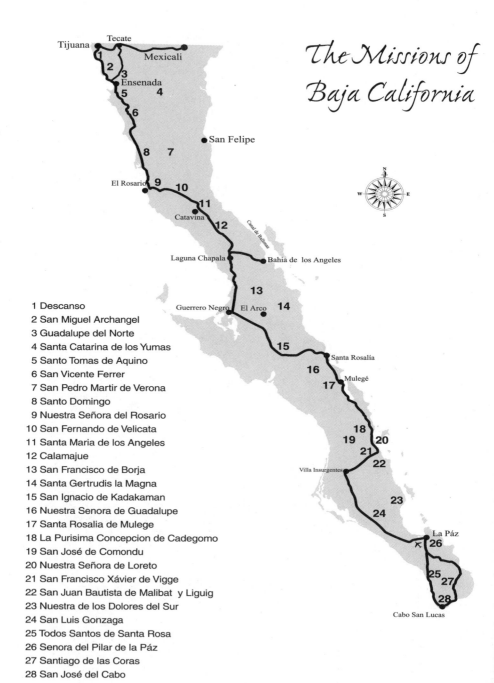

The Missions of Baja California

1 Descanso
2 San Miguel Archangel
3 Guadalupe del Norte
4 Santa Catarina de los Yumas
5 Santo Tomas de Aquino
6 San Vicente Ferrer
7 San Pedro Martir de Verona
8 Santo Domingo
9 Nuestra Señora del Rosario
10 San Fernando de Velicata
11 Santa Maria de los Angeles
12 Calamajue
13 San Francisco de Borja
14 Santa Gertrudis la Magna
15 San Ignacio de Kadakaman
16 Nuestra Senora de Guadalupe
17 Santa Rosalia de Mulege
18 La Purisima Concepcion de Cadegomo
19 San José de Comondu
20 Nuestra Señora de Loreto
21 San Francisco Xávier de Vigge
22 San Juan Bautista de Malibat y Liguig
23 Nuestra de los Dolores del Sur
24 San Luis Gonzaga
25 Todos Santos de Santa Rosa
26 Senora del Pilar de la Páz
27 Santiago de las Coras
28 San José del Cabo

"*California, majestic State of California, carest thou, on thine onward march, to recall the centuries when thou wert but an unknown part of those strange, mysterious lands, las Californias! Wouldst thou . . . hear the romantic story of thy mother, the First California, the California whose beginnings are thine own? Strange, strange indeed, California, that those brave days should be buried in oblivion, thine earliest heroes forgotten! Every camino, every mission, every harbor in thy southern Peninsula is rich with their memories, but alack, who knows aught of poor Lower California!*"

— *Arthur Walbridge North,*
" *The Mother of California,*" 1907

The Baja of Yesteryear

Baja Exploration Led to California

Baja Missions — 1697 to Present

Few Americans realize how significant the exploration of the Baja California peninsula was to the development of and eventual U.S. statehood of California.

The California chain of missions began in Baja in 1697, and, over the next 150 years, stretched all the way to northern California.

For the first century the word "California" only applied to the current Mexican peninsula. Unknown lands to the north were referred to as Nuevo California (New California) or Alta California (Upper California). Then, after the development of the northern area, the Mexican peninsula was called Antigua California (Old), and later Lower California (Baja California).

Today, the term "California" can rightfully refer to three states. In addition to the U.S. state of California, Mexico's Baja California is now divided into the two states of Baja California (Norte) and Baja California Sur (BCS).

Explorer Hernan Cortes, after claiming México for Spain and opening a route to the Pacific, sent the first European visitors to the Californias. His soldiers landed in La Páz Bay in 1533 and returned with tales of an abundance of pearls.

Cortes went to La Páz himself in 1535 and maintained a Presidio of soldiers for two years, but the harshness of Baja was noted even then as hostile Indians, hurricanes, illnesses and hunger forced them to return.

Other explorers traveled the Baja coast. In 1542 Portuguese Captain Juan Rodriguez Cabrillo, under the Spanish banner, visited not only the Baja coast but the Channel Islands off Santa Barbara, and sailed past the San Francisco Bay.

In 1622, Sebastian Vizcaino explored all the way north to Cape Mendocino in Nuevo California, resulting in many location names and the best maps of the entire west coast. But it was the Spanish soldiers and priests who developed the overland route by establishing settlements and missions throughout the (Lower) California peninsula. The missions were integral in the colonization of the harsh, semi-arid peninsula. They became the center of settlements in which the indigenous Indians could learn agriculture, ranching and social skills along with the usual heavy dose of religion mixed with forced cultural adaptations.

LORETO — CALIFORNIA'S FIRST MISSION

The historical capital of the Californias is at Loreto where a mission was established in 1697, becoming the only successful development in the Californias by the 17th century. Loreto is considered "The Head and Mother of the Missions of Lower and Upper California."

On October 19, 1697. Jesuit Mission President Padre Juan Maria Salvatierra landed at Loreto with a founding party. They went right to work to establish the mission and indoctrinate the Indians and immerse them in the European culture.

The Mission at Loreto was established in 1697

The Baja of Yesteryear

The Jesuits went on to establish 19 missions, from San José Del Cabo in the south to Santa Maria in the mountains above Cataviña in northern Baja. Three of those original missions became visitas, or visiting locations served from existing missions, and one, Calamajue, was soon moved to the Santa Maria site. Thus 15 missions were in operation before the King of Spain, for political reasons, expelled the Catholic Jesuit religious order from the New World in 1768.

From south to north, the 15 were:	Year established
San José del Cabo	1720
Santiago	1721
Todos Santos	1733
Los Dolores	1721
San Luis Gonzaga	1731
San Jávier (Xávier)	1699
Loreto	1697
San José de Comondu	1708
La Purisima Concepcion	1715
Santa Rosalia de Mulege	1705
Guadalupe (Guasinapi)	1720
San Ignacio	1728
Santa Gertrudis	1751
San Borja	1762
Santa Maria-Calamajue/Calamyget	1766

Other missions at La Páz (1720), San Juan Bautista de Ligui and Santa Rosa were abandoned and later served from other sites.

The Franciscan Order, under President Junipero Serra, took over the Baja missions. The timing was providential, because the Spanish Conde José de Galvez had just been given broad powers to secure as much North America land as possible for Spain, lest it fall into the hands of the English or Russians.

The Franciscans were a less-flamboyant Catholic order of priests with a three-knotted rope cinched around their waists. These knots allegedly signified their austere vows of poverty, chastity and obedience.

Using the missions as way stations on their trek north, Galvez' main party, led by Commander Gaspar de Portola, headed for Alta California. Serra, nursing a badly infected foot, accompanied Portola, and sent Padre

Juan Crespi to accompany the advance party, led by Rivera y Moncada.

In 1769, while the advance party reached San Diego to begin Alta California's famous mission chain, Serra stopped to establish the only Franciscan mission in Baja, San Fernando de Velicata, the ruins of which are just a few miles off Highway 1, near the El Progreso Rancho about 40 miles south of El Rosario.

During this time, the Dominican Order pleaded for equal participation with the Franciscans in the development of the missions in the Californias. Serra wrote to México City proposing that the Dominicans be given charge of all the peninsular missions and to establish new ones to complete the link between the two Californias, while the Franciscans continued north.

Serra must have known about the real estate axiom of Location, Location, Location, which the three knots could later have represented, as he guessed where the more fertile real estate was and planned to be a part of it.

In 1772, the plan that the Dominicans take over all the missions was approved by the Viceroy and that religious order went on to establish an additional nine missions in Baja's northern reaches.

The nine Dominican-founded missions, from south to north, were established at:

Mission	Year established
El Rosario	1773
Santa Domingo	1775
San Pedro Martír	1795
San Vicente	1780
Santo Tomás	1791
Santa Catarina	1797
Guadalupe	1834
San Miguel	1787
El Descanso	1817

The northernmost Baja mission was established at El Descanso (about 12 miles south of Rosarito Beach) and served an area north to Punta Descanso (Where Calafia Restaurant is today).

That marked the official boundary separating the Dominican Order to the south and the Franciscans to the north. This boundary was also designated in 1777 to separate the New Spain provinces of Alta and Baja California.

The current international border farther north between Baja California and the U.S. state of California was a result of the 1848 Treaty of Hidalgo which ceded Alta California to the U.S.

Serra, meanwhile, went on to become one of the Golden State's most important figures as his Chain of Missions led to the development along El Camino Real, the "Royal Road," the "Kings Highway," that still links many U.S. California communities.

The Baja missions, where it all began, saw the original establishment of 29 missions. They remain in various condition. Some are a pile of adobe rubble, while others are magnificent stone structures still used as parish churches.

The missions in the poorest present shape generally are the northern ones, and the two most northern Jesuit missions, Santa Maria and Calamajue. They were all constructed of adobe and all that remain are eroded walls, if that.

Many of the southern mission buildings were constructed of stone and some of them have changed little during their 250-300 years, some still serving as parish churches.

The three I feel are in the best condition are reached only by difficult dirt road: San Borja, Santa Gertrudis and San Jávier (Xávier). The best preserved one on the paved road is at San Ignacio. Other easily-reached missions at Mulege and Loreto are also well worth visiting.

Some historians see the Spanish padres in the altruistic light upon which they saw themselves (saving the lost souls of heathens). Others noted they were brutal, dominating masters who enslaved the natives, forced European culture upon them and subjected them to European diseases. In most cases it appears the intrusion of the padres upon the indigenous tribes was both, a blessing and a curse. Whatever their reasons or methods, the Spanish padres truly made an impact on all the Californias.

As for the buildings themselves, regardless of their present physical state, or their obscure locations, their historical importance is not to be denied. Their history is truly the history of the Californias.

THE FIRST CAPITAL OF THE CALIFORNIAS

LORETO, B.C.S. — 1697

"Cabeza y Madre de las Misiones de Baja y Alta California," reads the modest looking inscription above the main entrance. But its meaning is anything but modest. It translates: "Head and Mother of the Missions of Lower and Upper California." Above that inscription another reads "25 Oct 1697."

As the only development in the Californias in the 17th century, Loreto truly is the "Historical Capital of the Californias." Another inscription indicating that significant fact graces the nearby municipal building.

SAN BRUNO WAS FIRST SETTLEMENT

A broad arroyo swollen by rain water some "eight leagues" north of Loreto is actually the site of the first California settlement. In 1683, Padre Eusebio Kino, along with some Spanish soldiers and friendly Indians, constructed a presidio and mission at the site they called San Bruno. Lack of regular water forced abandonment two years later. Today only some weathered rock formations and a broad beach remain. Kayakers often set up camp amid the rocks and handful of palm trees, totally unaware of the spot's historic significance.

The Loreto founding party, which landed on Oct. 19, 1697, consisted of six Spanish soldiers led by Jesuit Mission President Padre Juan Maria Salvatierra. Under his direction, they constructed a church of stone laid in mortar of clay, all enclosed within a hardwood timber stockade topped by cactus thorns. Thatched palm leaves made the first roof.

Local Indians immediately were attracted to the mission. In learning the white man's ways, they were subjected to their visitors' religion, dress and culture.

With five additional soldiers and the help of Indians, work commenced on a permanent chapel, three small houses and storage and supply rooms. Hand-hewn cedar timbers were cut and dragged down from the mountains by oxen. The Roman bricks forming a decorative motif in the mission walls were contributed by an Italian patron and shipped over as ballast.

The stone Loreto Mission building of today was completed in 1704. By this time the padres had baptized some 200 Cochimi Indians.

CAPITAL OF THE CALIFORNIAS

The mission not only served as headquarters for the Jesuit mission chain for 70 years, but was, in effect, the capital of both Californias for well over 100 years. When the town was wiped out by a hurricane in 1829, the capital of Baja California was moved to La Páz and Loreto dwindled in importance.

The Indian population has long since disappeared. Much of the present Loreto population is made up of descendants of the early Spanish settlers.

In 1950 enterprising Padre don Modesto Sanchez Mayon was assigned to the Loreto Mission. One year he won a premium of $500,000 pesos in the National Lottery of México with which he graced the old mission with a new tower and made other repairs and improvements.

MUSEUM PRESERVES THE HISTORY

Now in a compound adjacent to the Mission is the historic Museum of National Institute of Anthropology and History. An unusual impressionistic statue of Christ on the cross carved from driftwood graces the courtyard along with rudimentary wine presses and an ox cart.

The priceless, old, renaissance oil paintings would be more fitting in Florence's Uffizi Museum than in this small Baja village, 703 miles from the U.S. border. Historical artifacts, including a boat hand-hewn from one log, are among the museum's attractions. The museum is open daily and charges a small fee.

A bust of Padre Salvatierra faces the historic mission from a plaza across the street. In recent years the main street nearby has been transformed into a pedestrian walkway, with small shops catering to the infrequent tourist.

Loreto is still remote, right off Highway #1 for those driving the peninsula, but a long way from a city; La Páz is 223 miles south. Aero California does provide one daily non-stop from Los Angeles to Loreto.

A FISHING PARADISE

Fishermen have long known about Loreto; dorado, yellowtail, marlin, sailfish, grouper, rock sea bass, roosterfish and many other species have been caught there.

It was November when Don and I checked into town, found a guide upon inquiring ($90 per boat per day - 2-3 people), and caught a number of dorado (mahi mahi) along with skipjack, bonito, sierra and barrilete. And summer is considered the better season.

Heading out to the fishing grounds, we noted the first glimmer of daylight slowly yielding to an explosion of color as the sun rose over the Sea of Cortez. Already, before the heat of day, Loreto's townspeople lined the jetty. We could see some lucky ones catching good sized roosterfish with live bait cast from shore.

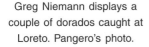
Greg Niemann displays a couple of dorados caught at Loreto. Pangero's photo.

For golfers, there's now an 18 hole golf and tennis center at Nopolo, just south of town. Snorkeling, scuba diving, whale watching and wind surfing trips can also be arranged at Loreto.

But Loreto remains a sleepy oasis where summer's heat forces a slow, laid back pace for locals and visitors alike. California's first city has changed very little, and a lot of people like it like that.

THE OASIS OF SAN IGNACIO KADAKAAMAN

SAN IGNACIO, B.C.S. — 1728

After driving south across miles of barren desert, the quaint, picturesque village of San Ignacio is a refreshing sight. A verdant oasis, replete with lagoons and thousands of date palms, it is the Baja California town that evokes the most impressive recall among travelers who drive the length of Highway One.

Dominating the landscape, and facing the shaded town square, is the imposing Mission San Ignacio, stone building well over two centuries old, is one of the best preserved missions throughout the Californias.

The current mission church was built by the Catholic Dominican Order in 1786. Constructed out of carved lava-block stone, it features massive four-foot thick walls that keep the interior cool, a feature still enjoyed as the Mission San Ignacio is an active parish church to this day.

Back in November 1716, Mulege's Jesuit Padre Francisco Piccolo visited the area the Indians called Kadakaaman (Creek of Reeds). Early Spanish travelers called it the Arroyo del Carrizal.

Piccolo stayed a month in the fertile valley, noting that the plentiful supply of water, complete with springs and an underground river which emerges as a small lake, had attracted large numbers of Indians.

It was 12 years later however, before a permanent mission was to be established. After studying the Cochimi language at Loreto, young Padre Juan Bautista Loyando arrived at San Ignacio with seven soldiers and numerous Indians on Jan. 20, 1728.

Padre Loyando, a wealthy man in his own right, donated part of his own fortune to establish the mission and become its first priest. With the many Indians in the area, he built a church and celebrated Easter services in the new church building that year.

First California date palms

It was Padre Loyando who arranged that the first Arabian date palms that arrived in Baja California in 1730 be planted at San Ignacio. As a result, three varieties of dates provided abundantly for the Indian families. Today's 4,000 inhabitants still rely on the date harvest from the area's approximate 100,000 palm trees.

The annual date harvest is celebrated on July 31, which is also the feast day of the town's patron saint, St. Ignatius of Loyola. Music and dancing augment the fiesta, where date products and a Date Queen, "La Reina del Datil," reign.

Despite the paucity of rainfall, the land near the mission is among the most fertile in Baja California. It wasn't long before many orchard trees, grapevines, figs and olives prospered along with the date palms. Cattle and sheep were introduced from other missions to help support the Indians, which at one time numbered about 5,000 in the area.

After four years, Padre Loyando was replaced by the veteran Padre Sebastian de Sestiaga from Mulege. Sestiaga (or Sistiaga) actually spent three years at Kadakaaman before Loyando established the mission. From 1725-28 in addition to establishing the site, he was preparing the Indians for their eventual baptisms.

Padre Sigismundo Taraval followed de Sestiaga, and then it was the noted explorer Padre Fernando Consag who was in charge at San Ignacio. During San Ignacio's first 25 years, it was the northernmost mission and a base for exploration into the wilds of the north.

Later, after the Dominican Order took over the Baja missions, Padre Juan Crisostomo Gomez, the Dominican Mission President, was based at San Ignacio.

Vaccine experiment saves Indians' lives

Padre Gomez earned distinction by experimenting with live small pox vaccine, saving the lives of 1,400 Indians. Only three or four San Ignacio Indians died during the epidemic that decimated the Indian populations at other missions.

While Padre Gomez was there, the mission enjoyed further good fortune when a Spanish Queen donated one and a half million pesos to erect storehouses, a parochial residence, soldiers' quarters and the beautiful stone church. Ruins of the outbuildings stand today, and the dominant stone

Mission San Ignacio is considered the finest example of hand-cut stone-work in the western hemisphere.

Date palms now cover the valley floor; thatched-roof houses on narrow streets surround pastel shops in the center of San Ignacio. A paved 1.1 mile road off Highway 1 make this mission and town among the most accessible on the peninsula.

San Ignacio offers overnight accommodations, campsites, meals, refreshments, gasoline, telephone service and limited supplies. Trips can be arranged in town to visit several cave painting sites.

There is a Hotel La Pinta on the road into town and an inexpensive, but modest, La Posada Motel, run by the Oscar Fischer family on a side street southeast of the plaza.

Next to the Pemex station at the turnoff from Highway 1 is the San Ignacio Transpeninsular Trailer Park Sites, which cost about $5.00, have water and electricity, but no shade. There are two smaller campgrounds in the date palms on the lagoon not far from the La Pinta. One charges $3, the other just $2.

I have never been able to drive past San Ignacio without stopping to at least walk the plaza, buy a few dates, take a few photos and revisit a few friendly merchants.

Highway 1 travelers approaching San Ignacio, their senses dulled from crossing the 90 miles of straight, arid Vizcaino Desert, are jolted to attention after rounding that last curve in the road. The visual delight of date palms and lagoon that make the San Ignacio oasis unique literally lures the traveler into stopping, resting and relaxing.

The 5,000 Cochimi Indians knew a good thing when they saw it.

SAN IGNACIO — HOW TO GET THERE

The oasis town of San Ignacio is about midway down the Baja California peninsula, 532 miles south of Tijuana, just 1.1 mile off Highway 1, in the state of Baja California Sur. It is 90 miles south of Guerrero Negro. The mission graces the town square and cannot be missed.

The belfry of Mission Santa Gertrudis

MISION SANTA GERTRUDIS LA MAGNA

ESTE SITIO FUE DESCUBIERTO POR EL PADRE JESUITA
FERNANDO CONSAG EL 22 DE MAYO DE 1751. LA PRIMERA
CONSTRUCCION FUE DE ADOBE CON CIMENTACION DE PIE-
DRA Y TECHO A DOS AGUAS, Y FUE EDIFICADA POR EL PA-
DRE SEBASTIAN SISTEAGA Y EL INDIGENA ANDRES COMANJI.
    EN 1752 LLEGO EL PADRE JORGE RETZ A HACERSE CAR-
GO DE LA MISION Y DE LOS 600 INDIGENAS QUE HABITABAN
ESTA REGION.
    SE CONSTRUYERON CANALES Y UN POZO ARTESIANO PARA
CULTIVAR OLIVOS, UVAS, DATILES, GRANADAS, HIGOS, TRIGO Y
MAIZ; PARA SATISFACER NECESIDADES DE ALIMENTACION, TRA-
BAJO, TRANSPORTE Y VESTIDO. SANTA GERTRUDIS CONTABA
CON VACAS, OVEJAS, CABRAS, MULAS Y CABALLOS.
    AL ABANDONAR LOS JESUITAS LA PENINSULA, LOS DOMI-
NICOS SE ENCARGARON DE TERMINAR LA CONSTRUCCION DE
LA IGLESIA DE CANTERA QUE VEMOS ACTUALMENTE, INICIADA
POR EL PADRE RETZ. CORRESPONDIO A FRAY JOSE ESPIN CON-
CLUIRLA EN 1797. LA DISMINUCION PAULATINA DE LA PO-
BLACION INDIGENA OBLIGO A CERRAR LA MISION EN 1822.

INSTITUTO NACIONAL DE
ANTROPOLOGIA E HISTORIA
BAJA CALIFORNIA

GOBIERNO DEL ESTADO
DE BAJA CALIFORNIA

VISITANTE: ESTE ES UN MONUMENTO HISTORICO
AYUDE A SU CONSERVACION

The sign a Mission Santa Gertrudis.

A typical Baja road leads to Mission Santa Gertrudis.

The Baja of Yesteryear

STONE CASKS CREATE WINE INDUSTRY

SANTA GERTRUDIS — 1752

Napa-Sonoma-Santa Gertrudis! Santa Gertrudis? Most wine fanciers might be surprised to learn that without the wine experimentation at Santa Gertrudis there might not be a Napa or Sonoma, or Mendocino either.

The Baja California Mission of Santa Gertrudis la Magna is known as the birthplace of the California wine industry.

Santa Gertrudis is unique for several other reasons as well: it was the first in the present state of Baja California Norte; for 10 years it served as headquarters for exploration to the north; and its graceful stone church in a peaceful remote setting makes it one of the most attractive Baja missions today.

Located 23 miles east into the desert from El Arco, Santa Gertrudis is just north of the 28th parallel which separates the two states of Baja California.

Mission San Gertrudis was named in honor of Doña Gertrudis de la Peña, wife of the Marquis de Villapuente. She donated funds stipulating that they must be used to establish a mission dedicated to Saint Gertrude in the land of the Cochimis.

The site for the mission, originally called La Piedad, was discovered in 1751 by the most adventurous of Jesuit explorers, Padre Fernando Consag. He established preliminary work by placing the construction of simple buildings under the guidance of a blind Cochimi Indian, Andres Comanaji Sestiaga, who was amazing in his accomplishments in spite of his handicap.

The walls were of mud and small stones and the roof was constructed of timbers across which were laid reeds or rules. As it rarely rained and the Indians preferred to sleep outside, these rough buildings sufficed in the beginning.

Dedicated in 1752

The mission was not formally opened until 1752 when Padre Jorge Retz, a robust German Jesuit, was sent there after spending a year in San Ignacio to learn the Cochimi language.

According to custom, the other missions contributed whatever could be spared of provision, cattle, horses, mules, sheep and goats for the new mission. Father Retz, ably assisted by the blind Andres Comanaji, built a substantial building of stone and lime mortar.

Father Retz soon found himself in charge of 1,400 Indians who had agreed to be baptized in this strange European religion. Some estimates indicate as many as 3,000 Indians living in the mission area in its heyday.

The settlers discovered a small spring and cut a canal 1 1/2 miles from solid rock to a small field that could be farmed after hauling in topsoil for the rocky surface.

This small aqueduct is still in evidence today; in fact just before arriving at the mission, the road crosses the narrow canal which is covered by large, loosely lain pieces of stone. I noted the water appeared fresh and ran freely in its ancient waterway.

California's first wine industry

The Jesuits planted date palms, olive trees and grapevines. There are still a few grapevines growing at Santa Gertrudis; no doubt these sprang from those early Padre Retz plantings, the ones that became known as the foundation of the California wine industry.

Earlier peninsular Jesuits had been making wine at a few other missions, some of it quite good and used for trading. But it was the industrious German Padre Retz who is referred to as the first California winemaker. This is because he produced such an excellent wine from the grapes of Santa Gertrudis.

The manufacture and storage of fine wine called for great ingenuity on his part. He enriched his soil with a fine loam brought in from distant arroyos.

Casks being unknown here, Father Retz had containers hewn from blocks of stone to be filled with the juice of the grapes. He covered these containers with boards and sealed them with a gum from the pitahaya trees. This ingenuity and care resulted in California's finest wine at the time. Grapevines from Santa Gertrudis traveled north as new missions were developed.

Life at Santa Gertrudis apparently agreed with Padre Retz because, it is said that he was a rather corpulent man. He was also somewhat infirm and, at best, had difficulty traveling. When the Jesuits were expelled from Baja California in 1768, Retz had a severely injured foot. So he had teams of his mission Indians hand-carry him 200 miles to the ship at Loreto.

CENTER FOR EXPLORATION

Santa Gertrudis, perched on a ledge in a small arroyo, became the center of the frontier region and base for further exploration until San Borja was founded 10 years later.

In 1768 the Dominicans arrived, completing the present stone church in 1796. They also built a campanile or belfry separate from the church. Bells are engraved "Santa Maria Magdalena 1739," planned for the abandoned mission of that name, and "Señor Sanyoso 1739."

Thick stone walls of Mission Santa Gertrudis.

Since 1918 Santa Gertrudis has been cared for by Doña Luz Pico Romero, Viuda de Arias, who received the keys from her mother-in-law, a part-Cochimi Indian. The widow supported her eight children from products of the mission's orchard.

Her children departed from the mountains, but one, daughter Trinidad, returned to care for the mission and the little farm. This manner of succession is typical at Baja's missions.

Santa Gertrudis is one of the more remote missions and will take a high clearance vehicle to get to. From El Arco the wide graded road narrows as it passes two ranches and enters a rocky arroyo.

201

IRRIGATION SYSTEM STILL IN USE

Date palms are in evidence near the mission, and you can see portions of the 200+ year old aqueduct. Cattle and horses bask in the small pond near the canal's terminus.

While the earlier adobe buildings have been reduced to crumbling walls, the mission chapel and belfry are in splendid condition. Thick stone walls render a cool interior which still has one room used as a chapel, and another set aside as a crude museum, complete with an original tabernacle in a glass case, an old crucifix and simple models of the church that were made by local children.

There is a small container for donations. This writer advises all Americans visiting these historic sites to perhaps leave a dollar or two to assist the caretakers. And please leave the place as you found it; never take anything, not even a rock or nail. As Sierra Club members would say, "Take only photographs; leave only footprints."

Despite the fine irrigation system, Santa Gertrudis was always plagued with insufficient fresh water, and the Indian population suffered greatly from diseases. By 1785 there were only 300 Indians. By 1822 the mission was finally abandoned due to a dwindling Indian population of fewer than 100.

Today the quiet arroyo is home to a few hardy families who still use a portion of the two-century-old irrigation system. They tend the dwindling old historic grapevines, olive trees and date palms along with their own crops.

The setting is a palm oasis in a desert surrounded by cirio trees, tall cardon cactus and chapparel. Colorful mountain cliffs stand guard over one of the better preserved and more attractive of the Baja California missions.

HOW TO GET THERE:

Transpeninsular highway to Guerrero Negro (444 miles so. of Tijuana); 17 miles south on 1 to El Arco cutoff; 25 miles on former paved road (now so full of potholes almost everyone uses dirt roads off to side) to El Arco; marked sign to Santa Gertrudis 23 miles away (most traveled road); road is good for first 17 miles, then has high crown and is rocky. Pass two ranches.

THE MOST INACCESSIBLE PLACE

SAN BORJA, B.C. — 1759

The very remoteness and inaccessibility of the rugged area around the Mission of San Francisco de Borja Adac was precisely the reason the mission was founded there. And the person who made that decision had not only never stepped foot in Baja, but lived in luxury as a duchess in Spain.

Señora Maria de Borja, the Grand Duchess of Gandia, might seem an unlikely benefactor to the peninsula's progress, but it was her donation that established three of the most remote and inaccessible missions of the New World.

Mission San Borja
is in a remote
mountain setting.

She learned of the Baja California missionary efforts from a soldier who returned to Spain and became a servant in her household. The servant who served in Loreto told her of the ruggedness and sterility of the Baja peninsula. He related stories of the trials and tribulations of the Jesuit padres among the Indians. He added that they were unable to help some Indians because they lived in far-off mountain valleys.

The Duchess was so moved by these stories she changed her will to donate a sizable amount to the Jesuit Pious Fund, specifically stipulating that the funds be used to establish three missions in the most remote reaches of this isolated peninsula called California.

She was from both a notable and notorious family. Aside from hereditary dukes from the Duchy of Gandia in Valencia, Spain, there were also two popes, and one canonized saint (San Francisco de Borja, a third general in the Company of Jesus).

As Borja is the Spanish spelling of Italy's Borgia, it was the Italian ancestors who gained the most fame. Two of the seven children of Pope Alexander VI, Cesare and Lucretia Borgia, became a brother and sister poisoning act dispatching notable guests with pharmaceutical adroitness. Keeping power in the family, Cesare and another uncle were made cardinals in the church.

Señora Maria de Borja died in 1747. From the original $60,000 Spanish pesos donated, with interest the amount had grown to over $70,000 by the time the three missions were established. From her funds, Mission San Borja was founded in 1759, the short-lived Mission Calamajue (Calamague) in 1766, and Mission Santa Maria in 1767.

San Borja is the best preserved of the three; only adobe ruins remain at the other two remote sites. Calamajue is in a wash west of Punta Final, and Santa Maria can be reached by a strenuous hike up a palm canyon from Catavina.

Among the stipulations Señora Borja specified when donating the funds was that one of the new missions be named for her canonized saint ancestor, San Francisco de Borja.

In seeking the remote regions of the peninsula, Mission President Padre Fernando Consag made exploratory trips northward in 1751 and 1753, but both times had actually bypassed what would be the eventual site for San Borja.

Later he and Padre Jorge Retz learned of a spring that could irrigate land at a place the Indians called Adac. The water was warm and smelled bad but was potable when cooled. It was a difficult three day's journey north of the established Mission Santa Gertrudis (near the current border of Baja California and Baja California Sur).

BUILDING THE EL CAMINO REAL

In 1759 Padre Jorge Retz built a road to Adac from Santa Gertrudis which was "30 leagues away" with the eventual plan to establish a mission there.

All of the roads that linked the missions led to Loreto and became known as El Camino Real, the Royal Highway. They were constructed by dedicated people in very difficult circumstances.

Arthur Walbridge North in his 1908 book "The Mother of California" discusses the road building:

"But no mountains seemed inaccessible to the padres. From the beginning of the 18th century their mission establishments had been extending out from Loreto like a great vine, well constructed roads representing its shoots.

"These highways, usually leading through rugged mountains and always through stony districts, were built with care and only by great labor; thousands of hands alone made possible their construction, and these, the hands of the Indians; Indians given one meal a day as their compensation, and — toward the end of the mission rule, at least — urged on by whips, 25 lashes being the penalty for lagging.

"The stones were removed and thrown up in a slight embankment at the sides, making a roadway from four to 40 feet in width, the average being over 15 feet."

Once the road to San Borja was constructed, Padre Retz erected a chapel, dwellings for the priest and soldiers, a storeroom, a small hospital and planted a modest cornfield.

The Mission President Padre Consag died in September 1759 and the plans to make San Borja an actual mission site were put on hold.

In August, 1762, Padre Wenseslao (Wenceslaus in some accounts) Linck (or Link), a native of Bohemia, was placed in charge at San Borja after months of studying the Cochimi language at Santa Gertrudis and the mission was then established.

There were 300 Indians in San Borja at the time, but soon so many arrived the padres could barely support them, even with help from other missions.

Padre Link was to have two assistants, both in training to establish their own missions. They were Padres Victoriano Arnes and Juan Diez, who later established Calamajue.

At San Borja, figs, olives, grapes and dates were planted, and cattle and sheep were raised. In fact, during my 1987 visit I observed a number of crops in the out-gardens. In the 1970s it was reported that one grape vine was 45 feet in length.

The Indians who were attracted to the mission soon became dependent on the padres for their sustenance. Prior to their arrival, in their native habitat the Indians lived on insects, lizards, rodents and other larger animals. The orchards, grain and livestock soon became an important source of food for all.

When the Jesuits were expelled from the New World in 1768, the Franciscan Padre Fermin Francisco Lasuen was given charge of San Borja on May 7, 1768. Inventory then included: nine outlying ranches, 621 cattle, 1,108 sheep, 722 goats, 96 brood mares, 136 horses, 12 saddle mules and 25 pack mules.

Lasuen, who later became assistant to Padre Junipero Serra and California Mission president upon Serra's death, replaced the original chapel with an adobe church, surrounding buildings and courtyard.

A MOORISH BUILDING OF STONE

In 1773 the Dominican Order of the Catholic Church took over the San Borja Mission, and in 1801 erected a handsome Moorish building out of stone that still stands today — just short of two centuries later.

An assortment of diseases almost wiped out the native population which peaked at 3,000 Indians, and by 1818 when the last resident priest departed, there were fewer than 100 Indians remaining.

The stone edifice that still stands today, although never entirely completed, is considered one of the handsomest of the peninsula missions. This is remarkable as it has not had formal maintenance since.

In the 1960s the bells from the tower were stolen at night by two men. One bell was engraved San Francisco Nsaga 1759 and the other Señor Saniocepth 1799. A small replacement bell now hangs in the belfry.

The mission dominates the still valley, rimmed by cliffs of red rock. It's the heart of a small oasis nestled snugly on a desolate mountain. I was surprised at the quiet, which provided the setting with an eerie, ethereal feeling.

A ranch house stands guard, but the occupants are not always there. I could not find anyone in the valley and my "hellos" bounced off the steep mountain walls to shatter the silence.

The old adobe Franciscan ruins, a cemetery and a spring are off to the right and rear of the impressive stone church.

The chapel is intact and still occasionally used by visiting priests. A circular stairwell of carved rock wends to a second level loft above the chapel. Remarkable stone work is visible everywhere. There's a water cistern with four inch thick walls carved from one rock! Detailed carvings grace window and door arches. Fallen statuary lies undisturbed amid a courtyard cactus garden.

The mission can be reached from the road to Bahia de Los Angeles or from Highway #1 at a small village called Rosarito, some 350 miles south of Ensenada. While only 22-23 miles either way, both are bad roads, trails in some spots, and will take an off-road vehicle 2–2½ hours one way. The Rosarito road is considered better.

The sandy, rocky road from the Bahia is dwarfed by huge cirios, cardon cactus and elephant trees in some areas as to render an unearthly presence. The road rises to hills of shale before descending through a wash to enter the mission valley.

There is talk about the Mexican government improving the Rosarito road so more people can enjoy this splendid example of stone architecture. Some Baja buffs, however, wince at the prospect of change that hordes of visitors would bring.

For now it is quiet, used only by a few neighboring ranchos and visited by few outsiders. A fiesta is held there annually on October 10 and mountain residents from miles around gather to celebrate and meet with neighbors and friends.

San Borja is desolate, serving as a proud monument and a reminder of those difficult times long ago. I enjoyed the solitude, the quiet dignity of a place that was once the cultural and social center of this mountainous area.

I left everything in its place. It reminded me of a ghost ship floating aimlessly in the ocean, without a hand aboard. It was easy to imagine it peopled with Indians and padres. Even disturbing the dust made me feel like I was violating the memories of those who built it.

I arrived on the bad road from the Bahia and left on the bad road to the west and Highway 1.

Duchess Borja requested an inaccessible place and she would not be disappointed, even today — almost 250 years later.

Spain Races Russians to California

Mission San Fernando Velicata — 1769

San Diego, Alta California's first mission, was established in the year 1769. When I learned that the Baja California Mission of San Fernando Velicata was founded that same year, I wondered about the connection.

How did Padre Junipero Serra, the Franciscan pioneer, lay the groundwork for two missions so far apart during the same year? Why was San Fernando the only Franciscan Mission in Baja during their five year tenure on the peninsula?

What was so important about hurrying north? Why did Serra literally "head for the border" from San Fernando, leaving the remaining nine Baja missions to be established later by the Dominicans?

The answers are mostly political and are based on Spain's decision at the time to claim as much land as possible.

Before 1768, the Jesuit Order had established 15 missions in Baja, from San José Del Cabo in the south to Santa Maria in the north. The Jesuit Order was abruptly expelled from the entire new world by Spain's King Charles III. The expulsion apparently was a result of reports, real or imagined, which reached the king citing resentment of their accumulated wealth and power. Thus, on Feb. 3, 1768, 16 Jesuits departed from Loreto after seven decades of incredible efforts in establishing a physical as well as spiritual foothold in Baja California.

At that time, the Franciscan Order had been responsible for missionary activity in northwestern mainland Mexico. They were hastily ordered to (Baja) California. Fifteen Franciscan priests, under the leadership of Padre Junipero Serra, landed at Loreto on Apr. 1, 1768. They were duly assigned to take over the existing missions.

Their timing was providential, because Spain had finally decided to establish settlements in Alta California. It appears that Russian fur trappers and explorers were working their way down the northwest Pacific Coast and were establishing outposts as far south as San Francisco. Spain had to challenge their intrusion.

Who knows what might have happened. Without that historic decision by Spain, Californians of today might be eating beet soup, drinking vodka and speaking Russian.

A POLITICIAN NAMED GALVEZ

The political climate comes to light by exploring the life of one man, an ambitious Spanish politician named José de Galvez. Galvez was sent to New Spain (Mexico) in 1765 by King Charles III, who thought he was a pretty good guy.

The Jesuits didn't think so, however, as it was Galvez who played a large part in their expulsion. The king gave him broad powers and also royal orders to organize an expedition that would head north and colonize Alta California, thwarting the Russian advance.

The incoming Franciscan padres found that, largely because of Galvez' influence, they did not enjoy the theocratic authority that the Jesuits had enjoyed for 70 years. They found they were pushed aside and their efforts secondary to the political and military leaders.

According to Pablo L. Martinez in his 1960 book "A History of Lower California," "The brusque and hopeless departure of the sons of Saint Ignatius de Loyola (Jesuits) had wrecked the process of development of European civilization in Lower California, and the missional system never recovered from such a great blow. ...they (Indians) saw that the real temporal power was now exercised by the commander of the troops. All this had a great influence in bringing about the lack of discipline that soon surged among the indigenous groups...."

Galvez cared little for Lower California and his aversion toward the Jesuit padres was noted by the Indians. Historian Martinez documented many frailties of the missional system so his denouncement of the Galvez attitude is even more revealing. He continues about Galvez, "Except for (his) conquest of Upper California, everything else was a complete failure."

Galvez arrived from the Mexican mainland to Baja on Jul. 12, 1768. He immediately communicated with Serra and explained why he had come. Serra proposed that when his Franciscans leave to settle Alta California, the other Catholic order, the Dominicans, could take over the existing missions.

Two by land and two by sea

Galvez' planned expedition north would be in four units, two by land and two by sea. For the trip, he had secured the two largest and strongest brigantines in western Mexico, the San Carlos and San Antonio.

Now instead of the religious leaders calling the shots, it was Galvez who directed what the Franciscans would do. He suggested to Serra that missionaries accompany the troops and initially establish missions at San Diego, Monterey and one place in between, with others to follow.

He wanted to use the then northernmost Jesuit mission, Santa Maria, as a convenient place to supply the missions to be established in the north.

The two land expeditions would both be under the command of Captain Gaspar de Portola, with the advance party led by Captain Fernando Jávier de Rivera y Moncada, then commander of the Loreto Presidio.

Galvez himself ordered Rivera y Moncada to stop at each mission on his way north and round up as many supplies as each mission could afford in the way of cattle, horses and other provisions. So each mission was duly stripped as the advance party made its way north to Santa Maria to await further orders. Many of the missions never fully recovered from such ransacking.

When Rivera y Moncada arrived at Mission Santa Maria he had with him 46 horses, 140 mules, 64 saddles and bags filled with supplies, 5 barrels of wine, 13 sets of cowboy leathers, 38 arrobas (an arroba is 25 pounds) of figs, 28 arrobas of flour, 340 arrobas of dried beef, 21 bushels of wheat, 23 arrobas of raisins and much more.

Forced to relocate

As Santa Maria had insufficient pastureland for the livestock, Rivera y Moncada was forced to relocate. He went north to a place first visited by Jesuit Padre Lick in 1749, a place the Indians called Velicata. He sent a report back as to his new location in December 1768.

From Loreto, Serra in February ordered Padre Juan Crespi to join the advance party, while Serra would later make the journey with Portola and the main party. For almost the entire journey Serra nursed a badly infected foot.

On Mar. 25, Rivera y Moncada, Padre Crespi, 25 soldiers, a guide, three mule drivers and a large number of Indians armed with bows and arrows left the Velicata valley and arrived in San Diego on May 14, 50 days later.

Back in southern Baja, Serra and Portola took different routes north and met in Santa Maria on May 5, 1769. They took the mission priest, Padre Miguel de la Campa y Cos, and headed for Velicata, a place also called "the well of the sweet water."

Portola and Serra arrived at San Fernando Velicata on May 13, 1769. The country around Velicata made a favorable impression, so much so that Portola and Serra resolved to establish a presidio and a mission in order to facilitate later communication with Alta California.

In his diary, Padre Serra describes the event, "On the 14th of May, the Day of the feast of the Holy Pentecost, in the morning a little hut of palisades was cleaned out and adorned. It was one that the advance party had left standing.

"In that hut the altar was arranged, the soldiers were drawn up under arms in the leather jackets and shields, and with all the neatness of holy poverty I celebrated the Mass of that great day with the consolation that this was the first of those Masses which must be continued with permanency at this new Mission of San Fernando, which dated from this day.

"The Mass was solemnized by the oft-repeated discharge of the muskets of the soldiers, the fumes of the powder in this instance substituting for incense, which we did not have because we could not afford it...."

Serra continues, "I named as the Missionary to this new Mission Fr. Miguel Campa (y Cos) who was very happy with his charge, knowing that many gentiles frequented the locality and seeing that this spot offers all the conveniences of land and water for those gathered in the future to form the Mission."

Serra and Portola then continued north to fulfill Galvez' order and establish the presidios and missions of Alta California, both becoming historical figures of great significance in California history.

HOME TO 1,500 INDIANS

Mission San Fernando became important as it is situated nearly midway between those missions on the gulf and those on the Pacific. It became home to approximately 1,500 Indians who helped raise sheep and cattle in the small valley. The mission flourished until an epidemic in 1777–1780 struck and wiped out the population. By 1818 the mission was abandoned entirely.

It is a remote location now, but quite accessible (only three miles) from the Transpeninsular Highway #1, some 40 miles south of El Rosario. A small modest wood sign announces the turn-off. The dirt road is easily navigated by most sedans. Another, slightly longer road from behind the Rancho El Progresso will also reach the site.

I often stop by San Fernando when I'm in the area. Back in the '70s, the adobe mission ruins were larger and more impressive than today. The remaining walls are crumbling rapidly.

The old caretaker who lives in the modest dwelling across the road proudly showed me and Don around on our 1995 visit. A more modern graveyard, in which the caretaker's father is buried, looked like it was constructed in the center of the old mission building.

The caretaker told us to continue driving past the mission for about a half mile to see ancient rock art. On the rocky cliffs, near where the road crosses the stream, petroglyphs are visible from the canyon floor. We scrambled around the rocks and found several examples of a culture much older than those Spanish missionaries. Some who study petroglyphs estimate the art to have been created from five hundred to 1,000 years ago.

The missionaries built an aqueduct which is still in existence. As the stone for the aqueduct was quarried from the nearby cliffs, it appears that much of the ancient art was destroyed at that time.

Palm trees and the ancient irrigation system grace the valley floor. There's an old corral, and quiet, lots of quiet. The small rancho rests beside the mission ruins, now grotesque pillars of weathered adobe. A paint-chipped sign, barely readable, Spanish on one side, English on the other, announces the significance of the ruins.

The friendly caretaker wouldn't let us leave until we shared a platter of sweet pitahaya with him. We both concur with him, the Baja Indians, and many Baja travelers, that the fruit of the pitahaya cactus is a most delectable morsel indeed.

We stood by the ruins to take in the silence. A few hawks circled the sky. The valley was still. The peaceful solitude was a throwback to the days before Serra, before the soldiers and mules and cattle, before the chiming of bells, the barking of dogs and the playing of children.

The desert quiet was probably enjoyed by those who came before, those who left their imprints upon the cliffs that overlook the valley. Once again I felt like the insignificant intruder in that wondrous land that is Baja.

THE LAST OUTPOST

EL ROSARIO, B.C. — 1774

The modest village of El Rosario, some 220 miles south of the U.S. border, could be considered as the birthplace of the northern state of Baja California Norte.

At most mission sites, communities were completely devoted to serving themselves, working with the Indians and growing crops. El Rosario alone quickly established itself as an important way station to those traveling the peninsula, to and from the capital at Loreto, to Alta California. In 1849, El Rosario even briefly served as the capital of the Northern District and was its largest town until 1870, and up until 1900 was still larger than either Tijuana or Mexicali.

Today the southbound Baja traveler drops down a winding road from a plateau separating El Rosario from the Pacific and encounters a small dusty town at a bend in the road. As the next town of any consequence is another 220 miles south at Guerrero Negro. Travelers stop there for fuel and other supplies.

El Rosario is actually two separate towns. Rosario del Arriba (Upper Rosario), the larger town on Highway 1, is the one most peninsula travelers are familiar with. There used to be two Pemex gasoline stations, one on the left as you arrive in town and another around the bend. In December 1996, I noted that the second one had closed and a large new station was in the process of opening, right next door to the always-packed, primitive first one.

There are a couple small modest motels, a few stores and bakeries and several restaurants, including the famous Mama Espinosa's, a small landmark that has served lobster burritos and lobster omelets to off-road enthusiasts for years.

Mama Espinosa

Doña Anita Espinosa, in fact, has become a legend among Baja travelers. As early as 1800 one of the first land grants in the area was made to Carlos Espinosa, a retired Spanish soldier. The Espinosa family became prominent in the fertile valley four miles from the sea and still is.

Doña Anita, an English-speaking daughter of a mining engineer, had married Heraclio Espinosa, the oldest son of the then village patriarch, and opened a small restaurant in the 1940s.

For years, increasing expeditions had been arriving at El Rosario (In 1905 only two parties, the author Arthur W. North and the biologist Nelson, made the journey; by 1927 the Auto Club of Southern California made its first trek there.).

After World War II, many more cars were attempting the trip and all of them stopped at the modest building that has not changed for the last half century, the one with the wooden sign that said, "Espinosa's Place, Gasoline, Beer and Soda, Meals, Rooms, Information, English Spoken."

The register she kept all these years is filled with names that comprise the lore that is Baja. Almost all of the off-road racers, including celebrities Steve McQueen and James Garner, have signed her register. Thumbing through the weathered old book on my first visit, I was surprised when my name jumped out at me. No, it was just my surname. It said "Gus Niemann." Yup, my father beat me here too.

In the early years Señora Espinosa kept tabs on those who continued on and monitored their progress through the informal Baja grapevine. For example, she once told me her brother owned the rancho at Laguna Chapala. Contacts like that and primitive but effective communication helped them know where travelers should be.

Doña Espinosa has seen it all, including the paving of the Transpeninsular highway and the multiplying of visitors. Her succinct comments about the road are echoed by many a long-time Baja buff, "Bad roads, good people; Good roads, all kinds of people!"

A first for the Dominicans

El Rosario, long considered the last outpost of civilization before one enters the "wilds" of Baja California from the north, was the first and southernmost mission established by the Dominican Order.

The Franciscans, after assuming control of all the former Jesuit missions, established one mission at San Fernando Velicata in 1769, and were heading north into Alta California.

Meanwhile the Dominicans had been pleading to the King of Spain, Charles II, for equal participation with the Franciscans in the development of missions in the Californias.

Franciscan Padre Junipero Serra, California Mission President, felt that a competing religious order was not warranted because of both the aridity of the land and the declining population of Indians. He proposed to the Viceroy that the Dominicans be given charge of all the Baja peninsula missions, including establishing new ones, while the Franciscans continue to develop missions to the north, in Alta California.

The first border between the Franciscan and Dominican operations was then set at La Mision (Just south of the present La Fonda restaurant). It was later moved to Descanso (near Cantamar), and ultimately to the Tijuana River, the religious boundary now dividing two countries for years.

El Rosario was established late in 1773 when Dominican Padre Vicente Mora arrived at a large and beautiful valley, called Vinadaco, or Vinaraco, by the local Cochimi Indians. After receiving permission from the Viceroy, the first mission foundations were laid in 1774 by padres not identified. The mission was called Nuestra Señora del Rosario (Our Lady of the Rosary).

The King of Spain helped establish the mission with a gift of $1,000 pesos.

This original mission had a large plaza with buildings on three sides and an adobe wall on the fourth. There was only one entrance to provide defense against any hostile Indians.

Ruins from the first mission are on a terrace on the right side of the valley facing west towards the sea, just over a mile from the present community center.

Inadequate water supply forced the mission to move downstream in 1802. This was called El Rosario de Abajo, or Santismo Rosario and was considerably smaller. The crumbling adobe walls of this mission can be seen off the side of the road on the right.

NUMEROUS MIDDENS LEFT BY INDIANS

As local Indians were within an hour's walk of the ocean, they lived largely on shell fish and fish speared or seined from the sea. Numerous middens (piles of shells) show evidence of this and the habitation of Indians along the banks of the Arroyo del Rosario.

The missionaries brought horses, mules, donkeys, cattle, sheep, goats and swine. The fertile valley was suitable for planting grain, and large olive and fig trees as well as date palms and grape vines of the variety imported by the missionaries still exist.

The two bells from the El Rosario Mission belfry were both inscribed "Santa Rosa 1788," having been brought north from the abandoned southern Baja mission of Santa Rosa de las Palmas. Today, one hangs in a small modern church near the second mission site. The other was sold to a small parish in San Ysidro, CA, just north of the international border.

The Indian population at Rosario numbered 557 in 1777, but by 1824 disease had reduced the population to 150. Today there are no known full-blooded Cochimi in the area, but their blood is evident in the current population.

To get to El Rosario del Abajo (Lower Rosario), turn right at the large Mercado where the highway makes a left hand turn. Make a left after a block, down a hill to the riverbed of El Rio del Rosario. You must ford the river, normally 2-6 inches deep, but it's a hard, sandy bottom and is crossed by locals all day long. I noted in 1996 that they had diverted the stream through a drainage ditch and fording hopefully will be a thing of the past.

One time when Ken and I were camped just down river from the lower village we spooked the largest covey of mountain quail I'd ever seen, about 50-70 birds. They flittered and fluttered and scooted away, but many hung around a nearby deserted building just daring me to do anything.

A FISH CAMP AT PUNTA BAJA

Beyond El Rosario del Abajo, a good dirt road leads to a fish camp at Punta Baja, seven miles away. Punta Baja is a cobbled beach with a very fine surfing point and the area's occasional surfers are rewarded with long point break rides. Oceanography students also conduct studies from a small building on the point.

A good dirt road leads south from Punta Baja along the coast. On another occasion, alone I made a campsite on the bluff overlooking the Bahia Rosario and the island of San Geronimo in the distance. It was a quiet, reflective site, peaceful and powerful where nature speaks with waves gurgling over the cobbles and coyotes baying in the distance.

Six miles south is the fish camp of Agua Blanca, a sea urchin (erizo) divers camp. On my most recent trip, I noted that all the pangas tied up for the night were equipped with the air tanks for divers.

A better and faster six mile dirt road leads directly from Agua Blanca back to town. Along the way you can see piles and piles of the spiny sea urchin shells, dumped by divers over the years. As the main industry has moved to town, the current piles are closer in, or right along the highway. Today's inhabitants are following in their ancestors' footsteps, also creating middens, not of shell, but of a more valuable animal — the sea urchin.

Back in Rosario del Arriba we stopped at what looked like a factory and entered. There were about 30 or 40 women, with

Women in El Rosario sea urchin factory.

safety masks and rubber work clothes cutting, gutting, washing and packing the sea urchins, preparing them for shipment abroad, primarily Japan where the roe is coveted by the sushi set. The manager graciously allowed me to take photos while the employees giggled and joked to overcome their nervousness at our intrusion.

El Rosario also has Baja's only decompression chamber for divers who develop problems working on the deep ocean floor.

The sea urchin industry has created a new economy for the residents of the lovely valley that mark the beginning of the "wilds" of Baja.

El Rosario is growing up but will never change in some ways. For over 220 years it has been an important stop for all who have traveled Baja.

Doña Anita Espinosa's daughter Roli is the current mainstay running the restaurant and modest rental cabins and RV hookups. Mama Espinosa, now in her eighties, still works hard and prepares annual Christmas and Easter baskets for the needy. She appreciates any contributions of canned food, etc.

The continued graciousness of the Espinosas and the entire community help continue to make this strategic location important as well as memorable.

HOW TO GET THERE

Highway 1, 154 miles south of Ensenada, 36 miles past San Quintin. Most visible ruins are El Rosario del Abajo; turn right at mercado where highway curves to left. Turn left at first street into riverbed; cross river to smaller town. Weathered adobe ruins are on right, past community center. Marked sign with peeling paint, in both Spanish and English.

MISSION SERVICES HELD IN CAVE

MISSION SANTO DOMINGO — 1775

While Thomas Jefferson was writing the Declaration of Independence and Napoleon Bonaparte was playing with toy soldiers, another drama was being played on yet another part of the stage called Earth.

The year was 1775 and the Franciscans were already making their mark on Alta California. In Baja the Dominican Order, which had arrived on the peninsula four years previous, was looking to establish their second mission, the 18th Baja mission overall.

It was one year after the establishment of El Rosario that a new mission was planned "a day and a half" to the north. Up the Pacific Coast some 23 leagues from El Rosario, the Mission of Santo Domingo was founded on or about Aug. 30, 1775 by Padres Manuel Garcia and Manuel Hidalgo. The new mission was named for the founder of their Dominican Order of Catholic clergy.

The mission's first location was in what is now called the Santo Domingo Arroyo near a large red rock that has become a familiar landmark as it is visible for miles. You can still see that rock from Highway 1 about one mile from Colonio Guerrero, some 10 miles north of San Quintin.

Services originally were said to have been held in a large cave in that rock while the mission complex was being built. Now swallows and other birds inhabit the many caves that speckle the huge, round granite rock that appears as if it had been dropped from space onto the sandy river bed.

The Santo Domingo River reportedly carries the heaviest volume of water of any stream on the peninsula, originating from the upper reaches of the San Pedro Martir range which attains an elevation of 10,126 feet at Picacho del Diablo.

A MOVE UPRIVER

During the summer months the lower part of the arroyo is dry, so in 1782 the mission was relocated four miles up river. There 120 acres were put under irrigation.

The extensive mission ruins are on the left of the road. The wide-spread foundations of this mission, as well as its unusually large cemetery, which was laid out in 1794, indicates a considerable population in the period of its greatest prosperity.

Santo Domingo was ravaged with smallpox in 1781, and later by a syphilis epidemic, and for a while the padres had a hard time keeping enough Indians to help harvest the crops.

In 1798 however, there were enough docile Indians to warrant a new large building for saying Mass, a granary, a kitchen and workshops

Records indicate that by the year 1800, Santo Domingo had a population of 257 Indians. The livestock included 166 horses and mules, 500 cattle, 1,100 sheep and goats and 30 swine. In that year the harvest of grain was 1,620 fanegas of about 220 pounds each.

The resident missionary of Santo Domingo also served at the visiting chapel of San Telmo, eight leagues northward. San Telmo was a cattle ranch which consisted of a few dwellings, a smithy and a carpentry shop. Ruins of those buildings have confused some visitors into thinking they were the Mission Santo Domingo. San Telmo is off the road to Meling Ranch and the Observatory atop the San Pedro Martir. Both Santo Domingo and San Telmo were closed in 1839 due to epidemics and totally abandoned in 1855.

BELLS STOLEN AT NIGHT

The buildings at Santo Domingo were still intact in the late 1920s, with bells hanging from a crossbeam at the mission's entrance. The bells were stolen at night in 1930 and the mission began to fall into disrepair.

A visitor in the mid-1900s also observed four large, three-foot tall and very heavy carved wooden saints in the community. It appears that in 1855 the mission's last padre, Father Tomas Mansilla, entrusted the wooden saint statues to the surviving eldest member of the parish, who would pass them on upon his death, thus preserving their safekeeping for the community. Originally there were five, but one had been loaned to a neighboring village for a festival and never returned.

The road from Highway 1 to the mission passes farms with broad fertile fields and scores of colorfully attired pickers, mostly Indians of the fertile San Quintín Valley. Multi-hued, brilliant bandanas hold their hair in placeand cover their nostrils as they stoop in the morning fog to quickly and deftly harvest the abundance of tomatoes and chilies the area now provides.

Past the bright red rock the arroyo narrows and a small settlement of houses neighbors the old mission ruins. A sign announces the two century old mission, of which many walls are still standing.

Arthur W. North, the author of "The Mother of California" and "Camp and Camino in Lower California," was seemingly the first American to visit most of Baja's missions in the early 1900s. Of Mission Santo Domingo, he reported that it was the best preserved of the Dominican missions.

Visitors in mid-century and in the late '80s found this to be still true. In 1949, authors Marquis McDonald and Glenn Oster visited the site by jeep. They reported that nearly all of the walls were still standing and some of the window and door apertures were still intact.

I later found continued weathering, yet the outline of the entire compound was still visible and many walls were standing. A large wooden door beam still stands, supporting two feet of adobe. Windows and doorways were still evident, providing framing for the weathered walls which once housed a thriving community.

Driving back out to the highway, I again looked up at the red monolith standing like a sentinel to the arroyo. I thought that while the later mission's adobe walls continue to crumble through the years, the padres' first mission site, that large rock, should stand for millennia.

How to get there:

Highway 1, 102 miles south of Ensenada, 7 miles south of Camalu, on the north bank of bridge crossing Rio Santo Domingo is dirt road with sign marked "Mission." Follow road to red rock and continue up canyon. About 5 miles from highway.

Several ranchos and farms are in the canyon so the road is heavily used. A chapel was build on this site, along with signs and walkways. A festival is held in the adjoining lot every August, 2–4 honoring Santo Domingo.

Capital of the Frontier

Mission of San Vicente Ferrer — 1780

The crumbling adobe walls of what was once the largest of Dominican missions, San Vicente Ferrer, are located just half mile west of Highway 1 and only 52 miles south of Ensenada, thus enabling this Baja mission to be within range of most Baja travelers.

Mission San Vicente was founded in October 1780 by Padres Miguel Hidalgo and Joaquin Valero under the auspices of the Spanish Governor of the Californias, Felipe de Neve.

Problems developed almost immediately. At about the same time, hostile and aggressive Yuman Indians destroyed two Franciscan missions on the Colorado River. It was reported that 70,000 Indians took place in these attacks; the Franciscan fathers were killed; whole families were massacred, and all the livestock was driven off.

In the same attacks, Captain Rivéra y Moncada, who led the advance party into Alta California for Portola and Serra, was killed.

Only two days journey across the Sierra Juarez, the fledgling mission of San Vicente Ferrer remained in a constant state of alarm. They did endure occasional, less successful raids.

For this reason, added to San Vicente by the governor was a headquarters presidio with lookout towers and walls to help protect all of the northern missions. It served as capital of the frontier up until 1849.

The existing foundation and remaining walls indicate a large area of buildings, and other ruins identify the presidio and extensive Indian dwellings.

Less than a year after the mission was established a severe epidemic of smallpox left many dead. Padre Luis Sales replaced Father Hidalgo in October 1781 and set about reviving the mission. He buried the dead and rounded up starving Indians to house them at the mission.

Records show only 83 baptized Indians in the first two years. The greatest number of converts was in 1785 when 257 were baptized. In the year 1800 the mission had 161 horses and mules, 750 cattle, 1,300 sheep and goats and harvested 906 fanegas of grain.

After the epidemic, Sales captured two Yuman Indian spies sent to scout the area. He reported that he sent them far away from their own country, and thus the mission was spared an attack.

Father Sales, who was also the chief chronicler of the Dominican era in Baja California, states in his memoirs that he despaired of the Indians' "natural inclination toward certain vices" and their disinterest in attending confession and communion. He lamented that the only way to keep them in line was by constant whippings.

Why is it that throughout history, it seems someone's always trying to forcefeed culture or religion onto someone else? Is it altruistic? Is it an insecure "they can't be good unless they're like me" complex?

By 1854 the mission system was on a decline. That was when William Walker and his riotous band from San Francisco captured Ensenada and then moved the capital of their newly established Republic of Lower California down to San Vicente. After about four months of occupancy, Walker returned to the states with his erstwhile army, sadder but wiser. The Mexican flag would continue to fly over Baja California.By 1867 Mission San Vicente was reported to be all but uninhabited.

Today, the rich earth of the San Vicente plain has made the area a small, busy farming center with a population of over 6,000. It is the first town of any size past Ensenada and 22 miles past the village of Santa Tomás.

Architetural rendering of what Mission San Vicente originally looked like.

The Baja of Yesteryear

Several small restaurants are near the town square which also hosts outdoor shopping stalls on weekends. There are two Pemex stations, a motel, a post office, tire repair, a hardware store and even a used car lot.

On the west side of the town square is a small museum of Indian artifacts and local history. San Vicente also has a State Tourism office on the north end of town.

The mission ruins are on a rise over the riverbed, about 1/2 mile north of the plain upon which the current town rests. There is an old cemetery, still in use, to the right on a little mesa that leads down to the mission. To the left on the same mesa is the foundation of the presidio, located where the Spanish garrison had a good view in all directions.

The Baja California Mission Committee has attempted to protect the walls from the elements with thatched roof coverings, and cyclone fencing to surround the area. They have also placed an informational sign in both Spanish and English near the ruins and an architectural rendering of the completed mission on a wall of an adjacent rest area. In addition, they placed a directional sign on the main highway.

While there has been some attempt to preserve this historic site, the setting is still primitive and mostly deserted. Its isolation belies its importance for almost 70 years as the headquarters for the entire northern Baja California area.

Marquis McDonald, who visited the San Vicente Mission in 1949, wrote, "It was very prosperous, noted for its fine gardens, vineyards and hospitality to the traveler. Now cacti grow rampant in the former gardens, and cattle graze peacefully among the debris. This was the largest mission we had seen to date and seemed to have been little disturbed.

"We were always depressed in the presence of these forlorn old ruins; and especially here, a dismal spirit seemed to permeate the surroundings, as a strong breeze soughed through the remaining walls like a mournful funeral dirge, adding to the effect."

How to get there

South of Ensenada 52 miles on Highway 1; marked exit ½ mile north of San Vicente, just north of arroyo; take right dirt road around hill about ½ mile to site on east slope of hill, past cemetery. Walkways are posted with signs, both in English and Spanish.

(I notice, in 1998, a new entry road that ends at the Mission grounds. Several full time workers and volunteers were busy excavating ruins and uncovering artifacts.)

U.S./México Boundary set at Descanso

Missions San Miguel/El Descanso — 1787, 1817

The northernmost of Baja's missions were San Miguel, established in a valley just south of the present La Fonda restaurant, and El Descanso, located in the valley of the same name just south of the Cantamar sand dunes.

The northern parish limits of El Descanso served as the boundary between the Franciscans and Dominicans, and more significantly, between the two Californias.

Back in 1772, when the Dominicans took over all the peninsula missions and the Franciscans were beginning to establish Alta California, a document was prepared and legalized that established the dividing line between the two religious orders as the arroyo of San Juan de Dios, later named San Miguel or La Mision where San Miguel Mission was founded in 1787.

Schoolhouse at the mission.

Ruins of San Miguel Mission are located behind the schoolhouse.

After founding their first few missions in the 1770s, the Dominican Order faced numerous problems during the next few years. In 1780–1782 a severe smallpox epidemic wiped out many of the docile mission Indians. Then there were various uprisings and raids on the missions by the more fierce Indians of the north.

King wants link between two Californias

But the King of Spain wanted a link between the two Californias and had given orders to the Dominicans to proceed immediately and create whatever was necessary to forge that link.

So in 1785 Dominican Padre Luis Sales went to the San Miguel arroyo first noted by Padre Juan Crespi in 1769 on his way to San Diego with Portola's advance party.

Unfortunately, due to attacks from the hostile Yuman Indians from the Colorado River delta, Sales couldn't establish the mission for two years, until Mar. 28, 1787. The mission and the valley was renamed San Miguel Arcangel de la Frontera (St. Michael Archangel of the Border).

Before El Descanso, Mission San Miguel originally served an area north to Punta Descanso (where Calafia Restaurant is today).

That marked the official boundary separating the Dominican Order to the south and the Franciscans to the north. This boundary was also designated in 1777 to separate the New Spain provinces of Alta and Baja California.

The current international border farther north between Baja California and the U.S. state of California was a result of the 1848 Treaty of Hidalgo which ceded Alta California to the U.S..

In founding San Miguel, Padre Sales was accompanied by Governor Felipe de Neve, Military Commandant of the Californias. The original location scouted was wiped out by a flash flood, so they found another place in the arroyo called El Encino (The Oak). After temporary shelters were begun, the governor took his leave.

After sowing crops and building houses, Sales moved the mission again, closer to the ocean. The new complex covered about 300 x 600 feet and consisted of a tile-roofed adobe church with two altars. Houses for soldiers and servants were also built.

According to the Tomás Robertson book, "Baja California and its Missions," Padre Sales opened a road northward to the Mission of San Diego de Alcala. "He brought into the fold a tribe of Indians living along this route, who, according to Sales, had been preached to by the Padres at San

Diego but had been perverse, had killed some soldiers, stolen their horses and done much harm.

"Sales brought their chief and his family to live at San Miguel Mission, as well as nine girls to be taught in the Mission school. Located as it was near the shore of the Pacific, the inhabitants of San Miguel had the advantage of securing fish and shellfish whenever they desired."

The mesa upon which the mission was built was an old Indian midden and currently houses a school. The Committee for Conservation of Missions has placed palmed thatched roofs over the adobe ruins but they are in the middle of a schoolyard. Several times I've noted the same thing observed earlier by the travelers McDonald and Oster in 1949, that of youngsters playing and digging in the 200-year-old ruins. (A cyclone fence in the center of the school yard now protects the ruins).

San Miguel is just inland on the old road south of La Fonda Restaurant. Just past the estuary, at the base of the steep hill, the school is on the left side. Cyclists who do the Rosarito-Ensenada 50-mile bike ride start changing gears as they pass the school, very few aware of the historic significance just to their left. Behind the school a huge cross has been erected to commemorate the site.

FORCED TO MOVE

In 1817 floods in the San Miguel Valley forced the mission to move. Five leagues (12 miles) north was El Descanso which was to become an important place in the U.S./México border region.

When Padre Junipero Serra went north in 1769 he left fellow Franciscan Padre Francisco Palou in charge of the peninsular missions.

In 1775, Palou himself headed north after delivering the Baja missions to the Dominicans. He wrote that on his 1775 journey north his party prepared a cross of hardwood timber at the La Mision arroyo and carried it five leagues (12 miles) north to a place opposite some high sand dunes (These would be the Cantamar sand dunes that begin at El Descanso.) Here they found a wide crevasse between high rocks which, Palou wrote, seemed placed there by God for the planting of his cross.

This became the Franciscan/Dominican boundary, the first separation between Baja and Alta California. As mentioned, the international boundary was later moved farther north.

Establishing El Descanso

In 1817, Tomás de Ahumada, the San Miguel Mission Padre at the time, established El Descanso Mission. El Descanso was so interlinked with San Miguel that for a while it was called Nueva (New) Mission de San Miguel and the padres administered both congregations, changing the base of operation from one to another.

México attained her independence from Spain in 1822 and other than a little stubborn Spanish acceptance of the new rule, there was little change among the missions.

El Descanso, the northernmost mission (about 12 miles south of Rosarito Beach), thrived for a period. An 1834 report indicated a population of 254, but most likely included San Miguel.

Records then showed 3,500 cattle, 1,500 sheep, 50 horses and 10 mules. Grain production was 600 fanegas, mostly corn, barley and wheat. In 1835 records showed only 24 residents.

The mission was later abandoned and study of the mission ruins showed former buildings surrounding a court. There were thick plastered adobe walls with fragments of red tiles remaining. Apparently the walls had disintegrated more quickly because the adobe was mixed with sea shells and did not hold together well.

A new mission chapel was constructed on the site over several years by descendants of the old families that settled the area: Cotas, Crosthwaites, Gilberts and Machados. Behind the chapel, parts of the old mission site are just barely visible. Here and there are clumps of adobe, or rises in the ground denoting a building outline.

The chapel can be seen amid some greenhouses from both the old road and the toll road, providing a picturesque setting in the tranquil valley (Descanso means restful place).

A padre comes twice a month to hold services, ringing the old mission bell to announce his arrival to the families of the El Descanso Valley.

To reach the chapel from the toll road, turn off at Cantamar, 12 miles south of Rosarito Beach; south on old road 1½ miles, past sand dunes. Cross under toll road by nursery in valley. Chapel with mission sign is about ¼ mile on left.

Historians also tell of a place five kilometers up Descanso Valley called "La Viña," where grapes planted by the padres grew so much better a little farther from the sea. In fact, one grapevine grew to over 50 feet in length with a trunk over 12 inches thick. It was destroyed by a storm during the winter of 1968–69.

Another ruin of Descanso lies southward across the valley near the top of a 150-foot mesa. From its strategic position it commands a view of the entire valley and the approaches from the south. Its 33x37 yard stone outline suggests a fort or guardhouse which agrees with the local tradition.

Allegedly within the stone wall was the foundation of a building some 12 yards square. Its plan is unlike any of the other missions, and was probably used more for sentry purposes.

New homes and a cemetery now line that cliff on the valley's south flanks, perhaps forever obliterating any physical links with the past.

I've also never located the exact site where Palou put his historic cross to separate the religious orders.

After the Mission was established at El Descanso, the missionaries used the Punta Descanso (Calafia Restaurant) as their northern boundary.

I've long been impressed with the marketing genius of the owners of Calafia. They have capitalized on the significance of their point, and by reconstructing replicas of several missions and sprinkling the area with artifacts, suggest that the Punta Descanso is of more significance than it really is.

They even built an old ship into the rocks below the point. I never did figure out the reason for that. Maybe people might believe that Columbus actually made landfall along our Baja coast.

Regardless, the ship that became part of an al fresco dance floor provides a romantic setting, and the mission replicas and artifacts do a good job of reminding visitors from the north of how the area's history is interwoven with that of their own.

Just think, if the U.S./México boundary was never moved, we'd have a 24-lane border crossing checkpoint squeezed onto that narrow Punta Descanso. Somehow I can't imagine that!

Paipai Indians Guard Mission Ruins

Mission Santa Catarina — 1797

In my Jeep, I turned off Highway 3 at the roadside town of Heroes de la Independencia. Bouncing up the good, solid-packed dirt road I thought about my destination, the ruins of the Mission of Santa Catarina. While its 1797 founding may seem ancient, outside of the short-lived mission at Guadalupe it was the last of Baja's missions and founded exactly 100 years after the first one at Loreto.

A lot had happened in that century with the founding of 25 missions by the padres of the three main religious orders of the Catholic Church: Jesuits, Franciscans and Dominicans.

That day in my Jeep it was 1987, 190 years after Santa Catarina had been established.

Ahead a small village sprawled amid huge, smooth granite boulders that dotted the countryside like a giant's marbles. Manzanita trees, chaparral, sycamore trees and a meandering stream lent a pleasing and lush welcome to this village of scattered buildings, many still built of adobe.

It is Paipai Indian territory and they still guard it with zeal. The road led me to a small village square. Several men lazing on a porch were roused into action and approached me as my open Jeep came to a stop.

They slowly sized me up as I inquired as to the whereabouts of the mission ruins. Seeing my emergency shovel protruding from the Jeep, I suspected they doubted my sincerity, afraid I would vandalize the site. Then one asked me about a blue canvas bag which contained a metal detector, a new Christmas gift which I played with in the desert. I did some tall talking about being a writer just wanting to visit the site and take a few photos, trying to assure them that I would disturb nothing.

Still suspicious, they said the ruins were on a nearby hill but I'd need a guide. So a one-eyed Paipai Indian named Faustino Espinosa jumped into the Jeep, ostensibly to show me the site, but more accurately, I gathered, to insure that no vandalism would occur. It was also a good way for Espinosa to earn a tip.

Paipai citizen shows the author outline of where the mission Santa Catarina once stood.

OTHERS ALSO RUN INTO PAIPAIS

I wasn't the first visitor so scrutinized by the Paipai tribe at Santa Catarina. Marquis McDonald and Glen Oster describe their visit in a 1968 book, "Baja, Land of Lost Missions" recalling their 1949-1950 Jeep adventure to visit all of the Baja missions:

"Located on the ledge of a small hill overlooking a shallow arroyo, there was a small cemetery below; and we found it to be still in use. Even the old graves had been draped in flowers by the Indians. While exploring the vicinity, we saw a large brick kiln recently unearthed by the Indians, with some of the small, flat bricks still remaining in the oven."

The pair set up camp and were later visited by the Paipai. "However, the chief and several of the Indians arrived just then and spent some time drinking coffee and listening to our radio, no doubt the first one some of them had ever heard....

"In El Alamo the miners had told us covetously that there were wealthy placer gold deposits in the vicinity of the mission, and that many of them had tried to secure permission to mine there but had always been refused by the Indians.

"It was also rumored that the Dominicans had produced much gold here. The chief told us that as far as he knew, the bells and all the mission's other artifacts were still buried in the ruins just as they were at the time of its destruction, and that the only article that he knew to have been dug from the rubble was a bronze mug which he had unearthed as a boy, but was since lost. No one had been allowed to dig in the ruins for at least 40 years — if ever."

McDonald and Oster went on to visit all the missions and sites by Jeep, horse, mule and foot. I was thus honored when late in 1987 I received a very complimentary letter from McDonald in Olympia, WA regarding my series on the missions in the Baja Times. A friend had sent them to him.

Our correspondence that commenced with his letter included a personal copy of his book. It had arrived shortly after I'd visited Santa Catarina and while reading it, I could relate to his adventure with the zealous Paipais, comparing my own experience.

The inland location (some 37 miles west of Santo Tomás) was selected because a few miles east of Santa Catarina is El Portezuelo, an old Indian trade pass over which the Spaniards planned to travel from the Pacific to Sonora and the gulf. By building a presidio and mission at Santa Catarina, they planned on patrolling from San Vicente on the Pacific to the deserts and along the Colorado River, areas occupied by Cucupah (Cocopa) and Yuman Indian tribes.

The Mission Santa Catarina area was first visited in 1794 by Sergeant José Manuel Ruiz, accompanied by Dominican Padres Loriente and Valdellon.

It was visited later when José Joaquin de Arrillaga, Spanish Governor of the two Californias, ordered Sergeant Ruiz and Ensign Bernal to explore for a place near the El Portezuelo pass with permanent water. The expedition left San Vicente, then the northern capital, on Oct. 18, 1795, went up the San Vicente Arroyo, and then the Canyon de San Pablo to the site of Santa Catarina.

The following year Governor Arrillaga himself left San Vicente by the same route, only continuing over El Portezuelo itself to the mouth of the Colorado River and returning from the north, over the desert, stopping at Mission San Diego in Alta California.

Changing the Name

Although Santa Catarina was the last mission established in Baja California to endure, its name is often different in various maps and resource materials with many calling it "Catalina." Apparently confusion of the Catarina/Catalina name comes from a name change the mission made during the early years.

Originally called Santa Catalina Virgen y Martir, the building was begun on Aug. 4, 1797 by Padre José Loriente, who was accompanied by Sargent Manuel Ruiz and several soldiers. The mission was formally dedicated on Nov. 12, 1797 by Padre Tomas Valdellon who officiated there during 1797 and 1798. An Indian baby girl born there on the dedication date was even named Catalina.

While the girl went through life as Catalina, the mission's name was soon changed to Santa Catarina, or officially Mission Santa Catarina de los Paipais, referring to the local Indian tribe. Some current books also refer to the mission as Santa Catarina de los Yumas, referring to Indians over the mountains.

Watch tower to fend off attacks

The mission at Santa Catarina was located on a stony hill near a year-round stream. An adobe chapel and a wall completely surrounding the site was constructed, including a watch tower on one corner.

As Spain was at war with England at the time, English ships were spotted off the Baja coast and the Spanish padres feared attack. Apparently the English did not consider the area worth the trouble and no attack ever occurred.

My research backed up more legends supporting what the miners told McDonald and Oster 50 years ago. One legend persists that the Dominican priests were particularly harsh with the Indian converts and forced them to work like slaves in secret gold fields.

In 1871 a rich gold field was developed in the area and miners at the time reported signs of much earlier mining work. The Dominican gold was allegedly cached near Portezuelo.

Nothing in the Dominican writings support this claim. In an 1808 report, Fray Ramon Lopez, Dominican Mission President, laments on the inability of most missions to pay an annual tax of 25 or 30 pesos to the

President for administration. Of Santa Catarina he states that they cannot give what they do not have. "The minister at Santa Catalina formerly was able to send something, but now he struggles just to make ends meet."

Not much was reported after that, and the mission operated for several more decades so anything is possible, I suppose.

We know they planted wheat and corn, but that the principal activities were raising cattle, sheep, goats, horses, burros and mules.

The Indian population at the mission went from 133 in 1800 to 223 the following year. By 1824 it was a robust 600, then dwindled to 239 in 1834. The mission was subject to continuous raids by hostile Yuman, Cucupah and Kiliwa Indians to the east.

In 1840, while then Mission Padre Padre Felix Caballero was at Guadalupe Mission and most of his converted Indians were off gathering piñon nuts, the mission was burned and 16 mission Indians killed by a hostile band of desert Yuman warriors.

Santa Catarina was never rebuilt. Only melted adobe mounds are left to barely outline the former mission grounds that rest on a rocky knoll next to a cemetery. Other research appears to support the Paipai claim to McDonald and Oster that its bells and other artifacts are buried in the rubble.

But the place is still guarded over by the Paipai and they dislike intrusion. The nearby El Portezuelo is now better known as "the summit," an important pass used in the Baja 1,000 and Baja 500 off-road races.

Several Paipai women in the area often have attractive pieces of pottery for sale. I noticed one of the ladies was wearing a Catholic rosary around her neck. Apparently the influence of the padres lingers on.

How to get there:

Take paved Highway 3 from Ensenada toward San Felipe. At 57 miles from Ensenada is a small scattered town called Heroes de la Independencia. in the center of town turn left on graded road five miles to Santa Catarina. Road to village okay for any type vehicle. At village inquire as to whereabouts of mission site.

Off the Beaten Path

Off the Beaten Path

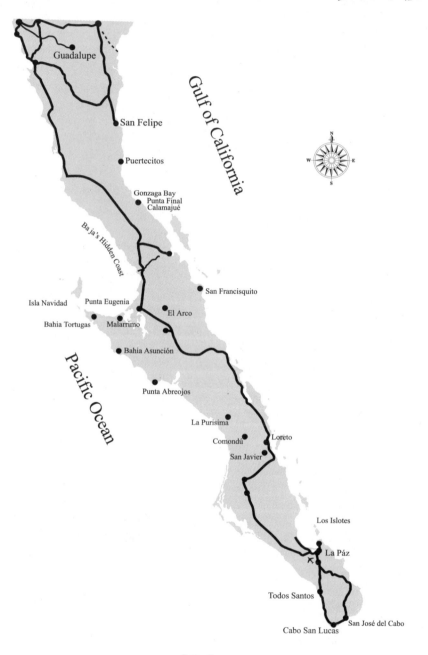

Guadalupe

Gulf of California

San Felipe

Puertecitos

Gonzaga Bay
Punta Final
Calamajué

Baja's Hidden Coast

San Francisquito

Isla Navidad

Punta Eugenia

El Arco

Bahia Tortugas

Malarrimo

Bahia Asunción

Pacific Ocean

Punta Abreojos

La Purisima

Comondú

Loreto

San Javier

Los Islotes

La Páz

Todos Santos

San José del Cabo

Cabo San Lucas

Baja Fever

"Baja California is a most interesting territory, and it is a friendly territory. Many of the people there don't have the individual wealth that we have in the United States. But they do have the dignity of men who are making an honorable living, who are close to nature and who have priceless integrity of character. Their poverty is only as to material luxuries. "There are rich people in Baja California, multi-millionaires, and there are peons. They all have something that we can well afford to study. They have friendliness and courtesy and inherent charm. "I hope to go back there next year for a longer stay."
— *Erle Stanley Gardner,*
"The Land of Shorter Shadows" 1948.
Gardner, who became famous for his Perry Mason series, made numerous trips into Baja over the 20 years following that first Baja book, resulting in 12 Baja-based books and a cave named after him.

A regular van in
Jeep territory.

Greg and Ken in 1996.

The Moorish spires of "Mision San Javier"

Baja Fever

SEIS LLANTAS (SIX TIRES)

GONZAGA BAY, B.C. — 1986

Seis llantas! Six tires! Six flat tires! In less than a week the rubber produced in Ohio fell victim to the rocky backroads of Baja by a 0-6 margin. The punishing roads won so decisively that I was even subjected to two flats at the same time.

It was June. My company had me in meetings all across the United States and I needed to get off the fast lane for a breather. I had Baja Fever so bad I flew directly into San Diego versus Orange County that Friday night.

Leila picked me up and we went straight to Cantamar. In the morning while she and local helper Manuel were rearranging furniture in the new room, I was loading my Baja-based CJ-5 Jeep with all my important toys. I was to set out into the wilds to escape from the pressures of civilization.

Ken had an ear infection so I was going alone. Undaunted, I set out with tent, sleeping bag, plenty of water, shovel, two extra gas cans, fishing rods and spears, metal detector, boogie board, inflatable boat, trusty camera and other indispensable emergency-related gear.

Objective: relax, unwind, maybe swim, surf fish, explore old missions and mines, take notes and photos for a few stories, check out a few beaches on the Pacific side below El Rosario, cross over to the gulf at Bahia Gonzaga by Punta Final, and drive up the treacherous gulf road to Puertecitos eventually reachinng San Felipe where my family and assorted Cantamar friends would be waiting later in the week.

BAJA'S LAST OUTPOST

On route to El Rosario, I stopped just a few times to poke around mission ruins at Santo Tomás, San Vicente and Santo Domingo. By late afternoon I was in El Rosario—for years considered Baja's last outpost of civilization—munching succulent lobster burritos at Espinosa's, a long-time stop for weary Baja travelers.

After camping on a deserted bluff overlooking the pounding waves near Punta Baja (south of El Rosario), I crossed the peninsula on Highway 1, and headed for the dreaded dirt roads that would take me up the gulf.

On the way I explored the Mission San Fernando founded by Padre Junipero Serra in 1769, lunched at the historic Rancho Santa Inez and drove out to the El Marmol onyx mine to pick up a few more large chunks of onyx that are scattered about the site. The beautifully streaked rocks look great in my gardens and the mine is only seven miles off the highway.

About 10 miles before the Catavina/Santa Inez area, I stopped to offer assistance to a Mexican couple whose tru ck was parked in the shade of a large boulder. In traditional Baja style, I refused his offer to pay for a gallon of gas we siphoned for him, figuring that favors have a way of catching up with you. Little did I realize I would be on the receiving end before the day was over.

Later, with a full gas tank and two extra five gallon cans of gas in the Jeep, I left the highway and set off across the dry lake bed of Laguna Chapala to begin my trek up the gulf route.

The road had recently been graded and seemed "a piece of cake" as it crossed the lakebed and entered the foothills near Las Arrastras de Arriola. I felt cheated; this was supposed to be one of Baja's worst roads. But even the vibrations from the washboard effect of the graded road were soon to take their toll.

My tailpipe in the road

Thump! Thump! Through the rear-view mirror, I could see some dark object in the center of the light-colored road even through the thick, white cloud of dust. I pulled over and walked back to discover a piece of my tailpipe lying in the road.

Picking it up, I considered the effect. It wasn't imperative for the operation of the Jeep, and I could get a welder to repair it later. It was certainly not serious enough to abort the trip. So I tossed it in the Jeep and continued onward.

The new graded road from the south to Gonzaga Bay was still under construction, and just as the bay loomed into view, a rustic sign directed motorists to shift over and get back on the old road.

Baja Fever

But the new road went straight as an arrow and lured me to continue on it. I stayed on the straight new road for about two more miles, and then it stopped. Just stopped! A large mound of dirt was piled at the end and beyond it, virgin desert. That's all, folks; backtrack to the old road.

Something about going backwards is alien to my nature, so rather than backtrack, I pulled off the berm and aimed for the gulf heading cross country across the desert. To keep environmental damage to a minimum, I followed the depression the new road would probably go. Dodging cacti, boulders and ocotillo, and following my nose, I eventually reached the old road which ran parallel nearby.

The construction caused me to miss the turnoff for Punta Final, but I wasn't too disappointed because I was planning on camping near Alfonsina's or Papa Fernandez's place, both on the northern end of Gonzaga Bay.

Alfonsina's appeared to be a cluster of homes on a sandbar off the bay. Heading for it, I was surprised at the depth of tidal water in the road. One roadbed was such a mini-lake that when I drove through, water flowed inside the floor of the Jeep!

Then I reached the lagoon entrance at the extreme south end of the appealing and inviting sandbar. I noticed residents had even lined the road bottom with rocks and boulders for entrance and egress, but it still looked deep. Apprehensive, I waded until my shorts were wet with deeper water still ahead. Wisely, I decided to pass on visiting Alfonsina's at this time rather than offer my Jeep up to King Neptune. I learned later that the highest tide of the month occurred the very hour I was there.

"I HEARD A POW"

I should have camped nearby and waited, because my tire troubles were about to begin. In the hills between there and Papa Fernandez's five miles away, I heard a "Pow" and felt the uneasy sway of a rapidly deflating tire on a loose gravel road.

Damn! I never did figure out what I hit, probably a sharp rock, but it was sharp enough to puncture both right side tires. And these were big, heavy duty desert tires.I wobbled as far to the right as I could and parked, allowing room for one vehicle to squeeze past.

I had one heavy duty spare tire at the rear of the Jeep, but only one. I also discovered that in my haste in leaving Cantamar I'd forgotten the jack. I'd loaded spare gaskets, fan belts and hoses but left the jack in the corner of the storage room.

My dilemma now was one tire and one jack short. Knowing Papa Fernandez's place had to be about two miles up, I started walking. Some sort of help would surely be there. I felt a little uneasy leaving all my valuables in the open Jeep, but knew from experience that the people who inhabit and visit the wild hinterlands of Baja California are among the most honest on earth.

Just as I hiked up a draw and a cluster of buildings on the gulf came into view, a large stake truck came up behind me, bouncing up the road I had just walked. The driver, a young, handsome athletic-looking Mexican perhaps in his early to mid-20's, stopped and opened the door for me.

I figured he'd give me a ride to the settlement, but no, he took me back to the Jeep to see if he could get me rolling again. He was immediately willing to help without my asking; it was just the thing to do.

The Jeep had six flat tires on the same trip, two at the same time!

Back at the Jeep, it soon became apparent that even his innate resources were not enough. As the right rear tire was only three quarters flat, we tried to see if it would hold air. He took a hose, removed a spark plug from his truck's engine, and used the compression of his running engine to inflate the tire. Unfortunately, it would not hold the air long, so we jumped in his truck and set out to find help.

THE FISHERMEN OFFERED TACOS

My Samaritan told me his family owned the Las Encantadas camp about seven miles up the gulf. But home could wait; I needed help. He drove directly to a small fisherman's camp of plywood shelters just to the south of Papa Fernandez's. Our fishermen hosts offered us sodas and fish tacos which we consumed before getting down to business.

No, no one had a patch. Yes, one of the fellows would help me change my tires if we could find a patch. With that information, and the willing worker also in the truck, we set out to find a patch and drove into "downtown" Papa Fernandez's, where a few small cottages ended at a hard-packed clearing adjacent to a small store and shady palapa. A couple of guys lounging in the shade tried to figure if anyone they knew might have a patch. An American appeared from one of the cottages. He offered a patch and refused payment saying, "Favors have a way of coming back to you."

My Samaritan and I went to the Jeep but discovered the patch was useless without a tube and the tire was tubeless. Great. We threw the flat in the truck and headed back to Papa Fernandez's to hunt for a tube. Everyone looked around the compound. Soon an excited little kid emerged from a small shed waving a well-used tube that already had about 17 patches on it. Success! Sort of.

My helper added yet another patch but now mounting the ill-fitted tube into the large Jeep tire became a chore even with the engine-compression method of inflating. A bubble developed on one side that four or five attempts wouldn't alleviate. We even dumped water, then oil on the rim so the tire would seat properly. It never did, but we decided to go with it, bubble and all.

Back at the Jeep we put my spare on the front and the mishappen monstrosity on the rear. I paid my two saviors for their now over four hours of concern, help and time. I had hired the helper outright and I believe the driver accepted money only because the other guy did. I was then advised that the only place in the vicinity that might have some spare tire components would be at Punta Bufeo, a small development about a mile before Las Encantadas.

I got on the road first in case of a problem, knowing my new friend would be following. The grading had not got this far and it was a brutal road. It was made worse in my mind by the constant expectation of another tire problem. Apparently the jarring road actually helped the mishappen tire to seat properly and I arrived at Punta Bufeo as darkness was setting.

CAMP ON THE BEACH

I set up camp on the beach and went for a quick dip to wash off the dust, and relax off the frustrations of a long day. I broke camp at first light and met the proprietor of Campo Bufeo as he was returning from the rocky Punta Bufeo where he'd enjoyed a successful dive for scallops.

After an hour of searching through his accumulated piles of rusting parts and scraps, we found an old Chevy tire mounted on a rim that had the correct number of lug bolt holes, and spaced correctly, but the axle hole would never have fitted over the protruding front axle on the Jeep.

"No problema," he said. "If you get a flat on the front, you take your rear tire and put it on the front, and put this one on the back." His broad smile and irrefutable logic prevailed and I bought the tire and rim for an absolute-emergency spare. I also bought a rusty old jack he came across and headed on my way.

It was 40 miles from Puertecitos and the Auto Club guide estimates that the very difficult road should take about six and a half hours. I set out full of anticipation.

Coming up the grade, Puertecitos to Gonzaga. Gus Niemann photo.

My father had told me about this road, which he called "Baja's worst." I longed to try it, to see for myself, to drive it. Bouncing along that rocky passage, I wondered if it was his influence on me that was so profound, or did we just like similar challenges. While I hardly approved of much of his personality peculiarities, I did find myself drawn to his pursuits of adventure. I realized that I'd never really thought about it before.

The heat bore down on the Jeep. By now all my ice had melted and after drinking warm sodas and water, I was salivating for anything with ice in it.

The 20 miles to Nacho's Camp was still bad; rocky ravines had to be traversed and sandy gullies negotiated. On a couple of occasions at rocky hills, I parked and got out to assess the road, to determine which tires I wanted on which rocks, trying to keep as much of the real bad stuff away from the right side as much as possible.

The volcanic cliffs north of Nacho's had been my greatest concern. They had a history of proving superior to many vehicles and I'd heard many horror stories. My father even had to get towed out after smashing his oil pan in there many years previous. Others have had to abandon their vehicles there. But by June, 1986, highway crews were busy blasting and widening what has once been described as Baja's worst through road.

Baja Fever

I felt cheated that the challenge was to come too cheaply. Yet I felt exhilarated that the end was in sight and I was about to do what I set out to do.

The road was not 100 percent complete and certain sections were still quite rocky and narrow, but not once was 4-wheel drive needed in that 20 mile segment.

ON FAMILIAR TURF

Puertecitos glistened in its quiet, small bay. It looked as large as Acapulco to me at the time. I felt relief as now I was on more familiar turf, having been to Puertecitos several times previous.

The town's sole restaurant was closed for meals, but they did have ice cold sodas. Upon inquiry, the owner reached into the cooler and set three different sodas on the counter. I chugged them all before she had the cooler door shut. She looked at me quizedly. I paid, smiled, tipped my cap and walked out.

North of Puertecitos, just like north of El Rosario on the Pacific, a more populous civilization reigns. That caring attitude so dominant down south has been regressed due to sheer numbers of people.

I stopped in the road to pick up a radiator hose someone had dropped. It could possibly come in handy to me, or maybe someone else. Or maybe its owner might be a few miles ahead. As I walked back to get it, a dune buggy manned by two laughing young Americans roared past, spewing dust all over me.

To the south, I did have a few tire problems. But now I found myself already missing that "help you" attitude that prevails where people are fewer. Those two whizzing past didn't even care if I was broken down.

About 20 miles out of San Felipe, I was going to stop to see if a friend was at his beach house. As I put my foot on the clutch, my foot went all the way to the floor. No clutch! It was probably something simple that had been jostled loose (like a loosened screw, which it later proved to be). But I didn't know. If it was serious, I was afraid that if I stopped I might not get going again, so I went for it.

I limped into San Felipe in high gear, shooting the few stop signs and feeling the engine lug in high gear as I slowed. I aimed the chugging Jeep toward the campground where my family and friends would be waiting.

They all heard my approach and rushed out to welcome me. I slowly got out of the Jeep and embraced my wife, looking at her through eyes damp with relief.

As I relayed the trip's highlights to Leila, Ken, Linda, Donnie and the others one of the kids said, "Look Greg, you've got a flat tire." It was the right rear. The poorly seated bubble tire knew exactly when to expire!

Later, the San Felipe tire shop sold me two apparently good, solid-looking used tires and we traded in the old Chevy tire and rim and my bubble tire. Well, with that last flat, the count was three. So how do we get six?

Well, first thing in the morning, the Jeep looked low on one side. One of the newly-purchased tires mounted on the right rear had gone flat. The tire shop then went to work on it and said they had found the leak and patched it. Four.

By afternoon, the same tire was three quarters flat again. I wobbled it back up to the tire shop and this time they replaced the whole tire. Five!

Two days later we all headed back to Cantamar. I was the last one back because I had to explore the Laguna Hansen, a pretty pine-rimmed lake high in the Sierra Juarez mountains above Ojos Negros, on the way.

At Cantamar, I began to unload the Jeep when I heard a hissing noise. I looked and could visually see the left front tire expelling all its air. I could see the cause, too. It was a large construction nail which I had just picked up on the cobbled streets of Cantamar. Six. Seis. Seis llantas!

The next week I was on a plane to Chicago and had time to reflect on my Baja trip. Did I unwind from pressures, or did I substitute a different type of pressure? Most of my business associates would prefer a pampering cruise or a week in an all-inclusive resort. They would deem me crazy.

But when you've got Baja Fever, there is no other antidote but to go. The way the people of Baja attack adversity with help and kindness almost makes the adversity welcome. The problem of six flat tires in Baja is addressed and remedied. There is no finger-pointing, responsibility-dodging, end-runs or subterfuge. While they may seem onerous, problems in the Baja outback beat complex corporate problems — any day.

When a Motorcycle Dies

Vizcaino Peninsula — 1987

I felt bad for Ken, his motorcycle seizing during its first mile off-road. It wasn't even his bike, just a loaner, and he was quite disappointed.

The 16-year-old's first motorcycle, a Yamaha 125, had broken down two weeks previously, and Pancho in Rosarito Beach had promised to have it running when we next came to Baja.

"For sure?" I queried, "We'll be down Friday and are heading way south early the next morning. We need the bike Friday."

"No problema," said Pancho, "I'll have it running good by then."

But when we arrived Friday, we discovered there apparently there was a "problema" and the bike was not ready.

Our plans unfortunately, were much more rigid than those of most Mexicans. My week's vacation started that day and son Ken and I had been planning and preparing for this trip a long time. We were going to put his motorcycle in the van, drive south of Guerrero Negro, head off-road at Vizcaino, and spend the week exploring Malarrimo Beach and the entire Vizcaino Peninsula.

It was a real blow because it was to be Ken's first real motorcycle experience off-road in Baja.

Pancho pointed to a yellow Suzuki RN400, about 10 years old, smiled, and said, "No problema, just take this bike for your trip and when you return I'll have yours ready."

His Suzuki ran well around the block in Rosarito Beach and we felt compelled to accept his offer. Otherwise, Ken would not have a bike to ride at all.

Off down Highway 1

So we loaded the bike into my 1982 Ford van and added our supplies and gear at Cantamar. Early in the morning, we said our goodbyes to our wife and mother, Leila, let our dog Taco excitedly jump in, and headed off down Highway 1.

It was August and there was plenty of daylight to allow us to get 400 miles to a camp site I like, near the Laguna Manuela fish camp at Punta Santo Domingo. It's on the Pacific, down a dirt road about seven miles from the Highway 1 village of Villa Jesus Maria, and less than 30 miles north of Guerrero Negro.

At camp, while Ken familiarized himself with the motorcycle and drove a few circles around the hard-packed lagoon area, I had enough daylight to clamber up the sandy road to the first of several coves that teem with fish. I caught a half dozen croakers before darkness made it difficult to find my way back to camp.

It was the morrow that we had awaited with anticipation. That would be the day we would head into Baja's remote Vizcaino Peninsula and hope-fully make it to Malarrimo Beach. Ken knew that once off-road he could ride the motorcycle and we would leapfrog each other, with me and Taco in the van.

In the middle of the flat Vizcaino Desert, an agricultural settlement had come into being over recent years. Here a graded dirt road takes off over 100 miles to the west ending at Punta Eugenia, Baja California's tip of the hook that curves northward into the Pacific.

At the edge of town we stopped and wheeled the bike down its plank.

Roared off in a cloud of dust

Like a matador before a bull fight, Ken methodically applied and se-cured his riding gear. Padding, belts, leathers, helmet and gloves were all put on and tightened and he was ready for a week of off-roading. But it was not to be.

He roared off in a cloud of dust and I planned to rendezvous with him later. But it was sooner, rather than later. He never got out of sight, first getting smaller and smaller with the dust billowing behind him. Then the dust stopped and his image started getting bigger and bigger, as if he was stopped. He was.

The engine on the bike had seized, its red hot pistons becoming stuck and immobile, necessitating a total overhaul before it would run again.

"Like a matador before a bull fight, Ken methodically applied and secured his riding gear."

Ken in motorcycle gear.

Not a quick fix in the desert. For the rest of the week the bike would become nothing more than about 250 pounds of strapped-in dead weight that had to be rolled in and out of the van every day.

I didn't say much as we bounced out the rocky dirt road that led further into the wilderness. I wasn't about to abort my trip and Ken knew that. I just let him settle his disappointment in his own quiet way.

With only the van, and with the weight of the motorcycle, we had quite an adventure ahead of us. To quote from the most current Auto Club guide on Baja California, "The trek onto the Vizcaino Peninsula should be attempted only by serious off-road adventurers who are equipped to handle the worst that Baja has to offer — isolation, poor roads, scarcity of fresh water, lack of facilities, frequent dust storms, desert heat and heavy coastal fog."

While we had plenty of water and other supplies, the crippled bike meant we were quite alone, with only one vehicle.

Our first destination was the most remote. It was the fabled Malarrimo Beach, that long, wide sandy north-facing part of the hook that serves as a dumping ground for the Pacific Ocean. Ocean currents swirl southward along the coast of Baja, and the "hook" quite literally catches whatever comes her way head on.

We'd read about explorers and other adventurers who'd found cases of Scotch, oars, entire dinghies, full bottles and items from all around the world — all washed up on that long, lonely beach at Malarrimo.

Off the Beaten Path

The biggest problem for most people is getting there as the fickle excuse for a road is often subject to periodic closures and is "iffy" even during the best of times.

After 72 miles of rough, rocky, graded road from the farm town of Vizcaino, we turned north onto the 27 mile dirt track that would lead us into Malarrimo. Ken was bummed about his bike, but even he was anticipating scouring the beach in search of booty.

We wound through some narrow arroyos and crossed a rocky plateau. A skeleton of a horse, its bones bleached white by the unremitting sun, reminded us of our isolation. It would take about three hours to traverse the 27 miles and get to the beach, and at first it was just a typical rocky Baja road. Then the road dropped down a cliff into a rocky arroyo. For about 30 yards or so on that hill the road was so severely eroded it looked impassable.

After getting out to survey the high points and deep ruts and to determine where the wheels should go, I decided to go for it. We bounced down onto the canyon floor.

Large sand dunes welcomed us as we neared the beach.

There was sand everywhere, especially on the road which now followed the bottom of the arroyo. At two spots of about 50-100 yards each, I was quite concerned. I revved the van up to a sufficient RPM and drove fast over the top of the sand. It worked.

MALARRIMO, JUNKYARD OF THE PACIFIC

Malarrimo turned out to be a long, wide beach, blinding white from fresh sand deposited by almost continual wind. Small dunes of sand gathered around clumps of beach grass just off the shore, and the larger sand dunes were just inland where the road ended.

We set up camp in the lee of a large dune and took off to explore. There was not another person nor sign of habitation as far as we could see up or down the long, gently curving beach. Nor would we see anyone the whole time at Malarrimo.

Taco enjoyed the romp and sticking her discriminating nose into the sand rife with goodies from far and near. There was beach junk from everywhere. We found light bulbs with Japanese symbols on them, old hatch covers and large wooden telephone line spools, fishing floats, oars, wooden boxes, military canisters and weapons boxes, ropes, rubber sandals, caps, helmets, plastic glasses from a cruise ship's New Years Eve party, plastic shampoo bottles, a half intact panga and much more. There was nothing of immense value, but it was fun to collect. Like a grab bag, we never knew what that half-buried, colorful thing protruding from the sand might be.

It was a desolate and interesting place. I skinny-dipped while Ken and Taco played in the sand dunes.

That night, after we cooked the croakers caught earlier, I started feeling uncomfortable, knowing there were a couple of rough places I didn't want to get stuck in on the way out. It would be a long walk to that one rancho 27 miles away. The van, while it had good clearance, was not 4-wheel drive, and we had the extra weight of the bike.

Thus we left early the next day while we still had plenty of water and supplies in case we got stuck. As it turned out, my concerns were for naught because we made it out of Malarrimo as easily as we made it in.

Back on the main gravel road it was about 30 miles to Bahia Tortugas, at a population of over 3,000 the largest town on the Vizcaino Peninsula.

The town, even though it rests on a barren plateau, is a pretty one. Scores of neat pastel-colored houses drop down past a picturesque church on a hill and past a large abalone cannery to end abruptly at the waterfront, from which a long pier juts out into the sparking blue cove. Children were diving off the pier and playing in the tepid water of the bay.

The almost perfectly round bay is the town's greatest feature making it one of the finest natural harbors on Baja's Pacific coast. The sailing and yachting communities know the place, and several boats bobbed just offshore in what the gringo "yachties" call Turtle Bay.

The locals were extremely friendly and especially curious to see outsiders who did not come by boat.

We enjoyed a hearty but simple restaurant meal and headed 16 miles out to Punta Eugenia to camp. We passed a cluster of houses at the extreme western point and continued around the point to a ravine where we could look out and see Isla Natividad, a short distance away.

THE MOMENT HE BECAME A FISHERMAN

I set up the fishing gear and offered a rod to Ken. "If you can't ride, how about fishing," I offered. He was still wearing motorcycle boots, but at least he no longer sported the rest of the gear. He shrugged, smiled and took it. That was the moment he became a fisherman. A few minutes later he was hooked.

It started to get dark and I headed to the van. I heard him yell and looked to see his rod almost doubled over with what was obviously a good-sized fish. Ken worked it and finally pulled a beautiful 6-7 pound cabrilla from the surf. Of all the fish Ken has caught since, that was the most memorable for me.

It signaled a change. It made him a fisherman. On that trip, rather than dwelling on missing bike opportunities, he welcomed fishing opportunities. The motorcycle boots came off, and he learned to assemble fishing gear, bait the hook and cast.

In the morning, from there we backtracked, passed Bahia Tortugas, and then turned south over a 37 mile dirt road over hills and down valleys to the charming little village of Bahia Asuncion. It seemed the whole town was out on the waterfront, either swimming in the ocean, or sitting in the shade of a few nearby trees.

We set up camp a few miles out of town and both went fishing. We caught several corbina and croakers. I caught a small ray and Ken had hooked what must have been a large one, because it took him up and down the shore line in its fight for freedom before finally snapping the line.

The road south from there is a sandy track that parallels the coast almost 50 miles to a village of La Bocana, which sits at the mouth of a small estuary. We stood on the bank of the narrow inlet at La Bocana and caught some nice 10–12 inch sand bass with almost every cast.

A van tire that had picked up a slow leak somewhere on the rocky roads, went flat as we were fishing at La Bocana. So we put to use a handy contraption for Baja, an air compressor that works off the car's cigarette lighter. It makes a whapping noise and takes a little time putting air in the tire, but works. The townspeople delighted in watching us repair the flat.

We drove another 10 miles to Punta Abreojos on the inflated tire and headed straight for a "taller llantas," a tire shop where we had the leak repaired.

Abreojos sits on a sandy spit between a point and a marsh. It's a small cannery town of about 500 with a few businesses and an airstrip to take their abalone and lobster to market.

The point creates outstanding waves and there were a few American surfers camped nearby taking advantage of them. We too rode the waves for a while before heading out of town to camp.

Just south of town is the Estero de Coyote, a separate estuary that abuts the northern part of the larger Laguna San Ignacio. A cluster of rustic cabins called Campo Rene sits on one of the fingers of land jutting into the mangrove-covered lagoon. We could see fish jumping all over the lagoon, but needed a boat to get to them.

Except for an old caretaker, Rene's was void of people. We noticed the tide rising and water touching each cabin, even completely swirling around a couple of the buildings.

The tide was rising all over, about to reach its high for the month, maybe even year, as we sought out a campsite. We splashed through the road flooded in several areas and headed into a place of low sand dunes near the mouth of the estero and not far from the pounding surf. I chose the highest hillock I could and would later be happy for my decision.

Rods in hand, we headed right for the mouth of the estuary by now swelling with ocean water from the unusually high tide. Casting out into the swirling current at the opening's deepest part, we were rewarded with outstanding surf fishing. We released most of them. We caught bass, croaker and corbina. I landed a large shovelnose shark and Ken even caught a stingray before we wrapped it up.

The incredibly bright evening skies of orange and pink began darkening as the sunset became barely visible through the clouds to the west. Exhilarated from such continuous fishing action, we hastened back to the hillock where we left the van. It was high and dry, but barely. We waded to the van which now rested on a very small island completely surrounded by water.

We could depart the next day during the low tide, but camping became a problem. Water lapped near the rear of the van and we couldn't take the motorcycle out. The cumbersome bike thus prohibited our crawling in the van to sleep, so we slept best we could in the van seats. It was a long and uncomfortable night.

But if you listened to the crashing surf, and relived that hot surf fishing action, it was worth it.

From Abreojos, we continued our loop of the Vizcaino Peninsula by taking the most direct way back to Highway 1, about 50 miles of hard-packed, miserable, aggravating, rocky washboard road, finally reaching the pavement about 20 miles north of San Ignacio.

Driving up Highway 1 we reflected on our experience. While some of the other roads were bad, the only real dicey area were those 27 miles into Malarrimo. And while the area is mostly barren, there were a few villages and towns. The townspeople we met were also some of Baja's most friendly and polite.

Most of all there were fish, at every place we stopped. And Ken learned a lesson too. While making the best of a bad situation, he learned to like it. While he still loves motorcycles, he now loves to fish too.

Fish from Shore in Baja Hideaway

The coarse white sandy beach, sparkling clear water, quiet balmy days and rustic cabins have made San Francisquito a real Sea of Cortéz hideaway. Located about the middle of the Baja California peninsula (at the 28th parallel which separates the two Mexican states), private plane people have known about it for years.

The small paved landing strip that ends right at the cabins has been a favorite stopping place for Baja enthusiasts en route via small plane to Loreto or La Paz. To many, it's been a fly-in destination.

Hundreds of miles from the nearest disco, Punta San Francisquito offers peace, quiet, relaxation, serene beauty, a gorgeous beach, swimming, snorkeling, and some of the hottest fishing in Baja.

Fishing is hot

Located in the heart of the Sea of Cortéz's famous midriff region (where the narrow sea forces an upwelling of the waters providing nutrients to spawn the fishery), I learned the waters teem with fish.

In March, April and May, white sea bass may be caught in the area, while July, August and September are good months for sierra and yellowtail. Dorado sometimes make an appearance.

In an August visit, Ken and I caught cabrilla, bass, triggerfish, scorpionfish, bullseye puffers, sting rays and a needlefish, all from the surf in front of the cabins.

But the hottest fishing is yellowtail; from May to October they are so dense you can sit on your cabin porch with binoculars and watch them boiling all over the bay in different locations.

They often come very close to shore chasing baitfish, sometimes close enough to catch with a heavy lure, other times just a short agonizing distance beyond the lures. We missed hooking any from shore, but one guy with the other small group in the area caught two in a few minutes that morning about 100 yards down the beach.

THE RESORT IS RUSTIC

Punta San Francisquito is located on a attractive bay and was established by Rodolfo Valladolid, now deceased. His son, Genaro Valladolid of Tijuana, continues to run the place, but is only in residence two weeks each month. The other two weeks the small resort is managed by Pepe and Fina Torres, who drive down from Tijuana with their three children every 15 days.

There is a small rustic bar (named Don Quijote), a dining room, small storage building (for plane folk) and 11 cabins. The bar decor includes one wall upon which several dozen yellowing business cards had been attached over the years. I added mine as looking for familiar names and companies is a fun diversion.

The cabins are hewn of stone up to about three feet and are virtually open above that. Canvas doors and windows can be secured in the event of inclement weather, or for privacy. The roofs are tin, covered with palm thatch. The porch becomes the social area. Beds are cots covered with a mattress, two to four cots per cabin. Bathroom and shower facilities are in two separate cabins.

Rates are $30 per night for two people, and $40 for three or more. There is a $5 charge for camping. (all prices are as of 1989). The place is run on the honor system, no key, no cash exchanged until you leave. If you want a beer or soda, you get it from the bar, and stroke tally on the clipboard with your room number.

Meals are served, but there is no menu. You let Pepe or the cook know you want dinner for two and at what time. We found the food delicious with the white meat from the manta ray served mojo de ajo (in garlic sauce) one night, and the dark savory meat (like beef) from the other side of the manta ray served the next night. The meals were $7.50 each, we discovered at check out.

A BEAUTIFUL COVE CALLED "THE PORT"

About a mile from the resort (down the runway and over a small hill) is a beautiful natural cove and a very small fishing village (called the port).

Off the Beaten Path

The locals were preoccupied with commercial shark fishing out in the gulf (the sharks never enter the cove) when we were there.

Two Americans live in the smattering of buildings, one a middle-aged man named Eduardo, and down at the other end of the cove on the hill is Deborah. She's a former New Yorker married to the head of the fishing co-op, Alberto Lucero. Alberto will also sometimes take sportsmen out fishing.

While Deborah's young children swim freely in the large shallow cove, she might be busy hand painting San Francisquito T-shirts to sell to the occasional tourists.

Another of Deborah's specialties is gourmet cuisine, an anomaly in this outpost so far from civilization. Guests let her know the day before that they wish to dine and the Mexican resourcefulness Deborah gleaned from 13 years in Baja pays off in a splendid candlelight dinner in a cluttered back-yard overlooking the cove. Deborah and Alberto also provide camping nearby.

Deborah in recent years has been active with her Citizens Band radio and has helped many an off-roader who has become stranded. She has also written several articles on her Baja experiences.

While I was there she was fretting an upcoming problem that is com-pounded by Deborah's chosen life style. Her mother was coming from New York to visit!

"Has she ever been to Baja before?" I queried.

"No."

"Anywhere in Mexico?"

"She's never been out of New York."

"You got a problem," I concluded, knowing that many New Yorkers consider anything west of the Hudson River to be the uncivilized outback. Even California, which they like to call "the coast" for some reason, is considered a cultural wasteland by many of them.

Deborah herself escaped the urban life where designer clothes are more important than values and friendship. She's in an incredible remote area; her mail even goes to San Ignacio (about 75 miles of dirt road and another 70 miles of paved road away). She has none of the conveniences coveted by the modern American household.

And she had to entertain her mother who was coming from America's largest city.

I found out later through the Baja grapevine that the visit went okay, but it was a lot briefer than planned. I would have loved to have been there just to see the reaction of someone who expects a deli on every corner.

Hard to get to

Not only is San Francisquito a remote outpost, it is very hard to get to without a private plane.

The best road is through Bahia de Los Angeles, where the pavement ends some 400 miles south of Tijuana. The 85-mile dirt road south from the Bahia has been graded and now takes about three hours. It is so rocky, most locals drive dirt tracks off to the side, lest they jostle all of their molars loose. It can be driven in a passenger car, and small boats can be towed if care is taken.

The other road, out of El Arco, is worse. The old mining town of El Arco can be reached off of Highway 1, south of Guerrero Negro. It's about 25 miles from the highway and while some maps show it to be paved, the pavement has worn off years ago and is so rutted most people drive the dirt road alongside it. It's not too bad to get to El Arco, but the 50 miles of dirt road due east from there to San Francisquito takes about three hours and is recommended only for high clearance vehicles.

There is a high crown most of the way, and there is one spot called La Cuesta de la Ley (the slope that rules) that will tax the skills of most drivers and their vehicles. It is a vertical rocky drop of 400 feet in only .40 of a mile that the Automobile Club once called a "harrowing plunge." A new track just to the right of the original was blasted in recent years, but when we were there recent rains had washed all topsoil off and it was a toss-up as to which was the best road. My kid dumped his Honda 250 on one of them and my van actually skidded down the other.

That's the way it is in Baja — some of the most attractive places are the most inaccessible.

Spectacular magenta and apricot sunrises explode from across the gulf, pelicans patrol the lucid turquoise waters, large fish boil right off the warm sand, and later in the day the whole bay takes on a warm orange glow before darkness sets in.

There's no disco; there's not even a store, nor a television, nor a gift shop. There's certainly no deli. There's hardly any people. San Francisquito is not for everybody — but to a long-time Baja buff, it epitomizes what the whole peninsula used to be like.

Baja's Hidden Coast

Baja California, México — 1992

The jagged rocks of the punishing road finally won, proving that rubber is weaker than rock, and the van wobbled to a halt. I was miles from nowhere and earlier Ken had roared on ahead on his Yamaha 500, a larger bike he'd graduated to.

Changing the punctured tire, I couldn't get good traction for the jack on the uneven, rocky dirt road. The plank I carry for such an emergency was mistakenly left at the last camp. Naturally, the jack slipped and the bumper would have hit me had I not anticipated the failure and lurched back just in time.

Ken, it turns out, was not ahead. He had made a wrong turn and soon, coming up from behind me, I heard his motor breaking the quiet desert stillness. With his help, we changed the tire and continued, vowing to stay closer together.

An accident, or getting lost there, could be fatal as travelers rarely come to this place, one of Baja's most remote desert corners. It might be days before someone would come along.

Baja California, an 800 mile peninsula, is home to two of Mexico's states. Baja California Norte greets millions of tourists in Tijuana, Ensenada and Rosarito Beach. And the southern tip of Baja California Sur has become a jet-setting playground in the Cabo San Lucas area.

Much of that vast area in between is one of the planet's most desolate regions. The narrow, paved Highway 1 runs the length of the peninsula and links the few, very small population centers. But to venture far off the highway often means you're quite on your own.

A REGULAR VAN IN 4-WHEEL TERRITORY

Our objective was to explore some remote beaches of the central Pacific coast area where difficult 4-wheel drive trails and total lack of supplies and people would make the journey not only adventurous, but onerous.

At Saturday mid-day we pulled the old Ford van off Highway #1, 47 miles south of El Rosario and 5.6 miles south of a rancho called Santa Cecilia. Son Ken, 21, had been waiting for this moment since we left Southern California Friday morning. He rolled his Yamaha out of the van, suited up, and after studying the map, took off.

I followed on the dirt road, replete with beautiful, yet harsh desert scenery. Giant cardon cactus, the ungainly cirio tree (which looks like a fuzzy upside-down carrot), large boulders, elephant trees and cactus of every species lined the smooth dirt road. It is a living desert too; before the end of the day I would see many long-eared rabbits, a rattle-snake, lizards, quail by the hundreds and even several groups of wild horses.

"THE QUIET WAS MOST AWESOME"

But the quiet was most awesome. I would stop, turn off the ignition, and just marvel at the stillness that pervades this area. I was the intruder. This rigorous land had been the same for millennia. It was no different now than it was in the 18th century when determined padres crossed it to establish missions on the peninsula and eventually into the U.S. state of California.

After 14 miles I came to a small rancho called Santa Catarina. Nestled in a draw with several scraggly trees and cactus fences was a rancher's shack. Walking out of the shack to greet me was a wrinkled old man who reeked of body odor. His big friendly grin revealed a mouth without a visible tooth, nary a one. I was surprised when he addressed me with a few English words mixed in with his Spanish. It certainly contrasted with his unkempt appearance. He indicated that Ken was 20 minutes ahead and that in five kilometers I should turn left at the road fork.

Shortly after the fork, the road deteriorated badly, hinting at the rugged days ahead. There were high crowns, holes caused by erosion, sharp drop-offs, steep canyons, and rocks, rocks and more rocks. Sometimes the road would follow a sandy creek bed in which maintaining a certain higher speed is required to avoid getting stuck. Sometimes the creek bed would be a rocky wash where you made your own road.

Fresh crab at a fish camp

Ken met me near the coast, where one road goes to the point (Punta Canoas) and the other to a seasonal fish camp. He'd been eating fresh crab Donated by newly-made Mexican friends at the fish camp. We set up camp down the beach from them.

Surf fishing, we caught two good sized croakers before dark and a couple of nice snapper and a surf bass in the morning. An American couple was camped way down the beach from us and would be the only countrymen, and among the only people, we would see all week.

Upon departure, we stopped at the fish camp and noticed that a van tire was low. We inflated it with my cigarette lighter pump, but noticed the valve was loose. Mexicans invented the art of repairing vehicles with available materials and the three of them immediately knew to look for a piece of wire to tighten the stem. That's all it took and we were on our way.

I averaged 7 miles per hour on miserable road getting to the little rancho of Santa Maria, 14 miles inland. It consisted of a well, corral, some horses and a small trailer providing the living quarters for the two middle-aged Mexican cowboys. Ken was there with them drinking an offered cup of coffee when I arrived.

While Mexican people are generally warm and generous, those in these remote locations are even more so. You couldn't pay them for coffee because not only would it be an insult, but because money doesn't mean anything to them. But they needed some matches, and we had an extra box. That, they genuinely appreciated.

The next four miles took one hour and taxed my considerable off-road skills. In fact, the next 20 miles back toward the beach took well over three hours, but that also included the earlier-mentioned repair of the flat tire.

Nobody home at Puerto San Jose

Puerto San José was an unusual place, a small village, nothing more than a few fish shacks really, perched on a rocky bluff overlooking a most beautiful lagoon and inviting sandy beach stretching way off to the south.

But not a person was there. We camped about a quarter mile north on a bluff and even the next morning the place was deserted, save a couple of dogs. I saw a utilitarian looking plank and having lost mine, threw it in the van.

Mornings along the hidden coast were damp and cool, but the sun burned the marine layer off by about 9 a.m. and continued to shine all day.

Continuing south on Monday, Ken and I met at each crossroad.

Cresting a hill I saw him in front of me, slowly getting up and lifting his bike. He was obviously hurt. The road dogged right at a hill crest and it appeared Ken went straight, hit a rock and ricocheted into a four foot barrel cactus which he took down with him.

His left arm was full of sharp needle-like stickers which took about 20 minutes to pull out. We bathed it in rubbing alcohol, bandaged it and continued.

The road got worse. It went through very rocky hills with occasional holes where large rocks had been. Rocks that rip gas tanks and mufflers are sometimes shaken loose and then finally removed by someone. But the resulting hole becomes a different type of hazard, jolting the wheel so abruptly your teeth could bite your tongue off. Off-roaders learn to drive tongue in and teeth tightly clenched.

Down in lower terrain, sandy stream bottoms demanded concentration and skill in keeping the van moving forward, a stressful task. I rejoiced at the occasional smooth spot where I would get in second gear and "speed along" at 20 miles per hour.

We approached a dry lake bed that looked a little damp. We stopped and Ken sailed across it on his bike, returned, and said, "It looks fine."

"I KNEW I WAS IN TROUBLE"

I decided to go. A quarter mile out, and only seconds after I passed someone's deep dig-out marks, I knew I was in trouble. The lake bottom got muddy, damp and very soft. I skidded a little and then the right rear tire dug in. Stuck!

The people in the earlier car stuck in the bog obviously sacrificed not only new Mexican blankets, all their firewood and sleeping bags, but most of their military clothing in order to provide traction to their wheels. It looked like a U.S. Marine corporal and PFC had spent many hours, probably the day before, digging out. They had to be almost naked when they left, considering all the clothing that remained in the mud.

From their tracks, it looked like they panicked when it got soft, made a big U-turn, and got stuck worse than I was in a yet-softer area on the way back out.

Off the Beaten Path

I paced off a circular area on the hardest ground in front of the van, planning where each tire would go within inches. Then with my new board, all their jettisoned clothes under the wheel, and Ken pushing, the wheel slowly became unstuck, I carefully kept the van to that paced-off hard ground and got off the lake bed.

An idyllic two mile long beach

We approached Punta Blanca, where an occupied 10x20 foot plywood fishing shack faced a cove. Nearby was another small house, built by an American artist and only used part of the year. To the south was a two mile long, beautiful white curving beach.

The fishing shack occupant, Amador, who dove for scallops, and his wife, Reyes, invited us to camp anywhere. Maybe we could go fishing in his boat in the morning. All right! All over Baja are fishermen who will take out anglers in their wooden 18-foot pangas for usually about $20. As dragging a boat over bad roads is impractical, I have often engaged such fishermen.

We camped at the head of the wide beach and in exhilaration I rode my mountain bicycle up and down the hard-packed sand. Aside from Amador and Reyes we were alone for miles. Later, the four of us fished off the rocks as dusk fell. Ken, whose arm was still bothering him from the cactus, lost a big halibut and Amador caught a beautiful 8-10 pound cabrilla. Later at camp, Ken and I feasted on a dinner of fresh fish and frijoles cooked over a mesquite fire.

In the morning, Amador and Reyes and their retinue of dogs came over to our camp and we used my van to pull his boat out across the sand. We loaded our gear and I drove the van back to camp. Then all four of us pushed the panga out into the surf.

The lonely coves along the hidden coast are void of people, but marine life abounds. Sea lions bark from their rocky headlands. Pelicans dive-bomb with startling splashes for their dinners and the fish are plentiful. In a few hours, we'd all caught a number of bass, cabrilla and croaker.

It was thrilling riding that panga over the waves onto a beach like a large surfboard. We then tied the van to the panga and tried to pull it out of the surf. Then when my van's clutch started burning pulling that boat back to dry land, we quit. Amador said, "No problema," and explained in Español how he'd let the tide and a rope do most of the work later.

By this time Reyes had lunch prepared in the shack. The four of us pigged out on delicious fish tacos from last night's big cabrilla, homemade tortillas, beans and salsa. Amador proudly showed us his meager treasures: a carved boat, a lamp, a grinder, a pistol. As neither he nor Reyes would accept any money from us, even for fishing, we gave him a couple of wrenches he needed, and her some candy, crackers and canned food.

To two lovely people who speak no English and who only see a truck that picks up his scallops twice a week, we also promised to return.

South of Punta Blanca when I could go fast enough for second gear, the trade-off was billowing dust, fine as baby powder, that swirled and entered the van from untold, unknown openings.

SIGNS OF CIVILIZATION

Signs of civilization started appearing, a well, a crumbling old building, a grave. The road dropped down a rocky hill, and near Punta Cono, we hit an improved, all-weather rocky road. My feelings were mixed between celebration that the worst was over and dismay at returning to a less pristine area.

We camped at Punta Cono and again at Punta Negra where we enjoyed surf fishing, surfing, motorcycle and bicycle riding, exploring the beautiful beaches and cooking fresh fish over open fires.

In six days travel we saw fewer than 10 other people and only two were other travelers. The graded road eventually turned to washboard, and after 191 miles of dirt, we rejoined Highway 1 and pavement south of Punta Prieta.

Punta San José and Punta Blanca showed us an idyllic part of México that, for now, remains an adventure, mostly because of the area's inaccessibility. In a way it's a shame there's so few people in the area, because the ones you do meet are among the grandest in the world.

A Loop Back in Time

Loreto Mountains, B.C.S., México — 1994

Take a time machine back 100 years or more. You need not go to Universal Studios for the "Back to the Future" ride. For the real thing, take a day-long driving loop into the rugged Baja mountains out of Loreto.

The graded dirt road, suitable for most high clearance vehicles, leaves Highway #1 just 1.1 miles south of Loreto. The mountain loop passes several historic missions, fertile, self-sustaining valleys and sleepy villages. It goes over country so high we could see both the Pacific Ocean and the Sea of Cortéz at the same time. The loop ends back on Highway 1, only 37 miles north of Loreto.

Don and I had been successfully fishing the Loreto waters and headed off to explore more of the interior. It was a 23 mile dirt road from Highway 1 to Mission San Javier (or Xavier). First the road wended though about six miles of low hills, then ascended rapidly up into the Sierra de la Giganta.

The stream bed of a picturesque palm canyon displayed remnants of the old road which can still be seen hugging the steep canyon wall. About half-way to San Javier is an oasis called Las Parras, with a stone chapel, groves of olive and citrus trees and several dogs barking over their domain.

Mission San Javier

From a high barren hill we dropped down into a fertile, narrow valley. Arriving in San Javier, we passed a few inviting blue-green pools that provide sustenance for livestock and the hardy ranching families who occupy this serene and secluded mountain village.

While I'd seen many photos of the Mission San Javier, its majestic presence still overwhelmed us as we rolled into town. Past small ranchos and a school, the dirt road ended at a long, wide plaza, almost like a boulevard, complete with concrete planters and curbs, leading directly to the stately mission.

San Javier (or Xavier) is considered one of the most beautiful and best preserved of all of Baja's missions. It alone is a delightful and rewarding experience.

After Loreto was established in 1697, Indians from these rugged mountains came down to visit the new settlement. Padre Francisco Piccolo followed them back to a place with friendly people, a stream and land to graze cattle.

With much difficulty he built a road and little chapel, dedicating the mission on Nov. 1, 1699.

During a drought in 1720 he was forced to move to a farm about seven miles south. There Padre Juan de Ugarte replaced Piccolo and built the current Mission San Francisco Xavier de Vigge. Costing over $1 million pesos, it boasts a stone belfry and Moorish spires. The intricate and detailed stonework is still outstanding. It was completed in 1758, some 240 years ago.

Black lava cliffs surround the quiet valley, providing a reverential stillness and stark contrast to the white domes of the mission.

The chapel is open, maintained regularly and features paintings, vestments and artifacts from earlier centuries. Don and I entered and saw an old woman busy cleaning. The devout old caretaker answered our questions while continuing to work, dusting centuries-old statues and gilt-edged oil paintings with reverence and familiarity. We left a few pesos in Donation.

Time stands still here, for this woman, and for all in this valley. Stateside California missions have gift shops and fax machines and computers to order and log supplies. Not here. Material possessions and modern devices are not only absent but are totally meaningless amid the simple life of this small Baja village. Love of family and a strong faith are the riches coveted and respected by these most unpretentious people.

From San Javier, we had to backtrack four miles to a junction and then head north 26 miles to the Comondus. The road passes a couple of small ranchos and a few goat herds and offers some spectacular views.

Two villages called Comondu

The Comondus are actually two villages, San José de Comondu and San Miguél de Comondu, about two miles apart. After the rough, barren, rocky high country, the lush valley is a welcome sight. San José de Comondu is reached first, with date palms and tropical foliage creating a "green carpet" welcome into town.

The original Comondu mission was established about 24 miles north of this site in 1708. It was moved to this village of San José in 1737. One stone building of the mission still stands next to the plaza and the original bells hang nearby. There is a small store across from the plaza.

The valley floor covers seven miles of lush vegetation, and two miles down valley is San Miguél de Comondu. It appears to be a larger village, but many of the buildings are no longer in use. Several workers can be seen climbing palms to harvest dates, and families nearby quietly and gently sort and dry them in the warm Baja sun.

Upon inquiry, visitors are led to a home where meals are prepared. No menu, but the food is good and reasonable.

Youngsters practice their English on travelers by yelling their halting "How are you's" and "What is your name?" from a schoolyard across the street from a chapel built as recently as 1905. Previously, a visita mission dating from 1714 was established there.

From the Comondus, one can head northeast to El Crucero and a shorter, although little tougher, road to Highway #1, or continue northwest to the villages of San Isidro and La Purisima.

Aqueduct graces San Isidro

We wanted to see San Isidro and La Purisima and left the Comondus on a winding rocky road. The oasis village of San Isidro, 16 miles north of San José de Comondu, lies in another remote and deep valley surrounded by high cliffs and rugged desert. Most interesting is an aqueduct built out of stone that runs alongside the road further irrigating the verdant valley. San Isidro, with a population of 600, has a few stores and a small cafe.

Aqueduct hugs the road near entrance
to village of San Isidro.

LA PURISIMA — MOST POPULOUS MISSION

Three miles down valley is the town of La Purisima, which greets a paved road from Cuidad Insurgentes in the south. La Purisima has such a feeling of remoteness and laid-back charm we felt cheated upon seeing the pavement.

La Purisima was established by Padre Nicolas Tamaral who, after first visiting in 1712, returned in 1717 to establish a mission. He had Indians help him build roads through the sierras from Mulege on the gulf to the Comondus and La Purisima. Soon, there were over 2,000 Indians and grain and orchards were planted to feed them.

The butte, El Pilon dominates La Purisima

While Padre Tamaral ruled the Indians with an iron fist, the mission was considered one of the most successful. In a 1730 report, it was considered by the padres the most populous and best cared for in the peninsula. Wonder what the Indians thought? The Indian population was decimated by disease and the mission was abandoned in 1822. Only a few mounds of adobe from the original mission remain.

The charming valley, overlooked by a dramatic butte called El Pilon, is fertile due to the elaborate irrigation system. Grown there are dates, mangoes, citrus fruits, corn, grapes, tomatoes, chilies and beans. About 700 people live in La Purisima and limited supplies are available.

It's about 30 miles back along good, high clearance dirt road to Highway #1, only 10 miles south of the southern tip of Bahia Conception.

Don and I were hot, dusty and tired when we rejoined the highway. We sped up the smooth asphalt road, heading directly for a sand-spit called El Requeson and a refreshing dip in the bay.

"The pavement feels good," said Don as we got into higher gears on the highway, "Do you think they'll ever pave those mountain roads?"

I glanced back up at the steep, rocky eastern escarpment of the Sierra de la Giganta. I thought about the timelessness of the remote villages and valleys. I thought about the warm, friendly people that prevail in the remote back country of Baja.

"I sure hope not," I said. "I sure hope not."

Calamajue — Beyond Punta Final

December, 1996

It was the bad water that drove the Jesuits to abandon the mission here after only months at the site. On this visit, we noted the water was mineralized, and now it was also deeper than my last visit. It was so deep Ken decided to stop and walk to determine where best to ford the muddy swamp.

It was Ken's first four-wheel attempt in the wilds of Baja and he did all the driving. Before he moved to Oregon, he'd covered much of Baja by motorcycle. Now he came south to visit, *sans* bike, but in a Toyota four-wheel drive pickup with camper shell. He was literally salivating to get some off-roading experience in Baja.

We chose the old mission trail road into Calamajue and then planned to join the rocky, graded road through Gonzaga Bay and up to San Felipe. From there we'd take the power-line road used in the Baja 1,000 in reverse direction to San Matias Pass on our loop back to Ensenada.

In my Jeep I'd been through the Calamajue road twice before. But it was early summer then and the road bed stream was only inches deep. Now, in December, and following an earlier storm, the stream swelled to about double its summer volume.

We picked up the Calamajue road off Highway 1 south of Laguna Chapala, about 13 miles north of the Bahia de Los Angeles cutoff. The road is initially a narrow, sandy wash, taking off through the desert to the east. It turns northward, among a thickening forest of large, multi-armed cardon cactus trees and huge twisting and bending cirio trees, their winter blossoms contrasting to their thousands of sticky spines and adding a sense of life to the desert.

I don't think Ken noticed the abundance of flora in the area, so intense was his concentration on the road, with its many ruts, patches of thick sand and occasional rocks. Let me say here that I quickly learned my off-road objectives are somewhat different from his.

While I truly like to test my skills on the most challenging roads, and I feel a sense of pride after negotiating a particular difficult spot, I most enjoy where the roads take me. And I love to soak up the beauty, or uniqueness of the wild country I drive through. Sometimes however, I will drive as fast as the road will allow, either in the interest of time, or returning on a road I've already been on.

Heading down Calamajue Canyon.

KEN LIKES TO ATTACK THE ROAD

Ken, on the other hand, likes to attack a road, every road, and "flat out" best describes his dream speed. Unfortunately this 25-year-old accomplished motocross racer was with his dad and this time sensibly tempered his speed accordingly.

I said little, just watching the desert fly by and holding my sides tight lest I suffer bruised ribs and damaged organs.

But he had to slow down once we dropped down into the Calamajue canyon. Year-round springs fed the valley floor with a trickling stream, soon adding palms, swamp grass and small shade trees to the harsh desert landscape. The road follows the stream bed, and numerous times we'd splash through water while swamp grass clumps almost obliterated the road and scraped paint on both sides of the truck.

A few cows grazed in the area, especially as the canyon widened and green meadows replaced the sandy desert floor.

An old, yellow Caterpillar skiploader provided a surprising bit of contrasting color, leaning up against a rocky embankment where it looked like it had been excavating. The rusting hulk with flat tires had not been there nine years previous. But that symbol of an outside world was the only change I noted in nine years. Change is slow in these remote arroyos of the Baja peninsula.

THE MEADOW WAS A MUDDY SWAMP

Ahead we saw a white limestone cliff at a bend in the road. Below the cliff, from which water tumbled in small waterfalls, was a large, wide meadow, now swollen with rain and spring water into a muddy swamp.

We stopped and got out. Tire tracks took off in several directions, their drivers obviously looking for the optimum spot to cross. Some got stuck and we could see where they had problems. It looked like the best course was through the deeper water. At least we could see the bottom there.

Ken, later acknowledging he learned this from me, sized up the situation. He tested some of the ground with his foot and visualized where each tire would go. I would stay outside and get a photo of him sailing through the bog.

I walked and jumped from occasional rocks to clumps of solid earth to a good location. The earth was crisp on top from the mineralized water tumbling off the embankment. It was like a pie crust and crunched when you walked.

Unfortunately, what looked like one solid spot was not and I was soon over my shoe tops in sticky black muddy goo. I was so ticked at my stupidity that when I waved Ken on, I forgot to open the camera lens. Thus the best photo of the trip was not taken. I pressed a shutter that would not click just as Ken got plenty of air over the bog in the best Baja 1,000 tradition.

He was elated over his success but we were both disappointed over my missed shot.

Parked on terra firma, we decided to survey the area.

The white, limestone cliff beckoned and atop it were several springs bubbling up vertically to heights of three or four inches, creating crystal clear pools that while the water cleaned my shoes, was salty and filled with alkali to the taste.

The entire cliff had been formed by this alkali spring, and while water in the canyon above this spot was potable, below the water brimmed with minerals leaving rings of white around former pools.

BAD WATER THWARTED MISSIONARY ATTEMPT

The deception of good water/bad water fooled the Jesuit missionaries too. Padre Fernando Consag made an exploratory trek into these northern wilds in 1753 and noted water at Calagnujuet (Calamajue). Later Padre Wenceslao Linck who established the Mission of San Borja to the south in 1762 also explored the area. When the second mission of the Señora Maria Borja Donation was planned, he recommended Calamajue. It was also about halfway between San Borja and an area called Velicata which had a number of Indians whose souls they wanted to save.

Thus in October 1766 Padres Victoriano Arnes and Juan José Diez arrived in Calamajue from San Borja. They were accompanied by 10

Spanish soldiers and 50 Indian neophytes led by Cochimi Chief Juan Nepomuceno. Even though the area was barren, they built structures on a rocky promontory and went about their work of trying to teach the local Indians their way of life.

They planted crops which subsequently died from the mineralized, salty water.

After only a few months, during which time they baptized 200 children and adults, they were besieged by problems. Failing health forced Father Diez to leave. Local Indians revolted several times against Padre Arnes, but Chief Nepomuceno and the mission Indians helped put them down and punish them. But it was the bad water that forced them to relocate the mission to another remote arroyo, Santa Maria, in May, 1767 after only seven months in Calamajue.

An interesting side note is that the exploration of Nuevo California (U.S. state of California) was planned in the area. Captain Gaspar de Portola, Commander of the Spanish Expedition to the Californias, passed through Calamajue on his way north to join Padre Junipero Serra, President of the Franciscan Mission to the Californias in May, 1769. The two leaders met and honed their plans at Mission Santa Maria and then continued northward.

A REMOTE THOROUGHFARE

We continued our journey down this canyon, so remote it seemed impossible to have been a major thoroughfare over 200 years ago. It's still a thoroughfare of sorts. On most of the years that the Baja 1,000 goes all the way to La Paz, the brackish waters of Calamajue are splashed by hundreds of off-road vehicles vying to be the fastest, and sometimes destroying the habitat in the process.

After the road expands onto a broad wash it turns up the canyon wall, leaving the arroyo for the rocky mesa. I recognized that point. A small weathered sign, no longer readable, indicates the old mission site is near.

We hiked to the site, which now only features a few rock walls and some mounds where walls once stood. A jeep trail can take you up the hill to the site. Someone has been here since my last visit. It appeared that someone had tried to excavate one of the wall mounds with hand tools. Also, some surveyors left their concrete markers on the four corners surrounding the site. I couldn't help but wonder if it would all be fenced to keep out those who would destroy historical areas.

We also explored the Molino de Calamajue, an abandoned gold ore mine on the lip of the opposite canyon wall near the road. Piles of rock outline the buildings and you can even see where a pulley or tram was located. An arrow scratched in concrete points to the mission site across the arroyo.

Back at the truck, our Peñance for challenging the road head-on was a broken extra can of oil. Ken's hydraulic jack had bounced and landed on top of it, squishing the oil all over the camper bed. Ken and I learned greater respect for those who help clean up massive oil tanker spills as we spent almost an hour wiping goo off our things.

Back on the road, we took every right turn to arrive at Campo Calamajue, a small, isolated fish camp, rather then continue straight to Punta Final and the more populated Gonzaga Bay. Imagine, being farther from and more isolated than Punta Final (The end).

SHANTIES LINE THE COVE

Soon we arrived at the campo, a large sandy cove with rocky promontories at each of the headlands. About 8-10 small fishermen's shanties line the cove. Pangas are neatly pulled up off the tide. A few fishermen are stretching and repairing their nets. A few others are sitting in front of one of the shanties taking advantage of the mid-afternoon shade.

There were about four or five families living at Calamajue this mid-December, with about half the places vacant. We were invited to camp among them and we pulled the truck up between two houses, a respectable distance from each.

One man said he heard on the radio that it was raining all along the Pacific coast. The sun was shining brightly here without a single cloud to mar a perfect, baby blue sky. The water was warm, about 70–72 degrees. That would be a lucky mid-summer day in the Pacific.

The fishermen tell us we can catch yellowtail and sierra from the shore. We try, and catch lots of the pesky bullseye puffers and some bass, but no sierra.

The water was so inviting, I snorkled, seeing several schools of small fish and the puffers. Then, right where the sand line turned to rocks, I saw a 1½ to 2 foot fish shaped like a sierra. It was too quick and too far for a positive identification, like the yellow spots, but I'm sure it was one.

A DAZZLING DISPLAY OF PHOSPHOROUS

Later, as the enormous tide sucked much of the water from the delightful cove exposing the bottom on the left half to be all rocks, darkness fell exposing a most unique phenomenon, the most dazzling display of phosphorous I'd ever seen. Every splash of the water rewarded us with a luminescence that reminded us of black lights on white shirts in a disco. Even walking on the wet cobbles produced a bright display that looked like we were rolling sparklers. Waves way out over the rocks were lit up. It was eerie and beautiful and apparently not unusual.

While we were drifting off to sleep in the covered pickup bed camper, we heard the pangas take off for their night runs. With only an occasional flashlight beam, we wondered how they could see.

Our answer came the next morning as they were unloading about 800 pounds of sierra from their nets. One fisherman told me the fish follow the wake of phosphorous right into their nets. Sounds like a fish story but I believed it.

Shortly we all looked out to the point. Fish were boiling like crazy, a frenzy that covered an area of about two football fields. The fishermen had finished their unloading and had refolded their nets. We were in the midst of negotiating a fishing run with one of them when the activity occurred.

They all dropped everything and pushed off, racing to the site of the boiling sierra. It wasn't a question anymore of a fisherman making a few dollars from a couple gringos when he could net many times that in minutes. We certainly didn't begrudge his decision. We knew if we stayed at Calamajue long enough one of them would eventually take us out.

We too joined the craze. We grabbed three rods, extra hooks and bait (frozen squid) and a few lures (Rapalas, Crocodiles and Candybars) and set off to the far end of the cove. After hiking around the cove and scrambling over the rocks, we reached the point where we could almost cast into the fishermen's boats. But they were already starting to move farther out, as that's where the fish were headed.

I had one nice strike on my first cast with a lure and then the sierra were out of range. Unlike the fishermen, we missed the sierra bite, so decided to bait fish, catching about a dozen nice triggerfish and a large parrotfish.

It wasn't the game action of the hard-hitting sierra, but we enjoyed the fishing.

We cleaned up our camp, gave a soda to a chubby little kid with an infectious and irresistible smile, said our goodbyes to those left in camp and headed for Gonzaga Bay. We didn't even stop at Punta Final. It just wasn't er, "final" enough for us.

The end of the land. Rock promontory at the tip of Cabo.
Baja Fever

La páz

and the cape

"Baja is forever a poem, the stark but lovely landscape, sunrise on the Sea of Cortéz, the sage filled fragrance of a desert breeze, driftwood smoke, gentle people, simpatico...

"Baja sings, and Mary and I have listened for a long, long time. Our memories of the beautiful peninsula are forever a part of our lives and of our love. They are our poem."

— *Paul "Panther" Pierce,*
"A Baja Love Song" 1985

THE MALECÓN

LA PÁZ, MÉXICO

Breezes brush the balmy bay;
Lovers stroll along the quay.
Lapping waves where children play,
The Malecón greets me this day.

Pelicans splash seeking prey,
Leaping fish ruffle the bay.
Maiden smiles on display,
Malecón's sun sets this day.

The sky explodes in crimson rays,
Darkness falls, but warmth, it stays.
The people of La Páz parade
The Malecón of this Baja bay.

by Greg Niemann

La Páz and the Cape

Papa and Maria

La Páz — 1975

The big Mexican jetliner from Tijuana dropped altitude like a rock in these cloudless and barren skies over La Páz. It was certainly more abrupt a descent than those by any stateside commercial carrier. These Mexican pilots don't pussyfoot around circling an airport waiting for clearance when there are only a couple daily landings.

Instead of the wide, sweeping airborne curves I had been accustomed to stateside, this jet dropped straight down. Then it made a hard left turn tilting the left wing tantalizing close to forests of tall cardon cactus and scraggly mesquite trees to approach the runway so suddenly that flight attendants were still standing as we touched down on the blistering hot tarmac.

This was my third stop here in the past year or so and each one featured a similar landing. The other times it was merely a brief stop-over on route to Mazatlan, a Mexican mainland port city in which I found beauty, solace and comfort in those months of single freedom following a 12-year marriage.

But seeing this city from the air had intrigued me and this time I planned to go beyond the frigid air conditioned comfort of their new airport terminal and spend a few days here. I'm glad I did too, for it precipitated a love affair with what remains to this day my favorite city. No matter how dicey the airplane landings are there!

The hard landings never changed either, as on my 1979 honeymoon, the pilot came in so hard and fast he had to abort just after his wheels touched down. As he made another pass, the landing gear just skimmed trees at the end of the runway!

I took a taxi to town and got comfortable at the venerable La Perla, a landmark waterfront hotel that was in the throes of some upgrading. They needed the modernizing then too; if they had a sign saying "Cortes slept here" I might have believed them. Since that 1985 trip, the whole hotel has long since been renovated and along with a great location, it is now a pleasant place to stay.

La Perla's open street-side coffee shop downstairs was the travelers' gathering place in those days. Sitting there, in about two days you would see every tourist in town walk by or pop in to eat. Which is how I met Pete, an attorney from Portland who lived on a houseboat on the Columbia River.

He was getting so serious with his girlfriend he had to get away to reflect. He needed time to try to determine what he really wanted. There are a lot of lost souls wandering around not sure what they want but hoping a change of scenery might be the impetus for action. We combined forces and together explored this capital city of Baja California Sur.

First visited in 1533

La Páz was first visited by Europeans as early as 1533, but hostile southern Indians killed several of the Spanish soldiers. In 1535 Hernan Cortes himself established a colony there but it was short lived.

In 1596 a new colony named La Páz (The Peace) was started by explorer Sebastian Vizcaino, but it too was later abandoned.

La Páz graces the southeastern shore of the large Bahia de La Páz and a pearl industry flourished as oyster beds were discovered there. During the 17th century there was enough pearl diving activity that La Páz pearls were coveted back in Spain.

Another regular colony at La Páz wasn't attempted until 1720 when the Jesuits established a mission there. The hostility of the Indians and the fact that many of the Indians died from disease forced the abandonment of the mission in 1749.

It wasn't until 1811 that the place became a permanent settlement. After a hurricane wiped out Loreto in 1829, La Páz became the territorial capital. La Páz was occupied briefly by American troops during the Mexican American War.

Pearls made a comeback but had become so rare by 1900, cultivation attempts had to be made. Cultivating didn't work too well and by 1940 the oyster industry at La Páz was finished.

Americans rarely visit this lovely city now opting instead for Mexican resorts like Cancun and Baja's Cabo San Lucas, both of which cater to a

La Páz and the Cape

more international crowd. La Páz has no golf course and outside of the few larger hotels, few merchants speak English.

Pete and I walked all over, along the Malecón (a seawall walkway separating the frontage road from the sandy beaches), up the narrow downtown streets that zig this way and that, past old, thick-walled colonial buildings, through Chinese restaurants, loud macho bars, small shops and large well-stocked department stores.

We romped through the mercado publico, the public market found in every Mexican and Central American city, where food, fruit, vegetable, meat and fish stalls provide the background scents while you explore clothing, brick-a-brack, hats and leather goods in a maze of vitality. It's all crowded together in tight quarters with narrow aisles and a bustling and clamorous crowd. It was a novelty to Pete who had never seen such a downtown market. I often seek these vibrant, intense hearts of every Mexican city to hone my bargaining skills, pick up needed supplies and enjoy the busy pulse of the people.

A central plaza across from a cathedral is also a Mexican mainstay, and the small, tidy La Páz plaza was alive with shoeshine vendors, young couples holding hands, children playing, and old men sitting and chatting under aged laurel trees which provided shade from the afternoon sun.

Wherever we went, the people were friendly and greeted us with big smiles. There were only a handful of Americans in town but we met several tourists from the Mexican mainland.

We went to a rowdy bar or two and ended up at a dark and loud nightclub where we danced with a couple of girls who spoke no English and their Spanish was altogether muted by the Mexican version of a hard rock band. Pete and I laughed and got drunk together, stumbling back to our separate hotel rooms in the carefree abandon of drunks on vacation.

The next evening we watched the locals stroll the Malecón, a regular nightly promenade. It seems the entire town delights in the dramatic La Páz sunset where bright bold colors reflect off the bay. Then the sun drops behind the distant mountains and renders a warm balmy evening. The Malecón is illuminated by moonlight from across the bay, residual light from the city and regularly-spaced quaint lampposts along the roadway.

As waves slap against the seawall, people stroll to see and be seen. Young girls, even some escorted by the mothers, were stealing glances and smiling at us, two blond gringos who had joined in their ritual.

Where we met Maria

That was where we met Maria. A lovely slender woman with big, dark flirting eyes, Maria was probably 30 years old, yet she was accompanied by her mother and younger sister.

She answered us in English when we said "Buenas noches" to her. She spoke pretty good English, which was surprising in this town.

After we exchanged names, we all tried to keep a conversation going.

"Portland, Oregon," Pete answered when queried as to where in the United States we hailed from.

"I live in Santa Ana; it's in Orange County, south of Los Angeles," I said.

"Orange County. Yes, I know. I have friend in Orange County. We write each other. He live in Laguna Beach," she said as her non-English speaking mother and sister sat on the wall nearby.

"I know Laguna Beach. My dad lives there," I added.

"My friend invited me up there some time," she continued. "He's real nice."

Yeah sure, I thought. That's what they all say!

"My friend Gus, he meet me here and comes back to see me," she added, "He drives all over Baja."

Gus? No. No, it couldn't be. Her friend just couldn't be my father! Then again, how many Gus' live in Laguna Beach? Where do I start?

"Uh, Maria, this Gus, what's he like?" I started.

"He's older and has a white beard, and he's real nice," she answered, a bit perplexed at my question.

Uh oh! Here I am in a city of some 100,000 plus people clear down near the end of Baja, flirting with an attractive girl and it looks like my dad beat me to her.

"Do you know if he has children, maybe a lot of them?" I tried, as now it was Pete's turn to be perplexed.

"Yes. He has nine children. Look, I have a picture of him," she boasted proudly, thus squelching any amorous thoughts either Pete or I might have had left.

While she was digging in her purse, I looked her in the eyes. Keeping my voice steady while still finding it hard to believe, I said, "Maria, I think I am one of those nine children. I'm Greg, the third oldest of your friend Gus's nine children."

"Really! Oh no," she exclaimed, "Greg. Yes. He tell me about you. You also sometime come to México."

La Páz and the Cape

I was dumbfounded. She knew quite a bit about my family, including stuff about me and the names and highlights of some of my siblings. Apparently when we kids were not around, the old man had a few good things to say about us.

Maria's mom and sister were then brought into the conversation, and once it was established who I was, a lot of excitement and hugging was generated.

If I was dumbfounded and Maria and her mama were stunned by this revelation, poor old Pete was floored, not only by the coincidence but also by all this immediate excitement establishing our relationship. He just kept shaking his head, saying over and over, "I don't believe it."

So I showed Pete a picture of my dad, courtesy of Maria. "Yup, he gets around," I muttered.

We exchanged numbers and addresses before we said our goodbyes and I promised to call my dad when I got home. In the morning I had a flight on to Mazatlan and Pete was later heading on to Cabo.

On the flight home, I'd reflected on this coincidence in La Páz. My dad traveled Baja quite a bit, and also flirted with women quite a bit. He loved women, especially younger ones. It could have been a win-win for them, with her "friend" helping her realize her American dream.

A few months later I was in Portland and visited Pete. We hit the local pub and went out to dinner. Pete was a great story teller and our Baja escapades kept getting more and more dramatic as the night wore on.

Gus Niemann stands under artist's pallet with painting of his likeness in Laguna Beach, California. Pallet is one of many displayed throughout town during Christmas season.

To his friends and pub acquaintances, my dad and I were already living legends, lecherous ones at that, but our chance meeting in La Páz did give him a different perspective on his life. His insecure, jealous girlfriend had given an ultimatum, "Your female roommate goes, or I go," she said, alluding to a nice young woman with whom Pete shared his houseboat in an absolute platonic relationship.

He next admitted to me, "So thinking about the freedom enjoyed by you and your dad, I let her go. It's wonderful; there's lots of women out there."

I was shaken by his statement but fortunately didn't have to live with the consequences. A little in awe, I wished him luck and headed back to California.

A few months later the phone rang. It was my dad. "Hey Gregory. Come on over. Maria, that cute little friend of mine you met in La Páz is here staying with me for a while. Why don't you come on by and say hi," he said, sounding upbeat and chipper.

"Wonderful," I thought, driving over to Laguna Beach. "Pete found his freedom thinking about my dad, and now my dad's relinquishing his free-dom — at least for now anyway, or until Maria moves on. What will I do?"

The next week, I took a plane back to La Páz. I found it a wonderful place to get a different perspective.

New seawall at La Páz

La Páz and the Cape

Honeymoon in Cabo

Cabo San Lucas — 1978

"Lisa and I are getting married on February 14," the caller said, "and we're going to Cabo for our honeymoon."

Good for Bob, I thought, but was stunned by his next comment: "We'd like you to join us there."

"Uh Bob, I mean a honeymoon? Isn't that kind of a private occasion?"

"We decided to make a party of it, so we're inviting several friends. Can you make it?"

I recovered sufficiently to consult my calendar and said something like, "February, yeah, I think I can get away. I'll let you know."

Bob, who had worked out of our San Francisco office, was a typical denizen of that city by the Bay, or just "The City" as they love to refer to it.

He was urbane, loved to party, and shared that image-conscience mentality so prevalent in Baghdad by the Bay. It was he who taught me to never, but never say "Frisco," and he who took me for romps through all the famous San Francisco watering holes, parking his chic sports car in some ungodly tight parking spaces on some ungodly steep hills.

The honeymoon was a flamboyant extension of a flamboyant wedding. A second marriage for both, and both in their forties, they decided to marry on Valentine's Day in the vast marbled rotunda of the stately San Francisco City Hall. The Cabo honeymoon party would cap a wedding distinctive even by San Francisco standards.

They all flew direct to Cabo. I flew solo from Tijuana to La Páz, taking advantage of the best rate. I also wanting to revisit my favorite Baja city of La Páz.

In a rented Volkswagen, I took the paved road from La Páz down the

130 miles to Cabo, past El Triunfo and El Bartolo, past the round sphere marking the Tropic of Cancer, past the old Cabo airport over 30 miles from the cape, past the quaint non-touristy town of San José del Cabo, and past the handful of hotels that led into the small village of Cabo San Lucas.

The honeymoon party was based at the new Solmar Hotel, over the rocks on the Pacific side. At Kilometer 0, where the paved road ended at the town's only stop sign, I turned left down the dirt road past the docks and toward the Finisterra Hotel on the hill. Once past the Finisterra turn-off, the sandy road went over a hillock where the long white, brand-new Solmar Hotel was anchored into rocks facing a white sandy beach.

The afternoon party was already in full gear, a non-stop spree of alcohol, appetizers, laughter, jokes old and new, and drunken gaiety. The poolside area was full and included about 18 members of the honeymoon party.

Bob and Lisa were delighted to see me and I was delighted I knew a couple of the others. Paul, there with his wife Harriet, also worked for my company, as did Charles, a Chinese-American from San Francisco. Most of the rest were Mary's co-workers and other friends.

As I had a car, Charles and I went to town and bought more booze, including a congratulatory wine bucket which we had sent to the newly-weds' room.

At the store Charles was amazed to hear me ask for things in Spanish. I reminded him that in San Francisco it was his jabbering in Mandarin that ultimately delighted our palates at some off-the-wall Chinese restaurant.

Charles insisted, too, that I share his room, using the other bed. After getting settled in, we rejoined the others at the poolside party. The afternoon turned to evening and everyone readied for a night of dinner and dancing.

That night about half of us found ourselves perched high on the rocks of the Finisterra Hotel where the tile dance floor looks out over the pounding ocean and under twinkling stars.

We drank, laughed and danced until the band stopped playing. Someone said, "Let's go to Rafaels." Sounded good to me.

We filled a couple of cars, cramming my little VW to beyond sober capacity and set out in search of Rafaels.

It was on the water, and I recalled instantly that I'd been there before. It was six months previous when Jon and I had driven the peninsula and culminated our drunken week by a blotto night at this place. Its uniqueness stirred my memory.

The entrance was like a cave. It reminded me of an old fort. Super thick, uneven walls led revelers up a few steps to an outdoors dance floor where tables and chairs were set snugly in grotto niches.

It's hard for me to describe the place accurately because both times I was so drunk I scarcely remember leaving. The first time I had danced with a couple of Alaskan girls, and on this night Harriet and I showed the younger set some suggestive bumps and boogies.

Raphael's at Cabo was once quite a lively place.

Back at the Solmar it was midday before any of us stirred, and then after lunch we started drinking anew. The entire time was a grand party but I didn't know how much more I could take. After two more days of fiesta and driving back and forth between Cabo's four or five resort hotels, I needed my time for introspection.

They'd have to finish the honeymoon without me, as quite literally my cup hath runneth over.

I said my goodbyes, jumped in my VW and found the old dirt road back to La Páz through Todos Santos.

Bob's Valentine's Day wedding and following honeymoon was definitely memorable. Along with the newlyweds themselves I too have never forgotten their anniversary date. And whenever I think of Cabo, I'm reminded o f a honeymoon that I attended that was not my own.

THE LURE OF TRANQUILITY

TODOS SANTOS — 1977-84

Paved in about 1984, the road south from La Páz to Todos Santos became an easy day trip. Leila and I and Don and Marie zoomed along the straight, undulating road in our rental car from La Páz. Soon the paved Highway 19 linkup to Cabo would be complete and I was hoping Todos Santos would be as charming and tranquil as I remembered. I was not disappointed.

I first saw Todos Santos in 1977 after coming up the dirt road from Cabo. That morning on a Cabo beach Jon and I were startled awake by huge, stinging red ants that had the audacity to enter our sleeping bags which were hastily and drunkenly just thrown on the sand.

He and I were on Cabo's Chileno beach, then a remote stretch of sand near a hotel, one of only a couple of buildings on what is now called The Corridor. After a crazy night in town, we pulled off the highway looking for a place to sleep. We promptly got stuck in the sand and made the best of it by camping right there.

To the delight of a few Mexicans walking past, we danced the ants off our bodies. While amused, the locals still exhibited the true Baja spirit and helped push our car out of the sand. After our profuse thanks, we left Cabo that morning.

The map showed a dirt road up the Pacific back to La Páz. After several false starts we finally found where the road left town and wound up a sandy ravine. Dodging the skinny cattle foraging in the brush we passed a couple of ranchos before reaching the Pacific near Migrino.

We immediately became enamored with the entire area. We cooled off by dipping in the ocean and strolled the peaceful streets of El Pescadero. I looked around the small hamlet trying to see what it was that appealed to my dad. He claimed that it and Todos Santos were his favorite Baja towns.

A profusion of tropical flowers and plants almost conceal El Pescadero's few rustic dwellings, most of them more picturesque than sturdy being simply constructed from mesquite branches and thatch or adobe.

Animals crossed the hard-baked roads while friendly residents stopped to wave as we approached. I could understand how the tranquility appealed to my dad, but noted yet again another paradox; how long could his gregarious personality tolerate such quiet, such peacefulness, such out-of-the-way obscurity?

My great-grandfather Bascom Stephens should have visited this area. It better fits his glowing description of a Baja not realized in the more arid areas of the north. Some of his alluring comments about the fertility of Baja actually describe this area.

From El Pescadero, we headed north and spent much of the day in the area's largest town, Todos Santos.

The town's only road-side restaurant, the Santa Monica, was closed. So was the old Hotel California.

But walking down a side street we found a simple thatched-roofed building, whose pastel walls tried to poke through a huge clump of bright lavender bougainvillea. A Dos Equis beer sign on the roof dwarfed the small print lettering which modestly proclaimed the rustic building to be "Restaurant Juanita's."

Chickens clucked beneath our feet pecking minute particles of food off the hard-packed floor as we feasted on a savory beef ranchero meal in the setting so characteristic of rural Baja.

I had revisited Juanita's on two visits the next year and established a relationship with the owner, who had learned English in Glendale, CA, a town I knew well.

LITTLE CHANGE IN SIX YEARS

Now, as we four entered town, I wondered if Juanita's would still be there six years later. It was the first place we headed for, and the only difference this time was that instead of chickens it was a litter of puppies crawling around our feet in anticipation of us dropping some crumbs.

Sated, we four strolled through town and I was delighted to see that it was still as peaceful, charming and laid back as it was previously. We toured the old Cine Manuel Marquez de Leon, a tidy, delightful theater neatly trimmed with paint and a pride of the community.

I noticed a few new businesses which blended into the timelessness of the place. One old brick building had a small hand-carved sign in front which indicated it was a Bed and Breakfast.

The proprietor was an energetic wordcarver who sold his crafts out of the building while his wife, an American, turned several rooms into whimsical and distinctive guest rooms. The place oozed charm and was a precursor for things to be.

Town square and theater in downtown Todos Santos.

The paved road from Cabo opened a few months after our visit, laying the groundwork for hordes of merchants and visitors wanting to escape the frenzy of Cabo.

According to the 1997 guide "Exploring Baja by RV," by Walt and Michael Peterson, "Todos Santos is now the home of a number of painters, potters, woodcarvers and other artists, plus a growing community of American expatriate retirees, artists, surfers and loafers. With its old brick buildings, tranquility and leisurely ways, the town is in dramatic contrast to 'Go Go' Cabo San Lucas."

The book lists several hotels and inns, a number of restaurants and stores, plus an RV park and Pemex station. Apparently the growth has not foisted too much damage to the delightful, picturesque town.

DEVELOPED IN 1724

Todos Santos, on a hill overlooking a broad, fertile arroyo one mile from the Pacific, was discovered by the Jesuit Padre Jaime Bravo who developed it as a visiting station from the La Páz Mission in 1724. Farming was introduced and the area is today still known for its delicious mangoes.

In 1733, Todos Santos became a separate mission and Padre Sigismundo Taraval was its first priest. It was named Mission Santa Rosa de Todos Santos in honor of the noblewoman Doña Rosa de la Peña who Donated 10,000 pesos for its support.

The mission was wiped out by rebellious Indians in 1734 but Padre Taraval and his two soldiers escaped, having been warned by faithful

Indians. The mission was rebuilt and repopulated twice, first by Guaycura Indians brought in from La Páz who were almost decimated by a smallpox epidemic, and then by Pericues from other missions. In 1748 the mission at La Páz was abandoned and Todos Santos received its entire population.

During the 19th Century the area was settled by mestizos. Sugar cane was introduced and several sugar mills were built to turn out small cones of panocha, a rich, dark brown sugar. The old mills still dot the valley today.

The original mission site is about a mile away at Mision Vieja and a few stones delineate the ruins. The large whitewashed church dominating the Todos Santos town square today was originally built in 1840, but was completely rebuilt since 1941 when it was wiped out by a hurricane.

The mission system declined during the 19th century and by 1840 only two missions remained active, including Todos Santos.

In 1841, after the secularization of the missions, Politico Jefe Luis de Castillo Negrette declared an act to distribute the mission lands. Padre Gabriel Gonzalez, Dominican Mission president residing in Todos Santos, strenuously objected, but to no avail.

According to historian Pablo L. Martinez in "A History of Lower California," Negrette had good reason for the act. "As is asserted in this document, the missionaries no longer had any neophytes, but they still kept developing for their personal properties the properties of the old missions. ... This priest (Gonzalez) had carried his activities beyond the church and had been converted into a farmer, merchant, cattleman, politician and father of a family."

The allure to the tranquility of Todos Santos is not a current phenomenon. Padre Gonzales went to the northern missions, but returned to his beloved Todos Santos in 1854. It was in Todos Santos he chose to live out his life and look after the multitude of children he had reportedly produced.

The area is rich in a history of attracting those who enjoy the laid-back life and the simple pleasures amid an almost perfect climate (The town straddles the Tropic of Cancer). Had my dad lived in a different era, I believe I could have been born here.

Every time I've walked the streets of Todos Santos, I've noticed scores of good-looking and active children waving at or following me. I envy their parents and ancestors for settling in that lovely garden spot. I note too that those kids could well have the blood of a Spanish padre coursing through their veins.

Odds are good that they do.

Lost in the Dump

Todos Santos — 1984

Sometimes it's hard to find the right dirt road in Baja. On the map, a single road might be shown leaving the highway to take you straight to the ocean a couple miles away.

That's the map. The reality often confuses the best of the Baja off-roaders. There might be four or five dirt roads taking off in the same direction within a half-mile area indicated by the map. Which one do you take?

Often the roads merge together and it makes no difference which one you start out on, but equally as often they don't. They might take you to a nearby ranch, or a well, or a corral, or twist forever, narrowing as they wind through rocky foothills, thus leading you far from your destination. Or they might end up in the village dump.

That happened to us. Even if you've found the road on previous visits, things change. New roads have sprung up nearby; landmarks have vanished and new ones might have developed or been constructed.

I knew an idyllic beach just south of Todos Santos I wanted to show Leila, Don and Marie. Confident, I whipped off the highway on the broadest, widest, most-traveled dirt road where the beach was sure to be.

Our road quickly narrowed and we found mounds of trash on either side of the car. Not to worry, I thought. There are a number of Baja towns where the trash is carelessly discarded by the side of main road. This ugly practice is most noticeable outside the pretty villages of the Vizcaino Peninsula.

As the road narrowed, and got bumpier, and the mounds of trash more formidable and more frequent, I began to get concerned. Trash was everywhere. We passed ripped up old mattresses that once dispensed comfort for an entire generation. Even rusty old vehicle carcasses that once provided valuable transportation lay browning in the tropical sun.

Plastic bottles and other nondisposable items lay in clumps, to cover the desert floor for decades, if not centuries.

The versatile and sturdy plastic bag replaced the prickly pear or pitahaya as the area's bloom. Ocean breezes have through the years swirled the flimsy bags in every direction, and many were snared by the sharp points of the desert foliage. Like airborne jellyfish, their presence blighted the vegetation.

The others looked at me. I grabbed the map again. "But it shows that the road was just past that curve," I blurted in an attempt at justification.

IT'S EMBARRASSING TO BE WRONG

It's embarrassing to be wrong, especially when the others count on my memory and sense of direction. Swallowing my pride, I tried to get out of there. I had to find a solid, turn-around place in that constricting location. It meant driving farther into the haphazard dump site, where we noted the age of the refuse by its effects from the sun.

We finally turned the little car around without getting stuck, went back to the highway, and found the correct road in the same arroyo, within yards of the dump road that had beckoned me.

The beach was worth it too. A beautiful lagoon nestled against a rocky outcropping graces the south end of its shores. Sugar-white sand forms a picture-postcard setting, with the beach dropping down a 10-foot dune-like cliff to the sparkling ocean.

We were amazed to see a couple of pangas on the top of the sand berm and a crowd of fishermen removing equipment from them. We wondered how they got up there. Then we saw several more pangas out in the ocean hovering just outside the breakers.

Suddenly, just after a set of large waves broke, we learned how they did it. One panga revved his outboard motor to maximum power and made a beeline for the beach. He was flying, as fast as he could go. The others on shore cheered him on. It looked like suicide seeing a boat come charging full bore toward land.

The panga hit shore hard, the skipper deftly lifted the motor and allowed the force of his forward motion to carry the boat not only across the sandy beach but all the way to the top of the berm. The boat bounced nd flew up on top of the hill before the forward motion stopped. The panga teetered on the brink for a few seconds before the others grabbed it, securing it to the top.

What a performance, we thought. The fishermen, who did this daily, even appreciated each other's efforts. We saw the rest of the pangas come in, all with the same daring maneuvers. A couple of them attained such speeds they needed no assistance at the top as they landed well up on the sand hill. They received appreciation from the others in the form of thumbs up signs and smiles. The peer appreciation was the motivation to excel at this game.

If one chose not to "go for it" and stop at the surf line, all would have to help drag the heavy 21 foot panga up from the tide. With such communal effort no one wanted to force undue labor upon their friends.

We enjoyed our stay at this beautiful beach, swimming and walking the shoreline. Kids from town were splashing and having a ball in the palm-lined lagoon just before it drained into the ocean.

On our way back out we wouldn't see the dump, but we all knew it was there. We were all thinking the same thing. This place really is a paradox. Here you have one of Baja's prettier beaches just down the road from the ugly eyesore of a municipal dump.

During a return visit in 1998, I noticed that the fishermen still work this pretty beach, called Playa Punta Lobos. They still bounce their boats up on the berm, upon their return.

However, unless they got lost like me, most people would never know about it.

Panga that didn't quite make the berm at Playa Punta Lobos.

La Páz and the Cape

THE FAME OF EL RANCHITO

LA PÁZ — 1978

Mention "El Ranchito" in the La Páz area and you'll always get a response. Women blush just hearing the words. Men roll their eyes, grin, and either knowingly, longingly, wistfully or wishfully often murmur, "Ah, El Ranchito, si, I have heard of this place."

Few in the La Páz area have not heard of El Ranchito, one of the largest and most famous whorehouses in Baja.

I initially discovered this house of ill repute on a trip to La Páz with Jon. After getting directions from a taxi driver, we drove out one hot May afternoon in 1977. The compound is a few miles south of town about a quarter mile into the desert from the highway.

The heart of the compound is a gravel courtyard with a fountain and a small shrine in its center. It is surrounded on all four sides by long, one story buildings like a motel. Looking around the four sides from inside the courtyard, I counted 66 closely-spaced doors facing the square. Small articles of clothing rested on the fountain's brick walls to dry in the tropic sun.

The famous El Ranchito in La Páz.

A few of the girls were up and about, performing their daily chores, laying out clothes, sweeping the gravel door stoops, or visiting with neighbor girls. It was a personal time, before the heavy makeup and provocative dresses that signified the long night ahead.

A pickup truck bounced down the road and pulled up. Three simply-dressed girls, who could easily have blended in with the townspeople, jumped down from the bed of the pickup. They'd been to market and began to carry in watermelons and other foodstuffs. They laughed and joked as they went about their business.

Anchoring the square compound on one end was the restaurant and bar. The loud music piped throughout seemed especially inappropriate during the harsh bright reality of daylight. The place was virtually empty with only a bartender behind the bar, a busboy mopping the floor and two girls sitting with a couple of cowboys at one table.

Simple folding, metal card tables and chairs, all adorned with brewery logos, filled the large, cavernous room. The concrete slab floor and general feeling of emptiness rendered the place a sad, vacuous existence. The odor of spilled beer and wet cigarettes seemed stronger in an empty room with music on too loud.

One could imagine that with the darkness of night, the place would put on its party face. The drabness would probably not be noticed when surrounded by scores of beautiful girls dressed to attract and lure their male patrons.

With nightfall, activity would increase until El Ranchito would become one of the most lively buildings in La Páz. Pickup trucks and cars from all over the area would find their way there. Taxi drivers would continually shuttle clients down that road to the famous place called El Ranchito.

IN A CAMPGROUND RESTAURANT

A year or so after my visit to El Ranchito, Leila and I drove the length of the peninsula. We spent a couple of days at a hotel in La Páz and another night in a Cabo hotel. Heading back north we decided to camp at a campground just north of La Páz.

It was a regular campground on the western shores of El Mogote, just a few miles out of town. There were trailer spaces and a restaurant with a bar. After setting up camp we went into the restaurant.

Earlier Leila had borrowed one of my T-shirts, and selected one advertising an Orange County chain of Mexican restaurants. With her shorts and the T-shirt I knew she looked good, but I really didn't quite expect the lascivious reception we got.

There were a half dozen Mexican businessmen in the restaurant bar, already far from completely sober. They were laughing and joking and all quickly became enamored with Leila.

They were bold and brazen, a couple even wanting to dance with her with me standing right there. Uncomfortable, we were forced to make a hasty departure. I had never seen Mexican men quite that forward, especially with someone else's woman.

Walking out the door, I heard one of them snickering and saying, "El Ranchito." Suddenly I realized what had provoked these guys into acting crude around Leila. Walking back to the campsite, I explained it to her. Back at the campsite she hastily took off my T-shirt never to wear it again. Emblazoned across the chest were the large words of that Orange County restaurant chain that suggested something quite different in the La Páz area, "El Ranchito."

... dates and mangoes grow in the fertile valleys near Todos Santos.

Big Tuna Fight Back

I held the rod tightly but could do nothing. The line was whirring off the reel as the big fish took the live mackerel bait and made his first run. W-r-r-r-r-r, the line flew off the reel. Soon I could see metal under the 50 pound line; in less than 30 seconds, I would be completely spooled!

Ysidro, the skipper of the 23 foot panga, hurriedly cranked up the 65 HP Evinrude outboard and headed in the direction of the fish. It finally stopped and I was able to retrieve some line. At that moment I felt confident I'd land this fish. I knew I was in for the fight of my life.

It's a big tuna

We were after tuna, and that's what Ysidro said it was — a big one! I fought; the tuna fought. After about an hour, there was a second run that almost spooled my line again. Finally, the big fish started circling under the small boat. I'd wind a couple of turns; the fish would pull it back out.

Another half hour and it looked like I was gaining. No, the fish made another run and took about half a spool of line.

The hot sun reflected off the glassy smooth Sea of Cortéz. Sweat poured off me as I battled the tuna. My arms started to feel like rubber and my fingers were pained and stiff. I never thought of quitting and stubbornly gained more line.

Finally, a few inches at a time, I secured the line with my fingers as I pumped and brought the big fellow up. As soon as he was gaffed I collapsed on the seat, totally spent, drained of strength, but with a sense of exhilaration unsurpassed in a lifetime of fishing.

2 HOURS, 10 MINUTES

The hand slapping after the big tuna came on board after a 2 hour, 10 minute battle, was genuine and welcome. My partner, Scott, had shared my excitement but patiently waited before we resumed fishing.

He was rewarded with a wahoo that tipped the scales at 60 pounds, the largest caught all month off the northern East Cape area of Punta Arena. My tuna weighed in at an even 100 pounds, also the largest in several weeks. We rounded out the exciting day catching and releasing some skipjack and needlefish

There were about 18 anglers that hot July day at Punta Arena. Pangas and guides were arranged through Bob Butler, an amiable American who runs a fishing fleet from his headquarters next door to the Los Arcos Hotel in La Páz. Our group of six was chartered through Boone and Crockett Expeditions of Long Beach, California.

We were told that tuna were running up to 100 pounds, with several 90 pounders caught the week before. My partners, all dedicated and serious fishermen, were excited. But on the first day only two tuna were landed, my whopper and a 50 pounder by a member of another group.

I only knew one of our guys before we met in La Páz. Earlier he had called me after a cancellation and I happened to be available and interested. The others flew out of Los Angeles to La Páz, while I opted for the closer Tijuana Airport.

DEDICATED FISHERMEN

That first evening, I realized these guys were really into fishing. I listened to them talk about equipment, tackle and past adventures. My vast myriad of interests precluded me from sharing their intensity. I just like to go fishing.

The first night we six, Scott, Jim, the taller Jim, Larry, Pete and myself, even though we had a 4:00 a.m. wakeup call, checked and rechecked equipment. They tied hooks onto feathers, crimped and double crimped lures and arranged all of the rods and reels. Each person had about five rods and reels. "I've got a 30 pound, a 40, a 50, an 80 and a 100," said one.

"That's about perfect," said another.

Up to that point I was pretty proud of my one rod, a 50 pounder with 50 pound line, which by the way, is the only one I used.

By 5 a.m. Bob Butler's vans take the fishermen out through the sleeping city of La Páz, southwest about 25 miles on pavement to the farming village called San Juan de Los Planes. Twenty minutes of dirt road later finds the panga fleet and friendly skippers at Punta Arena, just north of Bahia de los Muertos.

Author and the 100-pound tuna he caught on a panga fishing trip, off Punta Arena. - 1992

A WIND CHOP CAME UP

I landed my tuna on the first day. A wind chop on the second day prevented us from getting out past Cerralvo Island to the tuna grounds. Most pangas stayed close to shore that day, heading south to Punta Pescadero, or known dorado spots close in. We each caught 2-3 dorado that day.

My guys wanted tuna, and my early catch intensified their desire. In fact, one guy hooked a marlin, and said, "Damn it, I've got a marlin; I want tuna." Several of the others caught sailfish; in fact Jerry caught two, but my group practiced "catch and release" on all billfish.

On the third day the sea was glassy calm; the flying fish (voladors) were skimming above the deep blue swells, and the tuna were literally jumping out of the water. Large schools of 50 to 100 tuna would boil in front of us, leaping three to four feet out of the water. Then they would be behind us. It was truly a spectacular sight. We could see people in other pangas hooked up and fighting.

Scott had a strike and lost it and the Rapala lure he was trolling. He then hooked another one and after a 10 minute battle, lost it too. He really wanted tuna and it was good to see him getting the hot action. He and I decided to go after more wahoo once he landed a tuna.

The one that got away

That was not the way it happened. What happened was a fish story I'll remember all my life. Scott hooked another tuna trolling a Rapala with his 80 pound gold Penn reel, 100 pound rod and 60 pound line. After about a half hour standing battle, we realized he was into a big fish.

It was the hottest day yet, and Scott was sweating buckets. Back and forth the battle went on. Fighting a big fish while standing in a small bobbing panga is different from being in a large cruiser's fighting chair.

"Muy fuerte," said Ysidro, referring to the strength of the fish.

Scott hooked this monster at 9:05 a.m.. Twice he brought him to color (when you see the fish). It was so big it looked like a six foot shark, but you could tell he too was a yellowfin tuna. After two hours, he said, "I can't hold on much longer. Do you want to farm (buddy catch) this fish?

"Not yet. Go on," I said, "You can do it."

Forty five minutes later, he had to surrender the rod to me. I then fought him for another hour and 40 minutes, realizing that this fish, on heavier tackle, was much stronger than my earlier 100 pounder. Ysidro said the largest he'd seen in the area was 120 pounds, and we all estimated this one to be at least 150 pounds.

I brought him to color twice, and the giant tuna became more enraged at seeing the boat and quickly and disappointedly peeled out the hard-fought line. Even though we were using Scott's back harness, the strain on my long-suffering bad back was too much.

I gave the rod back to a refreshed Scott, who battled him for another 40 minutes. We were pulling harder now, but wanted to get him in. Finally and suddenly, the line snapped! The time was 2:13.

After 5 hours, 8 minutes, fighting two different heavier men, the big tuna broke loose, earning its freedom, and the respect of two tired anglers and a skipper who made the sign of the cross adding his testimony to the ordeal.

Back on the beach, the other four had all caught tuna in the 50 to 80 pound range.

Even though Scott and I earned plenty of respect day one with his big wahoo and my big tuna, we hated coming in empty handed. But we were drained of strength and in so much awe over the incredible struggle, we only grinned and said, "You should have seen the one that got away."

Swimming with Sea Lions

La Páz, B.C.S., México — 1996

"Listo?" said Jorge, motioning to Hugo and me as we secured our face masks and prepared to slip over the port side.

"Aquí? Los lobos marinos no molestamos?" I answered when the skipper asked us if we were ready. I was concerned about the sea lions, about 250 of them, many on the nearby rocks and many already swimming in the water Jorge intended us to snorkle in.

"No problema. Ellos no molestan."

"Yeah, no problema," I thought as I slid over the side anyway. Hitting the water with mask, snorkle and fins has added a new dimension to this life-long beach bum.

I was 55 years old before I began snorkling and loving it. Another new thing to do after retirement.

That first time at Playa del Carmen on the Yucatan got me excited even though just a few fish darted in and out of the coral. Sufficiently teased, I wanted more.

Some months later, in Australia, I took a day trip to Green Island on the Great Barrier Reef. That's the snorkling adventure that got me committed. Then, I took a snorkling trip out to Egmont Key from St. Petersburg Beach, Florida. I now go to the coves in nearby Laguna Beach, Ccalifornia, where I join neophyte scuba divers drifting over the rocky shelf watching bright orange garibaldis dart into kelp-covered crevasses.

But none of the trips was as exciting, nor as thrilling, as that day with the sea lions in the Sea of Cortéz.

I had lined up a solo three-night fishing trip to La Páz, at the southern tip of Baja, hoping to find a fishing partner in town.

On Tuesday I slid out of the house in darkness and arrived at LAX as dawn broke, well in time for my hellishly-early Aero California flight. I checked-in my encased rods and empty ice chest (always an optimist), and boarded. It was a kick seeing one of my articles about a Baja mission in the in-flight magazine, Baja Life.

In La Páz to find a partner, I not only placed a sign-up sheet at the Los Arcos, where I stayed, but literally left my name with every hotel and fleet in town.

I was about six weeks early for the area's prime fishing. In July and August, while the city of over 170,000 friendly souls bakes in unbearable heat, gringos invade for tuna, marlin and sailfish, the big three of Baja's game fish.

In late May, I could expect dorado, pargo, grouper, maybe wahoo and roosterfish, and an outside possibility of tuna, marlin or sails.

I wanted a 2-person panga (18 to 23 feet) and I wanted to fish the area south of Punta Arena, an hour's drive away. I did not want to fish locally and really didn't want a cruiser.

All day Tuesday I walked and talked. Pangas were going from $160 to $195 per day. I had planned on fishing two days, splitting the cost. But there were no takers. The town gets a lot of Mexican tourists, but most gringos go farther south to Cabo, with its American hotels, restaurants and five golf courses.

La Páz has no golf course, and most of the time you must speak Spanish. Surprisingly it has remained unspoiled. While I've traveled the world, La Páz has to be one of my most favorite places with beautiful smiles and friendly people.

Moisés at the Los Arcos suggested that if I couldn't find a partner, maybe I could just go one day, renting the boat for myself.

"Two days, two persons, half the fish. One day, one person, all the fish," the affable activities agent reasoned.

It sounded good to me. "I'll do something else tomorrow and maybe take the boat Thursday," I answered.

GAINED A SNORKLING DAY

I'd seen the snorkling information earlier and now, not to be dismayed about losing a fishing day, realized I was to gain a snorkling day. I quickly paid the $40, which covered a full day and included lunch.

At 7 a.m., I was ready, even thinking to buy a cheap throwaway underwater camera.

A couple of young guys picked me up in a dilapidated van, which took about three healthy slams to close the sliding door. The crack lines from the broken windshield fortunately did not impede the driver's vision too much. The van was rusted, like you see on the old cars in the U.S. northeast where salt on the roads has such a devastating effect.

As we headed toward Pichilingue and the peninsula north of town, I asked how many people there would be.

"Dos mas," the driver answered.

My wondering who the two might be was answered as we pulled up to the Palmilla Hotel on the outskirts of town. It was a man and a woman, mother and son.

Hugo was a 30-year-old travel agent from México City and his mother Petra would just go along for the boat ride. She was about my age with classical, fine-chiseled features, twinkling eyes and a big grin. Her hair, turning gray, was neatly tied back.

We approached a group of workers by the side of the highway, and in Mexican fashion, stopped while they all piled in for a ride out to the docks.

We sped out the narrow road to Pichilingue with the driver peering over the crack in the window and turning around all-to-often to talk to his passengers. The narrow road was shared by all sizes of trucks, even some that listed precariously to one side. On the return trip, I whispered to Petra, "El camino es mas peligro que la lancha," to which she nodded vigorously, grateful that I also noticed that driving on the road was the most dangerous part of the day.

We took a break from snorkeling to explore beautiful coves of Espiritu Santo Island.

The snorkling company does use larger boats and English-speaking guides. But for the three of us, it was just a small panga with a tarp for shade we boarded. Jorge, a skilled skipper, slowed for the larger waves as we bounced across the deep channel from the mainland to Espiritu Santo Island.

As we glided by the beautiful rock formations of Espiritu Santo Island, I thought how this island must delight a geologist. Large stratum of white sandstone interspersed with porous red rock created an eerie appearance. The coves looked inviting with white sandy beaches and shallow pea-green water.

La Páz and the Cape

We passed Isla Ballena (Whale Island) and the smaller crags called Islas Gallo and Gallina (rooster and hen) to Isla Partida, which was a short sand spit from Espiritu Santo. Jorge took the small craft under and through a couple of caves and arches on Partida's northern rocky cliffs.

He pointed to some rocks a few hundred yards away, Los Islotes, a sea lion colony. We were now 27 miles from La Páz and ready to enter the water.

The barking of the sea lion colony increased as we neared their home. They were all over, large males and smaller females and one misplaced elephant seal.

Still cautious, Hugo and I entered the water on the side away from the rocks and the majority of sea lions.

What an outstanding place to snorkle! While the water was a little murky in spots due to the current, you could still see 10 to 20 feet. The rocks jut straight down and fish of all sizes, shapes and colors darted in and out.

There were thousands of fish, from thick schools of inch-long fingerlings to schools of larger fish. There were more piscatorial delights on the other side of the boat, so we worked our way over there.

HE CAME STRAIGHT AT ME

A dark form moved over my right shoulder. I thought it was Hugo but he was in front of me. It came back — a sea lion. He came straight at me, then one or two feet away, he flipped over and swam away. Then others came, doing the same thing. They were playing, showing off for us, letting us know that this was their turf and they were by far more graceful.

About six or eight sea lions put on a display for us, coming as close as they could, then swimming away. It was an incredible thrill. Hugo and I surfaced, exhilarated, and smiled at each other. "Wow. Que fantastico!," he laughed.

"Si. Los lobos marinos viene mui cerca, pero no tocan," I exclaimed, saying that the sea lions would come very close, but not quite touch us."

He acknowledged and we went back for more. One little fellow would swim up close, look me right in the eye and then dart away quickly, as if to say, "Look at me."

I shot my film so fast, by the time Jorge pointed to an area nearby where there was an arch I had quickly run out of film. The arch was a gap between two rocky islands where there were so many fish it looked like an aquarium. The sea lions were still cavorting and there were thousands of colorful fish.

Though the water was still cool for May, after several dives we boarded, exhilarated from the experience.

It was a couple months later when I read that guides should instruct divers swimming among sea lions not to get within 15 feet of the rocks because bulls protecting their harems might charge you. Thanks, Jorge. No problema, huh?

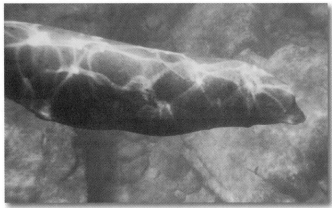

My swiming partner. "Un lobo marino."

Jorge then took us to a cove on Isla Partida for lunch. The only shade was a thatched palapa on the south end of the beach. We shared the palapa with a marine biology class from Prescott College who were kayaking the islands. They were the only people we'd see all day. We rested and munched burritos while I listened to the class. The ecological subject matter as well as hearing English kept my interest.

We left and entered a similar cove on larger Espiritu Santo, Caleta del Candelero (candlestick cove) where we snorkled again. While Petra and Jorge walked the beach, Hugo and I set off snorkling the shallow bay, gliding across the sand to some small crags.

Tiny, black fish darted amidst the white coral. Long, snake-like trumpetfish unnerved us at first, until we realized they'd leave us alone. We saw cabrilla, croakers, puffers, beautiful blue and purple fish with yellow tails (angelfish), damselfish, sergeant majors, triggerfish, a bright red and a bright blue starfish and an octopus.

Later we hiked inland over hot, blistering sands to a fresh water spring, the only one on the island.

Back in the boat, Jorge then took us to a rocky point at least a quarter mile out from another sandy beach. He pointed to the beach where they would be and Hugo and I jumped out. We slowly worked our way toward shore. Just this last spot alone was better than any other place I've snorkled.

We enjoyed the clearest water, over 30 feet visibility, while drifting over a large forest of white coral. Here again, fish of all sizes and colors were in abundance.

Back on the mainland for one last stop, Hugo and I hiked to a hilltop at Balandra Bay which offers a panoramic view of the large, sandy, bright green shallow bay. It was after 4 p.m. before I was dropped back at the Los Arcos, still on a "natural high" from swimming with the sea lions.

A FISHING BOAT FOR ONE

The next day Moisés was able to get me a great price on a boat, $140, which included transportation. At 5 a.m. a taxi driver named Estaban picked me up and we drove south past the village of San Juan de Los Planes to the point at Punta Arena. He even stopped at my skipper's home in the fishing village to ensure he was up and waiting at the boat.

José Lucero is the son of a fisherman, and his four brothers are fishermen, so his prowess of local waters was not questioned. I'd earlier asked Moisés about him not wanting to be stuck with someone who rarely goes out.

With help from a couple of brothers, we pushed off and headed south to Ensenada de los Muertos to net some bait. Schools of sardines patrolled the shallow bay and I handled the tiller while José adroitly threw the net from the bow. The fiberglass bait tank loaded, we set out straight east into the bright orange horizon.

At about five miles out, a couple of buoys mark an artificial reef. Each mile thereafter for a few miles has similar markers. Dorado (mahi mahi) love reefs. At the first buoy, a live sardine netted me a 25 pound dorado. All right!

Before the day was over, I caught a total of four dorado, the largest about 35–40 pounds, a couple of needlefish that I released and a 55 pound roosterfish. Back on shore only a few boats were returning, but two guys in one boat caught only a total of four dorados, two each.

Moisés was right. I caught so much I had to give fish to José and Estaban so I could close and seal my ice chest with all the filets.

Had I fished two days, it would have cost me more money, and most importantly, I would have missed the opportunity to swim with the sea lions.

Next time I go to La Páz, I'm going to go visit my lobos marinos swimming partners first, then I'll think about going fishing.

(ADDENDUM)

Moisés Cortes still runs, as of my visit in 1998, the sports desk at the Hotel Los Arcos. He uses several companies that take people out snorkeling or SCUBA diving. They all now leave from docks closer to town, either from the La Páz Marina or the Los Conchas Resort. The bigger, faster boats are now $45.00, all inclusive.

Make sure you're not playing second fiddle to SCUBA divers, though, by reminding Moisés that you just want to be with snorkelers. For $40.00 each, Don and I had a wonderful time in the same type of smaller boat I had before. Oh yes, the sea lions are still there!

Cabo San Lucas today.

La Páz and the Cape

CHUBASCO!

The tuna hit the bait hard snapping me out of my reverie. Fishing out of the La Páz area, we were north of Cerralvo Island at a seamount called El Bajo. Don Lund, the skipper Jesus, and I were drifting cut squid from our 23-foot panga, occasionally pulling the lines in to maneuver to another spot.

Most of the other pangas at El Bajo that day were commercial fishermen handlining for pargo and other bottom species. Of the other half dozen sportsfishers, we'd seen several tuna hookups. Us, we drifted and waited, basking in the hot, humid July sun.

The tuna hit so hard, I didn't even have to set the hook. The rod doubled over and my 50-pound line began singing off the reel. I tightened the drag a little lest I get spooled too quickly, while Jesus and Don pulled in their lines.

Jesus even helped with the 65 horsepower outboard motor, maneuvering in the same direction as the fish. I cranked the reel, gaining a little line. The big fish pulled the hard-earned line right back out.

It was a stand-off and we'd just have to battle it out. Tuna don't seem to tire, like marlin and sailfish, who after a few dramatic leaps in the air seem easier to boat. Pound for pound, tuna are the fightingest fish I've caught.

Don's 30-pound yellowfin tuna the day before took him a half hour to bring in. A few years previous, my 100-pound yellowfin tuna with my same equipment took two hours and ten minutes.

Tuna go straight down deep. They circle. They fight. They don't jump, and they don't give up. I was in for a battle.

The heavy, humid air along with the physical exertion had me sweating rivulets. My arms started getting sore.

Looking about, I noticed a heavy, black cloud out over the gulf on the horizon. The rest of the sky was bright blue with intermittent ivory clouds.

I battled the fish, gaining then losing, then gaining again for about 40 minutes. That black cloud was coming closer, and as it did the wind picked up. We all noticed the abrupt change in weather. White caps began to appear far out.

I'd heard of chubascos, those often-regionalized, abrupt, violent hurricane-like storms that strike without warning, but had never experienced their fury. I'd been surprised by wind and a quick, choppy sea before, but never a full-blown chubasco.

Several of the boats took off to beat the approaching weather. Jesus was concerned. He agreed we too should leave as soon as we brought the fish on board. I fought standing up, without a shoulder harness, just a leather rod butt belt for another 10 minutes. The storm got closer and the other boats were beating a hasty retreat.

Don offered to help, but I felt the younger, stronger 29-year-old skipper was our best bet. I handed him the rod, hoping he could bring the fish in before we had to leave. Jesus knew time was of the essence better than either of us, and began to try and muscle the fish in.

The rod doubled over to where I was certain it would snap. For 15 minutes Jesus fought and fought, gaining back some of the line. The storm was almost upon us now and we all knew a decision had to be made. The last boat had just left and we knew we had to go.

With Jesus holding the line taut I grabbed my knife and cut the line, releasing my huge tuna to fight another angler, another day.

Jesus quickly grabbed the tiller and made for Cerralvo, about three miles away.

The storm hit suddenly and the Sea of Cortéz got violent. Not only were white caps all around us, but the ocean swells were huge and powerful.

The rain came in sheets, drenching us completely. (My wallet contents had to be laid out to dry that night). With the rain came the wind. Don's cap blew off. The fish tank hatch blew to our feet. I couldn't see. My glasses were soaked and the salt water stung my eyes. My throat got sore from swallowing so much salt water which splashed over us with the wind and rain.

Visibility became minimal for all of us. Occasionally out of the dark cloud I could see the outline of the island which seemed so far away. Then it would disappear. I don't know how Jesus kept the boat in the right direction.

La Páz and the Cape

Wind-whipped waves came at us unrelentingly. The bow of our fragile panga would ride up one wave only to be slammed into the trough, jolting us with a slam. We held on for our lives, and sometimes the jolts were so sudden our hands would break loose of their hold and slam back down creating some very painful fingers and joints.

Sometimes the waves were so close the bow would slam into the next wave, digging in with a painful and scary jolt.

Some wave sets were huge, six, eight feet and more, and if Jesus did not approach them just right, we'd roll from side to side, coming close to capsizing.

I looked into the roiling water, waves furiously moving from east to west. The island was south, straight ahead. A strong swimmer might make it, but not in a storm like this. He would be swept far to the west, where the next landfall was many miles away. Plus we had no lifevests so survival would be iffy at best. If we tipped over, I vowed to do my best to hang onto the boat.

It took about a half hour of sheer terror before we reached the lee of the island and safety. We all looked at each other and could visibly see the tension slip away. Jesus breathed easier and it was only then when I realized this 12-year fishing veteran had been terrified.

"Señor," he said once we displayed tentative smiles and tried to relax, "Thank you for cutting your fish. I think five minutes more we would have been in trouble. We got out just in time."

We stayed close to the shoreline down the 12 miles of Cerralvo Island. The sun came out and it seemed peaceful. But ahead we still had about a five-mile storm-whipped channel to cross to get to Punta Arena and the mainland.

We headed into the chop and the waves were large and formidable. I looked back and Jesus made a circle of his forefinger and thumb, meaning "It's okay; it's tough, but nothing I can't handle." And he handled it expertly, riding the troughs when he could, and turning directly into the larger waves. On real big sets, he even throttled down giving us a more gentle ride up and down the roller coaster waves.

A small crowd had gathered on shore. It appears most gringos had fished south of the island and did not experience the full onslaught of the chubasco. Someone said that the fishermen on the last boat in before us had got out and kissed the ground.

As we told our story to other gringo fishermen, Jesus was relaying our experience to fellow pangeros. About the fish, Jesus said it was "Mas que 50 kilos," or more than 110 pounds.

I learned renewed respect for the strength of the yellowfin tuna, as well as greater admiration for the daring pangeros like Jesus. Most of all I looked at the fickle Sea of Cortéz through more weathered eyes. I will never again be casual about fishing there.

Cabo, 1998

La Páz, 1998

La Páz and the Cape

CABO REVISITED

CABO SAN LUCAS — 1998

As an aficionado of backcountry Baja, where outside influence is minimal, and warm, gentle Bajacalifornios dominate, I have shunned Los Cabos, the resort megopolis at the peninsula's southern tip for over 21 years. My last visit was in the '70s and I decided to check it out during the summer of 1998.

After fishing out of La Páz, a city I visit regularly, fishing partner Don and I rented a car for a two-day loop to San José del Cabo, Cabo San Lucas and Todos Santos.

Heading down the gulf 130 miles to Cabo, I'd noticed little change in the small hill towns of El Triunfo, San Antonio, Santiago and Miraflores.

But on the coast, at Los Barriles, the town's extensive expatriate colony became obvious as a pink mini-mall now graced the entrance to town.

I'd expected vast changes at Cabo; after all, I'd seen many photos and magazine ads. But I wasn't prepared for "The Corridor." The minute we got south of the international Los Cabos Airport, I knew I was in a different world from that of several decades ago. It was once a sleepy little airport way out in the countryside on a lonely road. I was amazed at how much the entire area had been built up.

From the airport south, the road now becomes four lane with occasional pedestrian bridges — necessary because it's one long suburb the entire seven miles into San José Del Cabo!

I'd always enjoyed San José, traditionally a larger town than Cabo with minimal outside intervention. Narrow streets, sturdy square buildings and a small but dignified town square made it seem worlds away from a tourist enclave. Just south of town the stately Hotel Palmilla has graced a picturesque point for decades.

Now the San José town square is surrounded by T-shirt shops, trendy restaurants and wandering tourists. A new Presidente Intercontinental Hotel abuts the peaceful estuary, and the area's first golf course rose on the former barren plain between town and the bay.

The verdant course is but one of many developments between the village of San José and the water's edge. Many new hotels (Posada Real, Hotel Aguamarina, Fiesta Inn, Holiday Inn, Howard Johnson, etc.) line a strip between the golf course and the beach.

Since that first nine hole, par 35, 2,900 yard course was completed in 1988, four additional 18-hole championship courses have opened in Los Cabos, two of which were designed by Jack Nicklaus. Major tournaments have already come in and two more courses are under construction.

The new wide four-lane highway skirts greenery and the continued construction of more greenery. Hotels and condo developments now dot the remaining 20-mile corridor from San José del Cabo into Cabo San Lucas.

The most striking new building I found was the Hotel Westin Regina Resort, whose use of bold colors and dramatic arch design make it anything but commonplace.

In the seventies "The Corridor" housed only three tourist hotels: the Palmilla, Hotel Cabo San Lucas and the Twin Dolphin. The town of Cabo San Lucas itself had the Hacienda, Finisterra, the newly-opened Solmar and the basic Hotel Mar de Cortéz downtown. San José del Cabo had none. There were no condos nor time shares anywhere.

Imagine driving into downtown Cabo in the '70s: the two-lane road passed the old air strip (which is now a marina), continued straight, past the Mar de Cortéz Hotel and ended at Kilometer 0 by the small square. All other roads were dirt, even that going up to the Finisterra Hotel.

The new marina gave need to a Marina Blvd. which houses most of the restaurants, including the popular Giggling Marlin. Plazas, malls, hotels, shops and restaurants now encircle the marina. There were no homes on hills in the '70s; now Pedregal de Cabo residents can look down on upon the old, the new, and the continuing construction still underway.

While Los Cabos may have become too touristy for my personal taste, it certainly has a lot going for it. It's a great place for the timid to sample Mexico, with much more to do than other Mexican resorts like Cancun.

Big game fishing was Cabo's main attraction for years. The "Marlin Capital of the World" is still world-class and boasts several major fishing tournaments.

As mentioned, Los Cabos has also become a world-class golfing destination. I learned there are countless other attractions, however, besides fishing and golf.

Along with enjoying beautiful resorts, broad sandy beaches, fine dining, elegant shopping, art exhibits, and a pulsing night-life which now includes cabarets, a Planet Hollywood and a Hard Rock Cafe, other activities have followed.

It seems there's always something different to do; snorkeling, SCUBA diving, sailing and yacht charters, kayaking, boat cruises including glass bottom boats, catamarans, tall ships, dining and sunset cruises, and whale watching, parasailing, sightseeing plane rides, beach volleyball, hiking, horseback riding, and motorcycles, scooters, mountain bikes, and ATV rentals and tours.

Todos Santos, 1998

A wide range of packages and accommodations await the tourist. Aside from a handful who arrive by boat, and fewer still who drive the peninsula, they arrive by jet.

Los Cabos Airport is now served by Alaska Airlines, United Airlines, Continental Airlines, Mexicana, Aeromexico and Aero California.

We took the shorter, now-paved Highway 19 (100 miles) back to La Páz. Rather than hunting for a dirt road leaving town the back way, this new road up the coast was easy to find and was most direct.

On the way, we explored the mountains, driving up several dirt roads into the Sierra Laguna, one of the rare pristine environments left in Mexico. The 7,000 foot elevation mountaintops receive over 40 inches of annual rain and the vegetation clinging to the slopes becomes an unusual mix of desert, sub-tropical and alpine flora, a refreshing change from the lower elevations.

We stopped in Todos Santos, a town Don and I'd visited together with our wives about 10 years previous. While there was change, it was very subtle. The same old, low-key buildings now housed a handful of low-key art galleries and shops. An outstanding Café Santa Fé was even hard to find in an old building facing the square. The old Hotel California (1928) now sells T-shirts with the words of the immortal Eagles' song on it, but the town otherwise has changed very little.

We drove north along the beach to a small settlement of newer homes, many constructed by Americans. We found the old Juanita's Restaurant, which is closed and now used as a storeroom. We drove into the lush valley floor and joined a few other townspeople by scooping up handfuls of succulent mangoes which had fallen off the trees.

We visited the new Culture Center and a couple of simple, small art galleries. We enjoyed the languid pace of the town and, while it had grown to include more restaurants and a few more amenities, it was basically still the same old Todos Santos.

Cabo daytrippers sometimes drive up to enjoy the tranquility of Todos Santos. I just hope it stays like it is — the vitality of the resorts of Los Cabos should be enough for everyone.

La Páz and the Cape

Bikers in Rosarito-Ensenada 50-mile ride passing through Cantamar.
Leila Niemann photos.

Baja Fever

Baja
Sports

Baja Fever

"But not everyone who visits Baja California falls in love with it. Nearly every place along both its coasts is a fisherman's paradise, but everyone doesn't fish. There are a variety and an abundance of game in its wilderness areas the like of which few American hunters can imagine, but hunting is not everyone's favorite sport. Its inland oasis villages and its seacoast towns are remote and tranquil, compared to anything one can find in the United States, but everyone isn't looking for a place to 'get away from it all,' at least not quite everyone. We think, that the majority by far, who spend awhile in Baja California are sorry they can't extend their stay just a little longer. Some return year after year and a few, more favored by the gods than the rest, manage to spend whole seasons— or even longer—in the peace and quiet of this land of mañana."
— *Ralph Hancock, Ray Haller, Mike McMahan, Frank Alvarado.*
"Baja California," 1953

"The Hill" Taunts Thousands

Rosarito-Ensenada, B.C. México, 1994

I was only a third of the way up "the Hill" and worried. My legs felt heavy. My ninth time on this bike ride and I was prepared the least.

I was once again riding the Rosarito-Ensenada 50 Mile Fun Bike Ride, which draws about 8,500 to 10,000 entrants to Baja each April and September. The old road between the two Mexican towns is closed to traffic as enthusiasts on tandems, mountain bikes, road bikes, bikes pulling kiddy carts, and roller skates fill both lanes in their quest to get to Ensenada.

The course record is a tandem timed at 1:55. Best single finish ever was timed at 2:01. Some top riders come close to the record every year, but most entrants finish in from 4 to 5 hours.

Through the years, the ride has attracted some top cyclists, including Ironman John Howard and Pete Penseyres, winner of the Race Across America. Last year two sons of Mexican President Ernesto Zedillo brought their mountain bikes from México City to ride in what has become one of México's premier cycling events.

A decade ago, mountain bikes made up only about 10 percent of the total. Today that percentage has shifted to over 50 percent. With the notorious potholes a thing of the past, Bicycling West, Inc. expects that future rides will attract more street bikes.

Over the years I've steadily improved, and last year following physical therapy to strengthen weak knees and other muscles, I logged my best personal time (3:31).

Everything went wrong this year. Lack of physical therapy, trips out of town and a week-long illness left me unprepared. The couple of 8-10 mile bike jaunts I was able to get in were not enough preparation for a 50-miler.

Then my regular partners, who had already signed up, canceled. At the last minute my real-estate oriented wife had to work and was unable to come to Baja and provide assistance. So I was on my own.

I too would have canceled but I had promised to do a story and get photos. Plus, a former co-worker and his family were at my Cantamar rental, one block from my second home, 12 miles south of Rosarito. I had offered him guidance on his "first venture south." So I was determined to do the ride.

To aid my transportation problem, the co-worker said, "My family will take me and my son to the Rosarito start and then they'll all go straight to Ensenada. My daughter and her husband are coming to México in the morning so he can do the ride. We'll have two cars then, so we can give you a ride from Ensenada, but we just won't have room getting you to Rosarito."

BUMMING A RIDE

"No problem," I said, knowing that some of my Cantamar friends usually do the ride and I could tie in with them.

Cantamar friend Larry Hayden was to ride again. In his group were three young women riders. His brother Gary, a non-rider, would drive my van which was larger than their wagon. All six of us with our five bikes drove to about a half mile south of Rosarito, where Gary could turn around easily, go back to Cantamar, park my van, and then get his wagon across the old road before the thousands of riders blocked it. He would then head for Ensenada to pick up that group. I would return with my co-worker. Got that?

In Rosarito, as Larry and the girls signed up, I volunteered to return to the van with all the T-shirts. Sounded simple. But we were running late. I took a few photos of the thousands lining the boulevard in lycra-clad splendor while the others registered.

Finally I had five T-shirts, a sweatshirt from one of the girls and sunglasses from another. Loaded down, I balanced my booty the half mile on my handlebars. But my van was gone! It was almost 10 a.m., the starting time, and all the vehicles had to have deserted the area.

So the ride started and I just continued south, balancing my load all the way to Cantamar. I couldn't see my speedometer/odometer. I couldn't even shift as one hand had to balance the load.

The first 12 miles is a pretty flat ride, with a few gentle rolling hills. It is the area where you can get the most speed. The burden was most unwelcome but I still made decent time.

Knowing now I wasn't "shooting for time" became a blessing as my competitive nature gave way and I was able to slow down and "smell the flowers." I could and did stop and take photos along the way. No longer was I out to "break my record," which my lack of training would have prohibited anyway. I could be excused for not pushing to the limits.

American residents along Baja's Gold Coast gather in front of their developments to wave, yell, drink beer and enjoy the passing spectacle. Cantamar had its usual crowd of well-wishers, including a sheepish and apologetic Gary. After tossing the unwieldy pile of shirts at him, I continued pedaling unimpeded.

A RESURFACED ROAD

It was a gorgeous, warm day. The newly resurfaced road was a big improvement over the legendary potholes of the past. You could raise your field of vision from the pavement to enjoy the crashing waves and the many local Bajacalifornios lining the route, along with the local kids who love to "high five" the competitors.

Enterprising vendors gathered roadside to sell sodas, Gator-ade, fruit and goodies. One wag had a sign offering Preparation H, a not-so-subtle hint at the pounding the posterior takes on such a long bike ride.

THE HILL CLIMBS 800 FEET

After La Fonda, the road turns inland, drops down into the beautiful La Mision Valley, crosses a bridge at mile 23 and starts climbing. This is the infamous "Hill," two miles of steady climbing up a 7.5 percent grade. Cyclists pump up 800 feet along the steep walls of the canyon to the plateau above.

When my legs felt heavy, I dismounted for photos, hearing only the occasional clicking of gears and the panting of breath as hundreds passed, grimly challenging this "monster" they'd heard about.

A few had already started walking their bikes. Later on, many more would be pushing rather than pumping.

Back on my bike, I thought I'd see if I could get to the top without dismounting. About halfway up a sharp pain stabbed my calf. Cramp! Charlie-horse! It hurt to move. It hurt to stop moving. Whoah, this is no fun!

I stopped to let the pain subside, took a few more pictures, and started pedaling again. Once again, a stabbing pain. I better walk the rest of the hill.

I felt a little foolish walking the bike, but I was not alone. The far right side of the road was full of "walkers" by now. Besides, I didn't want to cause further damage to my leg.

The walking helped. I had shaken off most of the pain, by the time I reached the top, and could ride from there on.

I enjoyed the plateau this year. Winter rains had blessed the hillsides with a green carpet sporadically dappled with multi-hued wildflowers.

But the recent moisture brought critters one does not associate with the barren Baja hills. Bugs, insects and butterflies made my glasses and teeth look like the front end of a Buick after crossing Florida.

Cyclists hit "the hill" about midway through the ride.

At El Tigre two beautiful, winding, steep downhills speed you back down to the ocean. I particularly look forward to those downhills and enjoy hollering "On your left" as pure momentum creates a heady exhilaration. But today light headwinds from the ocean slowed everyone down.

"I could really feel that breeze today," Hayden later told me. "I usually hit 40-42 on that hill, but 38 was my top speed today."

After the old road merges by the toll gate, it's a fairly level eight mile romp to the finish. But April's headwind even made that a challenge.

A FINISH LINE CHALLENGE

Still another challenge at the finish line added to my frustrating day. That of finding my party. We were to meet at the "heads," the statues of Mexican leaders that are hard to miss. On a map, I even showed the riders in my co-workers' group where the "heads" were and how they were past the finish line (Meta) which was north of town.

Everyone rendezvoused there except the co-worker's son. He passed me just before the downhills so I figured we two would finish around the same time and then wait for his dad. But no. 3 o'clock came, 4 p.m., and by now the dad was in. 5 p.m. We looked all over. At 6 p.m. his wife and I were headed to the ambulance to see if maybe he had been reported injured. As we approached the Fiesta at the south end of town and the near-empty streets, we saw him.

He was exceptionally hard to spot as he had removed his purple shirt which we had been scanning the crowds for. And he was standing under a banner a well-meaning, but errant sponsor had strung up by the Fiesta that said "Finish." Somehow he missed the real finish north of town, missed the "heads," and figured he was in the right place.

After we explained, he said, "Oh, I was wondering why everyone slowed down coming into town."

Between the load of shirts, the headwind, the bugs and the horrific cramps, I think the worst was not getting my salt-encrusted body into a shower until 7 p.m. After the "Hill," just thinking of a hot shower is a luxury.

Montaña Grande Challenges
Mountain Bikers

Rosarito Beach — 1988

They called it "Montaña Grande" which means "big mountain" in Spanish. You would think that knowing the race was called "Big Mountain," I should have realized it was out of my league, but I was lured to attempt it. Why? I couldn't answer. I asked myself that question every nasty one of those 20 miles through the dusty, rocky and steep hills and mountains east of Rosarito Beach.

It was the first of what developed into an annual event called the Montaña Grande Mountain Bike Ride sponsored by Armando Carrasco Productions. Carrasco, a former official from the Tourism Office, would later run his events under the "Too Much Fun" banner.

I was bicycling more and enjoying it to the point where I started getting cocky. Only six weeks earlier, I'd finished my fifth Rosarito-Ensenada 50 Mile Fun Ride in my best personal time of 3:47.

Just two weeks earlier, I completed a 100 mile Anaheim-San Diego ride, and before that, the Orange County Classic, and...and I thought I was ready for a dirt ride. I had recently purchased a new mountain bike, that I rode mostly on pavement, until then.

I read about the Montaña Grande. Being a part-time resident of nearby Cantamar, this event was right in my backyard. I'd forgotten how steep my backyard was! I wanted experience riding in the dirt, so I signed up.

I couldn't coax my buddies into accompanying me on this one. They clearly used discretion by sitting it out. So on that crisp, clear fall morning, I drove to town, wrote a registration check to Armando Carrasco

323

Productions, got my bib number, map and colorful T-shirt, and headed for the start line in front of the Rosarito Beach Hotel.

I realized immediately I was in for an ordeal. Instead of the thousands of cyclists of every age, shape and size who line the main boulevard for blocks and spill over onto the sidewalks for the Ensenada ride, there was just a small group assembled.

There were only about 150 young, healthy riders. Most were in their early or mid-20s, or less than half my age. Their T-shirts bespoke their experience: Mammoth, Big Bear, Desert-to-Sea. I recognized their logos to be challenging mountain bike rides.

Not dismayed; intimidated, yes, but not dismayed, I pulled into the line-up and began concentrating on a good ride. Even the pretty Mary López Gallo of the Rosarito tourism office who joined other dignitaries on the platform didn't distract my concentration.

Hugo Torres Chabert, Rosarito's top official and owner of the Rosarito Beach Hotel, then rendered a brief welcome. He saw me in the line-up and with his normal serious frown, just shook his head. He knew I was crazy.

Then instructions were bellowed by Carrasco over the bullhorn and Torres prepared to drop the flag.

We're off! We immediately left the pavement for the dirt road across from the hotel. We all jockeyed for position as the dirt road narrowed and went under the toll road. It required utmost concentration. It was like the strategic hole shot in motocross where all riders reach that first curve at the same time yet only one leads after the curve.

When you're in the pack, you pick a spot and go for it, hoping you won't get bumped or knocked down. As we hit that first steep hill south of the arroyo, I was still in the pack. It was a mad scramble as most of the riders dismounted and we grabbed the bike frames and carried our bikes up the rocky dusty trail as fast as we could run.

Soon the crowd thinned. Most of the younger "animals" quickly got ahead of me and my problems abated to merely keeping the bike on the trail. I was careful not to hit rocks too big, or too sharp, or ruts too deep or too slippery, or to fall, yet still go as fast as I dared.

For many riders, flat tires took their toll; it seemed especially so in the first mile or two. I passed one fellow who was knocked out of the race early with a broken frame.

Speed was essential, but preserving the equipment was paramount, as in all off-road races.

Early on I came upon an attractive girl with a flat tire. "Can I borrow your pump," she pleaded.

"Sure," I said as I gallantly proceeded to assist her. The trophy dash never entered my mind anyhow.

It did hers, however, as she hastily remounted and sped away, hollering a sincere, "Thanks a million."

We followed brightly-colored fluorescent ribbons tied to bushes and fences as the route wended south to the Lienzo Charro rodeo grounds. Sometimes we followed dirt roads, other times horse trails, and sometimes the route just went cross country. Before the day was over we would ford several shallow streams and climb several steep hills.

The uphills were tough; we put our bikes into the lowest gears and gave ourselves a workout. On dirt, however, there often came a point where the wheels spun as traction gave way on the gravelly slopes. That's when we had to dismount and "hike and bike" as they say.

A couple of downhills were so steep we had to gingerly walk our bikes down or risk going head over heels. When we could we pedaled down hills. Sometimes I would go for it, going all out down a long, steep hill and praying I could stop in time for the hazards that surely lay at the bottom. Those fleeting moments of dodging rocks and ruts at speeds over 25 miles per hour provided the pure exhilarating "natural high" this sport offers.

I got hot, dusty, tired and sore and realized that each mile completed on the dirt is tougher than several on the pavement.

We came to the steepest uphill yet; it surely had to be the "big mountain," a couple hundred yards of 25 plus degree slope — to me it looked like 45. A sign at the bottom and officials at the top offered free beer to those who could pedal all the way up it. They could have offered me ownership of the entire Tecate Brewery and I couldn't have made it.

I never did learn if there were any beer winners. I think not, as I joined a procession of sweaty folks pushing those by-now super-heavy bikes up that rutted, rocky road.

Less than five miles to go I passed the girl I'd aided earlier. She was sitting on the ground at the base of the last big hill. "I just can't go on," she answered to my query. "I started getting dizzy so I thought I'd better stop a while."

"Wise," I said and reassured her that a support wagon would be along shortly. What bothered her the most was that she was in line for the third place women's trophy at the time.

The course continued its way north, up and down hills, past Morelos town, ranches, greenhouses and re-entered Rosarito by the polo field.

While no trophy awaited me, I proudly panted across the finish line in front of Papas and Beers, a co-sponsor of the event. My time of 2:35 placed me 92nd out of 125 riders. All I wanted to do was finish, so I was quite pleased.

The winner blazed the demanding course in 1 hour, 20 minutes. The second place finisher came in at 1:23. The third place trophy went to a fellow who complete the course in 1:36.

The women's race was won with the time of 1 hour and 53 minutes, barely edging the sencond place, who ended at 1:54, and third at 2:00 even.

Those who had other mountain bike races under their belts felt that Rosarito's Montaña Grande was a challenge. According to the women's race third place finisher, Monika Fack, "Big Bear had more uphill, but this ride was rockier; it required a much more technical ride."

And was this rider humiliated into checkers and the NFL for future autumn weekends? Who knows. Maybe next year I can beat two hours!

THE GRANDDADDY OF DESERT RACING

THE BAJA 1,000 — 1994

"Wow," said Ken, "They look great this early in the morning."

That they did. The Tecate Girls, a trio of lovely girls in bright mini-skirts with the "Tecate" beer logo emblazoned across their midsections, were helping flag off racers at the start of the Tecate SCORE Baja 1,000, the "Granddaddy of Desert Racing."

The famous Baja 1,000 is the annual November pilgrimage to Baja that brings out desert racing's finest stars along with thousands of support crew personnel and spectators.

Every third year the race is a purists' 1,000 mile dash from Ensenada to La Paz in the south. On off years it's an approximate 1,000 kilometer version looping the northern sector of the state of Baja California Norte.

The 1,000 kilometer version, like this year, offers many more accessible spectator areas, is much easier to pit and support, features a start and finish in roughly the same area, and conserves fuel.

Regardless of the route, each year the excitement begins to build Thursday afternoon as visi-

The author and the Tecate Girls

327

tors wander among the cars and product booths on "contingency row" downtown. Friday the race starts. Many spectators choose to leave early Friday morning and head out of town to find a place where the highway nears the race course. There they position themselves for the arrival of the race.

It's one thing to see these powerful vehicles on television, but to have them blast right by you is an experience one never forgets.

The booming roar of the finely-tuned big engines as they approach cannot be duplicated electronically; the speed with which they travel over marginal trails is awesome; the vehicles are sturdy and specifically designed for the rough stuff, yet they still take incredible beatings with parts and fenders littering the course.

Most admirable is the daring of the drivers, with life or death decisions made in micro-seconds, and the demanding course constantly bruising backs, spleens and kidneys.

You really don't need to know who they are, nor who is winning. Just find a curve or hill or long straightaway, get comfortable, and feel the experience, feel the power.

Don't position yourself downwind, however. Not only will an exciting sensory experience envelope you, but a thick layer of dust will, too.

Crowds of well-wishers always jam the starting line, in Ensenada again this year, to view modified cars and trucks that even most Americans can ill afford, and to catch a glimpse of, or get autographs from, a pre-race favorite. Thousands more line the course, especially in areas near villages and highways.

TECATE GIRLS WAVED THEM OFF

This year Ken and I watched the motorcycles depart in regular intervals about two hours before the cars and trucks. It was still dark out as the first motorcycles rolled up to the start line and the officials and the lovely Tecate girls waved them off.

Son Ken, 22, was right. The girls looked fresh and attractive, especially considering they had been up and smiling a couple hours already.

After most of the bikes were on their way, we broke away from the start (and the Tecate girls) and headed east into the mountains.

Driving directly into a brilliantly rising sun up the hill to Ojos Negros had already caused some racers trouble staying on the road. My vision was impaired even with visor and polaroid glasses. Squinting into the sun, I shared the road with motorcycles, quads and ATVs dashing around me in spurts.

One motorcyclist was momentarily blinded enough by the sun that he hit a rock and went right over his handlebars. He was able to continue the race, shaken and bruised.

Once the sun rose, it turned into a beautiful, crisp, clear, but windy November day. The wind was welcomed by both drivers and spectators as it quickly blew the dust away rather than have it linger and settle like a thick, choking soup on the roads.

While the Ojos Negros area is now a small town and the population center of a large farm community, over 100 years ago it was at the center of the gold rush, with the boom town of Real del Castillo to the north and the canyons of the greatest mining activity around El Alamo to the south.

Those miners of 1889 who endured a long and difficult wagon or horseback journey through these mountains would have been amazed at the speeds these same trails were being attacked by those seeking the "gold" of a finish line many miles away.

I'm sure my great-granddaddy who drew some of the maps outlining these trails would have cheered the crowds now brought to Baja by this "Granddaddy of Desert Racing."

JAMMED WITH TRAFFIC

From Ojos Negros to San Felipe, Highway 3 was jammed with traffic heading east all morning. Support crews raced ahead bringing riders to ride later segments. Families, friends and spectators jockeyed to pit stops or other optimum viewing locations.

Usually called "off-road" racing, "desert" racing best describes the event as existing roads and trails are used thus protecting the peninsula's pristine environment.

We noticed pit crews from the professional Chapala Dusters or Checkers teams to the factory teams, to the smaller one-person crews, racing ahead to get in position for when the riders neared the highway.

Suppliers, and other sponsors were out in force. They are well aware of the marketability of "Baja proven" advertising.

At checkpoints were the major pit areas, most of them close to Highway 3. The contours of sagebrush, ocatillo, chapparal and cactus are dwarfed by the mini-cities that had sprung up within their midst. Large semis, trucks, trailers and campers were strategically placed to await the racers. Generators keep the "cities" alive as riders and drivers blast by through the night.

While the motorcycles leave earlier, many are still on the course, especially the quads and smaller bikes when the first of the powerful cars come roaring into view. You can tell the 4-wheel leaders are nearing by the distant clouds of dust being kicked up and the helicopters which thump-thump overhead following the lead cars.

Baja 1,000 participants have a big following in México. Their machisimo is respected and their vehicles admired. While I see Americans in every crowd, the majority are the locals who arrive from even distant locations to line the route.

The race crosses Highway 3 after going through the old mining town of El Alamo. Near that intersection is a steep hill. Literally hundreds of spectators gather at this hilltop to await these powerful vehicles.

We joined the crowds in whooping as almost all of the contenders got "lots of air" at the crest of the hill.

Families of Mexicans had been waiting for hours, some grilling tortillas and carne asada over small open fires, others drinking beer straight from quart bottles of Tecate. When the riders arrived, spectators dangerously crowded the course to cheer them on. The roar of the crowd seemed to be in direct proportion to how high, or how much air, each car got.

It has been my favorite spot over the years. After I'd photographed most of the 4-wheel leaders literally flying over the hill, Ken and I left and continued on toward San Felipe where we would see a lot of these vehicles emerging out of an arroyo at the bottom of the San Matias Pass.

At the bottom of the pass, from the highway we went down a narrow, rocky road and dropped a short distance into the arroyo. A number of spectators' cars were pulled off the highway and others came down the dirt road as far as possible.

I was down at the bottom of the arroyo watching a different type of race here. The arroyo bed was thick with sand and the cars flying down were sashaying back and forth like fish swimming in water. Great volumes of sand flew into the air with each car and their tires kept digging deeper and deeper ruts into the course.

Ken was ahead, yet suddenly I heard my name called from behind me. Looking back, I saw a most incongruous vision approach in the heat of the desert, a mirage so to speak. The three Tecate Girls, still in miniskirts, hose and high heels, were making their way past a mesquite bush, and crossing the rocks and sand in my direction.

Behind them, emerging from his white "Too Much Fun" tourist Bronco, was Armando Carrasco, former Rosarito Beach tourist official and long-time promoter of events in the area. It was he who had called me. He was grinning from ear to ear and carrying a chest of ice cold beers.

"Look what I brought," he beamed.

I wasn't sure if he was referring to the beers and sodas he offered or the fact that after half of Ensenada had lusted after these Tecate Girls, all three end up with him in the middle of the desert over 100 miles from Ensenada.

Everyone's attention was diverted from the sandy arroyo track to the sidelines. I noticed spectators perched on rocky crags had now aimed their binoculars in our direction.

The girls whipped out a boom box and talked to us while standing in the sand, rocking to the beat of the music, nursing cold products from their sponsor, and occasionally glancing at the cars roaring down the canyon.

While Armando told me the story how he was "asked" to escort the girls and show them some of the race, Ken was in some sort of heaven. He finally realized it wasn't a mirage when the girl most smitten with his youthful good looks wrote her phone number and address down for him.

All the way back to Ensenada where we would wait for race results Ken was giddy and excited. This gal lived in Tijuana and he had a date with her the following day.

Now most guys who go into the desert to watch a race would count on the chances of meeting a gorgeous female that weekend as slim to none. Something about Baja — anything can happen.

Lots of fans come to see the Baja races.

Baja Sports

Huge crowds highlight Baja 1,000

To a dog, heaven is a dense forest of markable trees, or a vast field of uncountable sniffables. To a football couch potato, it's a holiday weekend with a surfeit of television games that overlap each other. To an off-roader, it's miles and miles of wide open spaces — like Baja.

Off-road participants and fans get afflicted with Baja Fever every November, at the world's most famous off-road race — the Tecate SCORE Baja 1,000.

While the off-roading visitors had Baja Fever, for the locals it was more "Baja Mil" fever.

The Baja 1,000, or "Baja Mil" in Spanish, alternates from an approximate 1,000 kilometer loop around northern Baja to a purist's 1,000 mile one-way dash to La Páz. Normally, both versions begin in Ensenada. Mexicali had not seen the race since 1972.

In 1993, "The Ironman" Ivan Stewart climaxed his best season ever by handily winning the Baja 1,000, even beating the motorcycles in elapsed time. But the biggest Baja 1,000 story of the year was people — as thousands lined the course to watch the Mexicali-based race.

The huge crowds were even more of a story than Stewart or the difficulty of the 762.4 mile course, which prevented all but 24 percent of the riders from finishing. Only 70 of the 250 entrants completed the race due to a combination of tough terrain and sporadic downpours that turned dust to mud, and dry lakes into slippery skating rinks.

CROWDS CHANT "IVAN, IVAN"

Stewart had to carefully thread his way to the finish line as a sea of 15,000 delirious fans crowded Boulevard Lopéz Mateos at 10:25 p.m. waving their arms and chanting "Ivan, Ivan."

"Ironman" Ivan Stewart Signs authographs for fans at Baja 1000.

At the victory stand, Stewart addressed the fans, "I have never been to a race where the people have been so hospitable and enthusiastic," he said, adding, "I can't get over the size of the crowds. They were all over the course, and of course here in Mexicali....I do believe the people here are more excited about our racing than anywhere else."

OVER 400,000 SPECTATORS

Police estimated that more than 400,000 spectators watched the race from some vantage point. For a one-day event, this may have out-drawn the Indianapolis 500, acknowledged as the largest spectator crowd ever assembled for a sporting event.

Adolfo Yee Chek-ng, President of Mexicali's Convention and Tourist Bureau (COTUCO), commented on the first Baja 1,000 in Mexicali in 21 years, "Mexicali is very proud to have a race of this magnitude. It is important for us to expose Mexicali to the companies in the auto industry, the manufacturers of tires and automobile parts. We believe the race will have a great economic effect on the community."

At every Baja 1,000 I've attended, I've always been amazed at the crowds, and this year it seemed even more overwhelming. The desert roads south of Mexicali were jammed all day, as support crews raced ahead with back-up riders, families, friends and spectators. Pit crews, large and small, were everywhere.

Joining the desert caravan were the suppliers, with wares ranging from tires, spark plugs, oil, wheels and shocks to fuel. This was their opportunity, their big chance to develop a reputation or to continue one. This one race is most important to them. If successful, their future advertising can boast "Winner of the Baja 1,000." If not successful, well, they can still advertise "Baja Tested" or "Baja Proven," with the magic of the land transferred to all that the name "Baja" implies.

THE IRONMAN

Ivan Stewart, 47, a big crowd favorite in Baja, drives solo and had earlier this year won the Parker 500, the Ultra Wheel 500 and the Baja 500. He was declared the season's overall 4-wheel champion in his Toyota Special V-6 truck.

In addition, he was reconfirmed as the "Ironman," collecting two Valvoline Ironman trophies for winning both major Baja races with no relief driver.

I've watched Stewart win a number of races, including several Baja 500s. Invariably, this big friendly blond man will sign autographs and banter with his admirers. Then he turns introspective to mentally prepare for the race. He gets in his car and goes over every detail, no matter how trivial. Intimately knowing his car and equipment is just another edge he uses to help him win.

With an elapsed time of 13 hours, 29 minutes, 11 seconds, he also beat all the motorcycle competitors. His time over the fastest motorcycle entry of Larry Roeseler-Danny Hamel-Ty Davis, on a Kawasaki KX500, was approximately 28 minutes. It was Roeseler's 9th Baja 1,000 2 wheel victory, and the first time it wasn't enough for the overall win.

Stewart was elated and said, "I've been wanting to beat the bikes here for 20 years."

MANY FOREIGN ENTRANTS

The Baja 1,000 is increasingly luring a broad range of entrants from all over the world. Riders and drivers from 15 states were joined by entrants from Canada, Denmark, France, Israel, Japan, México, England and Wales.

A large Japanese contingent now creates record motorcycle entrants where "Beat the Baja on a bike" has become a cultural vendetta. Riders come on junkets from Japan, buy a specially-prepared Honda 600 in the U.S. and make time for one quick pre-run before they tackle the big race.

Then they take their dust-laden motorcycles back home to display, still encrusted with Baja mud and dirt, at local Japanese businesses proving that the rider had indeed survived this Mexican adventure.

The race was covered by media representatives from Australia, France, Germany, Italy, Japan, México, New Zealand, Portugal, Qatar, Sweden, the United Kingdom and the United States.

British racer James Tennant said, "The course was great, but it was absolutely exhausting."

British driver Graham Roberts summed up why the Baja 1,000 is still considered the world's premier off-road race, "This is definitely rougher than Paris to Dakar."

The 1993 Tecate SCORE Baja 1,000 had something for everyone: a grueling course that ended up knocking out 76 percent of the entrants, huge crowds lining the Mexicali-San Felipe corridor, inclement weather, entries from around the world, and a 47-year-old champ who deserves to be called "Ironman."

Fans come south of the border for the Baja-1000

Lots of excitement.

Baja Sports

BAJA'S BEACHES LURE SURFERS

BAJA CALIFORNIA — 1998

"In New York they have therapy. Out west we have Baja," quipped Longboard magazine editor Scott Hulet in a recent issue featuring surfing "down south."

To many, the Baja Fever is endless series of unbroken waves.

That mindset is well earned as world-class surfing beaches in pristine settings run the length of Baja's

Eight hundred miles of Pacific coast. Legendary right point breaks from Calafia in the north to Abreojos in the south have continued to beckon several generations of surfers.

While right points dominate and create seemingly endless wave sets that have made Baja a surfers' paradise, there are enough left breaks, protected by kelp paddies and/or rocks and reefs, to get most "goofy footers" drooling.

What most surfers like about Baja, aside from the endless variety of surfing breaks, is the remoteness of most areas. Not only are there fewer surfers to fight over waves but a sense of adventure is often attained in just getting to this Baja surf.

In some cases the adventure is very real indeed. Some years ago four Cantamar youths "in search of the perfect wave" wanted to surf Isla Natividad, a small island near the tip of the Vizcaino Peninsula. With trepidation they took an irregular commercial flight out of the tiny Ensenada air field. In a dilapidated, old prop job that had been resurrected from the moth balls, they droned south for hours to Natividad. There they spent a week camping and surfing on the tiny island with few amenities.

"But the waves were awesome, man," they reflected.

Baja Coast.

Surfers have known about Baja since the sport came over to the mainland from Hawaii. Many surfing legends have invaded Baja to hone their skills over the years. Nowadays, several excursion companies offer surfing packages for those who:

1. Don't know where the good spots are;

2. Don't want to risk damage to car or self by jostling over impossible, axle-breaking, killer roads;

3. Want to make the most out of a three-day trip by flying, yet are leery of periodic commercial flights.

4. Want everything set up and planned for them;

5. And want coaching and/or instruction.

Baja Surf Adventures takes their neophytes to a surf camp about 100 miles south of Ensenada. In addition, BSA offers central Baja excursions.

More ambitious is Baja AirVentures, a fly-in surf adventure run by Kevin Warren, a 25-year Baja veteran. Over 3,000 of his more than 4,000 flight hours have been logged in Baja, shuttling people to remote surf and fishing spots.

In 1987 he spotted an airstrip and perfect waves peeling off an obscure point on Magdalena Island, a 70-mile long strip of sand and rock sheltering Magdalena Bay, almost seven hundred miles down Baja. He and his brother Steve built an island base camp there.

The "If you build it, they will come" philosophy gave birth to the new company and now Baja AirVentures is a fully certified FAA –135 international air carrier, with two aircraft featuring state-of-the-art navigation equipment.

Baja Airventures also offers camps in the wild central Baja area, a series of "dynamite" coves and bays collectively called the "Seven Sisters," and the aforementioned Natividad Island, long regarded as one of North America's most powerful beach breaks.

SURFING THE BAJA

Surfing in Baja is not restricted to those out-of-the-way places reached by air or "roads from hell." The most visited surfing spots are between the border and Ensenada, only 75 miles away.

Many have learned how to surf on Baja's waves. At Cantamar, where occasional large wave sets can sometimes intimidate me and other body surfers, I have seen several generations of young people take those first hesitant steps in learning to balance their bodies on projectiles gliding across the water.

If you were to ask the surfers where they go in Baja, they'd tell you about some of the more popular spots. From north to south, they are:

At the border, there is a delta break right off the Tijuana River estuary. Between the border and Rosarito Beach there are fine beach breaks at San Antônio Del Mar (KOA) and Baja Malibu. Surfing is spotty with occasional nice beach breaks all along the broad beach at Rosarito and in front of Rene's. South of town there's a rock reef at Alfonsino's and a reef break at Popotla.

K–38 (38 kilometers south of Tijuana) was perhaps the most legendary of Baja's northern surfing venues. Every weekend throughout the year surfers of all ages crowded the rocky point, rough camping on the bluff above. Even though condos have crowded their converted vans off the point, the surf at K–38 is still outstanding.

Surfing at Raul's restaurant just to the south is popular and features a fine left and right reef break. Surfers often find solid beach breaks all along the coast south of Raul's: Cantamar, The Dunes, Campo Lopéz, Alisitos and La Fonda. In addition there are reef breaks at the Halfway House and Salsipuedes.

San Miguel, just north of Ensenada, has such a fine right point the Tecate Longboard ProAm tournament is held there each year. It's a PLA event sanctioned by the Association of Professional Surfers.

South of Ensenada, the area around Colonet and Camalu features a number of popular reef breaks. Along with Punta Cabras, Cabo Colonet and Cabo San Quintín, they include what surfers call Cuatro Casas, Roberts Lefts and Rincon de Baja.

I get a kick out of surfer-designated place names. They're colorful, descriptive and you won't find them on maps. Over time, most beaches end up with several names and surfers rarely know the proper ones. I've talked to hordes of surfers who tell me they've been to Cuatro Casas (4 houses), yet only a handful have any idea that it's near the village of Camalu.

Even in San Clemente, the beaches called "Old Man's" and "Hole-In-The-Fence" are more expressive than their proper designation. From San Quintín all the way south to Cabo are any number of legendary surfing beaches, many of them reached only by those roads from hell: Punta Baja, Punta Canoas, Punta Blanca, the Seven Sisters area, Punta Santa Rosalita, Turtle Bay, Punta Abreojos, Punta Pequeña, Scorpion Bay, Magdelena Bay, Punta Conejo and Migrino.

Many of Baja's beaches have become firmly entrenched in surfing folklore. At any given time, winter or summer, there are scores of surf bums prowling Baja along the Pacific coast looking for that "perfect wave." Surfers who call southern California home have quite an option, with world class beaches on both sides of the border.

One easterner after his first trip to Baja told me, "I can't believe it. Californians have all these beautiful beaches — and they have Baja, too." I didn't ask how much his therapy cost.

Baja Fever

Epilogue

Baja Fever

"As an individual he is neat and with him it is a case of individual enterprise, analogous perhaps to his love of colorful costume and gay mood. In any event, from whatever the cause, it gives to even small Baja villages something of the charm of the little old towns in the hills above the sea, in southern France. Isolation, poverty and primitive facilities take on a certain dignity. To come upon such a village after traversing mountain or desert is to feel that it belongs. It may not be progressive but it has character and individuality."

—Joseph Wood Krutch,
"The Forgotten Peninsula," 1961

Epilogue

Baja Fever

Symptoms and Antidotes

An acquaintance who learned I was a Baja buff commented that she and her husband had gone to Baja the previous summer. "We had a great time," she said, and then added, "but it sure was nice to get back across the border to the good old U.S. of A."

Obviously, that couple was not inflicted with Baja Fever. With those who have this chronic disease, the comfort is crossing the border going south. I will concede that it is nice getting the car in high gear on the wide multi-lane U.S. freeway after leaving the border congestion, but I am saddened each time I cross going north, not relieved.

I know I'm back in a land where precious minutes and seconds are all-important, where material goods and status mean more than character and family and friends. Where I know I will be busy just managing my daily affairs.

Going south has always been great therapy for me. Especially after a busy week in the business world, I could cross the border and immediately start slowing down. My heart would start beating slower in Baja. My attitude began mellowing. Within a day my self-regulatory watch would be put in a drawer until we had to leave. It's easy to lose track of time in Baja, even lose track of days, because you're not compelled to count.

The slower pace of Baja offers a sense of timelessness, and those who can jump off the corporate merry-go-round long enough to enjoy it rarely regret it. The wife of one manager we took to Baja continues to marvel that she had never seen her Type-A husband as relaxed as he was that weekend.

John Steinbeck described the feeling well in his "Log From The Sea of Cortéz" when he said, "The matters of great importance we had left were not important....Our pace had slowed greatly; the hundred thousand small reactions of our daily world were reduced to very few."

BAJA IS UNIQUE

The stories in this book have been just a few examples of my lifetime's wanderings south of the border. I limited them to Baja instead of including many mainland México adventures because Baja is unique, even to the rest of México. There is more desolation in Baja, there are more Americans and a greater influence by them especially in the border regions, and there is a greater feeling of remoteness, of being apart from mainland México among all who live there.

Early tribes of those who crossed from Asia to populate the Americas had lived in Baja California and left their legends in art work on the walls of obscure caves in distant mountain valleys. The confines and harshness of the peninsula had entrapped them and they and their descendants did not develop the more refined cultures of those who settled elsewhere.

As I write this, the village of Loreto is celebrating its 300th birthday. It celebrates the time in 1697 when the Europeans first arrived on the peninsula to gather the indigenous Indians into villages.

For well over a hundred years Spanish padres and soldiers tried to populate and tame the barren and wild peninsula. Then after the Mexican independence, more colonization attempts were made.

About a hundred years ago the Mexicans were aided by Americans, English, French and Russian groups, each of whom tried to establish colonies, large and small.

As we have learned, some of those attempts would be considered hostile takeovers if we were to apply today's current corporate terminology. The hostile attempts all failed and for that the Baja Buff is lucky. Then again, would a different ownership have developed the Baja peninsula any sooner? Probably not.

My great-grandfather was early in his glowing praise for a land that at the time was barren and forbidding. Indeed even today much of it still is.

But today the tourist dollar has created a wealth not imagined by those early gold miners and settlers. The Gold Coast of Baja California has grown so fast in the past decade alone that all projections by even the most bold economists have been overshadowed.

Epilogue

The growth in the extreme north and south, spearheaded by the American tourist dollar, has made the two peninsular states among the wealthy states in México.

WILD AND UNTAMED LAND

There is still a lot of wild and untamed land in central Baja. As more and more of us seek these out-of-the-way spots, the Mexican government is right behind us, grading and paving the roads and providing economic opportunity for its citizens.

I have over 200 books on Baja California in my library, from very old tomes to those of recent vintage. Many are written by adventurers who made the trek by burro, or horse, or walked, or bicycled, or jeeped, or kayaked. As we learned, my father too romped all over the Baja peninsula. Those who came before me are the people who have become the Baja legends.

Perhaps as more and more roads are paved, and coves and little villages opened up, another generation might use the term "legends" to those of us who are now visiting and exploring the territory.

Baja is one of the few of the earth's last outposts, certainly the only one accessible to so many people. It abuts directly against the most affluent part of the most affluent state of the most affluent country on this planet. Nowhere else in the world is there such a collision of cultures, values and lifestyles separated only by a fine line on a map.

Baja is right next door and those who cross the border in either direction whittle away at the profound differences between the countries. The Mexicans learn our way of life and we are foolish if we in turn cannot learn from theirs. We have much to gain.

Past the border regions, the rocky, desolate, dry peninsula still provides adventure and excitement for those who enjoy a different pace, who can shun the cruise ship and the mega-resort for solace and a more rugged time. Baja is truly the last outpost. Even a generation from now visitors yet to visit will someday be known as Baja legends. But first they have to get a taste of Baja Fever.

Baja Fever means different things to different people. To some it's just laying poolside at the Rosarito Beach Hotel waiting for another coco-loco from the bar. To others it's riding horses on the beach or haggling with the vendors in front of the hotel.

To some it's being surrounded by a group of mariachis with trumpets challenging the acoustics of a small cantina, or pigging out on succulent spiny lobsters, hot fresh homemade tortillas, beans, rice, and a chilled Bohemia beer.

To others it is wolfing down fish tacos at a small Ensenada street stand and later enjoying a margarita at Hussongs or Papas and Beers.

To some it's bouncing down a dirt road to discover a wide, broad beach with long, unbroken wave sets rolling in from the southwest all day long.

To others it's fishing, sailing, bicycling, off-roading, hang-gliding, parasailing, windsurfing, hiking, golfing, shopping and surfing. Baja is what you make it.

Baja Fever begins with an itch, an internal gnawing. It comes when you need to wind down, and you know it. When you check your calendar to see how long it's been since you've been in Baja.

Baja Fever is infectous when you know that you have to get down there again, and soon. And when you get your fix, when you seek the only-known antidote — you go.

You know you are truly afflicted when you feel as I do and note a sadness upon leaving Baja, not relief. You know you will soon again catch Baja Fever, and you'll return.

Ken Palfenier surf fishing at Gonzaga Bay.

Epilogue

Greg Niemann at kilometer "0" in Cabo San Lucas. - 1998

"As my journey began at Tijuana, there let it end. As I write these closing lines there comes over me a flood of recollections—of gorgeous sunrises and sunsets, of evenings about the camp fire with copperhued brave or swarthy Mexican telling of days that are gone—of nights on the lone deserts with the glittering stars, and white moon close overhead." ...Yes, you are right I do 'miss — my chaps, taps and latigo straps.' Perhaps yes. God willing, I'll come again."

— Arthur W. North,
"Camp and Camino in Lower California," 1910,
after seven months in the saddle covering over
2,500 miles throughout Baja in 1906.

ABOUT THE AUTHOR

Greg Niemann is a life-long Baja buff with a home in Cantamar, Baja California, México. He has traveled and camped all over the Baja peninsula for over 50 years.

Niemann holds a B.A. in Journalism from California State College at Los Angeles (CalState-LA), is an Accredited Business Communicator, and was a public relations/communications manager with UPS before he retired with over 34 years of services. He has been a newspaper columnist and still contributes regularly to several publications.

Most of his regular weekly and monthly columns have been Baja-related, including those for *La Fiesta*, *Orange County Leisure* and the *San Clemente Journal*.

He has had many articles published in most of the Baja tourist publications, inlcuding *Discover Baja*, *Baja Life*, *Baja Sun*, and the *Gringo Gazette*. He was a regular contributor to the *Baja Times* for over 12 years, which included a series on the Baja Missions and coverage of all the Baja off-road races.

Greg and his wife Leila are real estate investors living in San Clemente, California.

A Note from the Publisher

When two or more cultures clash, languages, music, eating habits combine, modifying, sometimes creating new cultural standards. The popular vernaculars always include vestiges and influences of the assimilated culture, or signs of an emerging one.

Baja Fever contains a great deal of Spanish words, native names, and colloquialism used in the southwest of the United States of America, as well as in Baja California, México.

We chose not to use the traditional method of italicizing or identifying such expressions, as "of another language," since they are now part of the Southwest vernacular, and understood by most of the readers interested in the subject of this book.

We also have chosen to use the original spelling of some names and places.

OTHER TITLES FROM
MOUNTAIN N' AIR BOOKS

ADVENTURE GUIDES

Cross Country Northeast
John R. Fitzgerald Jr.
ISBN: 1-879415-07-0 $12.00

Cross Country Skiing in Southern California
Eugene Mezereny
ISBN: 1-879415-08-9 $14.00

Great Rock Hits of Hueco Tanks
Paul Piana
ISBN: 1-879415-03-8 $ 6.95

Mountain Bike Adventures... MOAB, Utah
Bob Ward
ISBN: 1-879415-11-9 $15.00

The Rogue River Guide
Kevin Keith Tice
ISBN: 1-879415-12-7 $15.00

ADVENTURES, LITERATURE

A Night on the Ground, A Day in the Open
Doug Robinson
ISBN: 1-879415-14-3 $19.00

High Endeavors
Pat Ament
ISBN: 1-879415-00-3 $12.95

On Mountains and Mountaineers
Mikel Vause
ISBN: 1-879415-06-2 $12.95

Rock and Roses
Mikel Vause, editor
ISBN: 1-879415-01-1 $11.95

The View From the Edge:
Life and Landscapes of Beverly Johnson
Gabriela Zim
ISBN: 1-879415-16-X $17.00

COOKING (BEARLY COOKING)

Cooking with Strawberries
Margaret and Virginia Clark
ISBN: 1-879415-26-7 $10.95

EATING OUT

The Nose Knows:
A Sensualist Guide to great Eating Joints
in the Greater Los Angeles Area
Lloyd McAteer Battista
ISBN: 1-879415-23-2 $13.00

HIKING AND HIKING GUIDES

Backpacking Primer
Lori Saldaña
ISBN: 1-879415-13-5 $12.00

Best Hikes of the Marble Mountain and
Russian Wilderness Areas, California
Art Bernstein
ISBN: 1-879415-18-6 $16.00

Best Day Hikes of the
California Northwest
Art Bernstein
ISBN: 1-879415-02-X $13.50

Best Hikes of the Trinity Alps
Art Bernstein
ISBN: 1-879415-05-4 $17.00

Portland Hikes, 2nd Edition
Art Bernstein and Andrew Jackman
ISBN: 1-879415-22-4 $18.00

So... How Does the Rope
Get Up There, Anyway?
Kathy Myers and Mark Blanchard
ISBN: 1-879415-17-8 $10.00